Simulation

Simulation

A Statistical Perspective

Jack P. C. Kleijnen *and* Willem van Groenendaal

School of Business and Economics
(Faculteit der Economische Wetenschappen)
Tilburg University
(Katholieke Universiteit Brabant)
Tilburg, The Netherlands

JOHN WILEY & SONS

Chichester · New York · Brisbane · Toronto · Singapore

Original Dutch version published under the title of *Simulatie: technieken en toepassingen*. Academic Service, Postbox 81, 2870 AB Schoonhoven.
Copyright © 1988 Academic Service

English translation copyright © 1992 by John Wiley & Sons Ltd,
Baffins Lane, Chichester,
West Sussex PO19 1UD, England

Other Wiley Editorial Offices

John Wiley & Sons, Inc., 605 Third Avenue,
New York, NY 10158-0012, USA

Jacaranda Wiley Ltd, G.P.O. Box 859, Brisbane,
Queensland 4001, Australia

John Wiley & Sons (Canada) Ltd,
22 Worcester Road, Rexdale, Ontario
M9W 1L1, Canada

John Wiley & Sons (SEA) Pte Ltd, 37 Jalan Pemimpin #05-04,
Block B, Union Industrial Building, Singapore 2057

Library of Congress Cataloging-in-Publication Data

Kleijnen, Jack P. C.
    [Simulatie. English]
    Simulation : a statistical perspective / Jack Kleijnen and Willem
van Groenendaal.
        p.   cm.
    Translation of: Simulatie.
    Includes bibliographical references and indexes.
    ISBN 0-471-93055-5 (paper)
    1. Computer simulation. I. Groenendaal, Willem van. II. Title.
QA76.9.C65K5913   1992
003′.3—dc20   92–7364
                                                                    CIP

British Library Cataloguing in Publication Data

A catalogue record for this book is available from the British Library.

ISBN 0-471-93055-5

Typeset in 10/12 pt Times by
Dobbie Typesetting Limited, Tavistock, Devon
Printed and bound in Great Britain by
Courier International Ltd, East Kilbride

Contents

Preface

This book is meant for those readers who wish to acquire a basic knowledge of simulation. It gives a survey of problems that can be analysed by means of simulation, especially problems in economics, business administration, management science, operations research, and mathematical statistics. It also shows how to analyse simulation results. This analysis makes it possible to obtain more general conclusions when using simulation. Moreover, the efficient design of simulation experiments is discussed. For all these topics there is specialized literature, but this literature is often too difficult for the novice. After reading this book, however, the specialized literature becomes accessible. Thus this book prepares the reader for the application of the simulation technique in practice. Therefore the problems and pitfalls of practical applications are outlined. Understanding the examples discussed in this book requires a basic knowledge of business administration and operations research. Understanding the techniques presented in this book, requires knowledge of elementary computer science, mathematics, and statistics.

Depending on their background and interests, readers might skip some chapters. Chapter 1 gives some simple examples of simulation and a few definitions. Chapter 2 evaluates pseudorandom number generators. Practitioners, however, often rely on the generator implemented on the available computer. Chapter 3 shows how pseudorandom numbers are transformed in order to sample from statistical distributions such as the normal and the Poisson distributions. In practice there are subroutines for sampling from classic distributions, so readers in a hurry might skip Chapters 2 and 3. Chapter 4 is important for readers interested in economic and business applications. This chapter also introduces Forrester's industrial dynamics or system dynamics. Chapter 5 covers classical operations research applications such as inventory and queuing systems. Chapter 6 presents computer programs for more complicated queuing systems, and briefly discusses special simulation languages. Chapter 7 is an introduction to the later chapters. It shows how simulation is applied in mathematical statistics, for example to investigate the robustness of regression analysis. The next two chapters set this book apart from other textbooks on simulation. Chapter 9 shows how statistical designs such as 2^{k-p} designs can be applied to select the combinations of factors (parameters and variables) to be simulated. The results of such experiments are analysed through analysis of variance (ANOVA). Chapter 8, however, presents ANOVA in the more familiar terminology of regression analysis. This leads to so-called metamodels, namely regression models of the input–output behaviour of simulation models. Because the specification of the metamodel determines the experimental design, regression models are presented before experimental designs; see Chapters 8 and 9. Chapter 10 answers the question: given the experimental design of Chapter 9, how long should the simulation program run? In other words: how many years or how many customers should be simulated to obtain accurate answers? To improve the accuracy of the simulation response, this chapter also gives a few variance reduction techniques, such as common and antithetic random numbers. Chapter 11 gives some information on verification and validation of models. Chapter 12 mentions literature sources and professional societies in the simulation area.

The reader (and instructor) may follow a different path through the book. Chapter 11 on validation and verification may be read immediately after Chapter 6 on simulation software. Tactical issues, discussed in Chapter 10, may be examined before strategy issues, discussed in Chapters 8 and 9.

This book is based on nearly twenty-five years of experience in teaching simulation to students in management science. During the last few years this course has also been taught to students in information systems; they have indeed been able to follow the statistical parts of this book. Though this book has a statistical emphasis, the authors are no statisticians: their education was in management science and econometrics. The simulation course is taught during 13 sessions of 90 minutes each; so the total course takes 19.5 lecture hours. Besides this textbook there is a 3.5 inch disk with a collection of exercises in Pascal. These can be used by the teacher for demonstration purposes during the lectures. The exercises on the disk are to be solved by the students, using whatever type of computer is available, and closely follow the chapters of the book. After doing the exercises, the student should be ready to start simulation projects in practice.

This text is an adaptation of a book originally published in Dutch under the title *Simulatie: technieken en toepassingen*, Academic Service, Schoonhoven, 1988.

We received many useful comments from Bert Bettonvil, Rommert Casimir, René van Nistelrooij, and Richard Veltman (all at the Katholieke Universiteit Brabant), Brian Ripley (University of Oxford), and Mark Johnson (University of Central Florida). We also acknowledge comments from Jerry Banks (Georgia Institute of Technology), David Kelton (University of Minnesota), H. Mollema (F&H), Bob Sargent (Syracuse University), Tom Schriber (University of Michigan), Rob Sierenberg (Sierenberg & de Gans), Bernd Brink and Kees Takkenberg (Katholieke Universiteit Brabant), and Jac Vennix (University of Utrecht). Their comments on earlier versions enabled us to remove many inaccuracies from the manuscript.

J. P. C. Kleijnen
W. J. H. van Groenendaal

Tilburg, January 1992

Chapter 1

Introduction

Chapter 1 is organized as follows.

—1.1 Some examples
  A few simple examples illustrate the type of problems that can be solved by means of simulation.
—1.2 Some definitions
  A number of concepts are defined to distinguish simulation from other methods and techniques.
—Appendix: Algorithms for the computation of estimated means, variances, and correlations.

The examples illustrate the following topics:

(1) macro-economic models;
(2) inventory models;
(3) management games;
(4) mathematical statistics;
(5) numerical integration;
(6) queuing models.

Sample surveys on the application of quantitative techniques in management show that in practice linear programming, simulation, and simple mathematical statistics are used most often, whereas more advanced techniques are hardly employed; see Ledbetter and Cox (1977).

1.1 SOME EXAMPLES

EXAMPLE 1.1: MACRO-ECONOMIC MODELS

We begin with a simple macro-economic model that consists of three equations, namely one equation for consumption C, one for investments I, and one for national income Y, given governmental expenditures G:

$$C_t = \beta_0 + \beta_1 Y_{t-1} \qquad (1.1)$$

$$I_t = \nu(Y_{t-1} - Y_{t-2}) \qquad (1.2)$$

$$Y_t = C_t + I_t + G_t. \qquad (1.3)$$

Suppose we know the coefficients β_0, β_1 (marginal consumption), and ν (accelerator), the values for future governmental expenditures G_t with $t = 1,2\ldots$ and the historical values Y_0 and Y_{-1}. Then we can use this model for straightforward calculation: substitution of Y_0 into (1.1) gives C_1; substitution of Y_0 and Y_{-1} into (1.2) gives I_1; substitution of C_1, I_1 and G_1 into (1.3) gives Y_1; in the next round, substitution of the computed value Y_1 into (1.1) leads to C_2, and so on. Obviously the calculation sequence is not arbitrary: first we calculate consumption and investments; only then can we determine income. So the sequence of solving the equations is important. Figure 1.1 gives the time path of income for one particular combination of coefficient values, governmental expenditures, and starting values. Figures 1.1 and 1.2 illustrate the effects

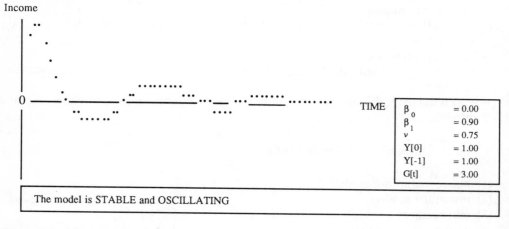

Figure 1.1 Macro-economic example

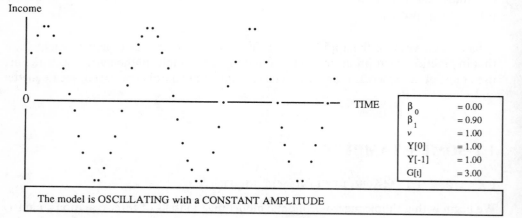

Figure 1.2 Macro-economic example; accelerator effect

of changing the accelerator coefficient ν from 0.75 to 1.00: the income oscillations change from a decreasing to a constant amplitude.

Equations (1.1) and (1.2) usually do not hold exactly, that is, in principle we should add disturbances or noise to these equations. The usual assumption is that this noise is distributed normally. In simulation we account for noise by sampling from the specified distribution for each period, and adding the sampled values to the expected values for consumption and investments respectively; that is, the model becomes

$$\underline{C}_t = \beta_0 + \beta_1 \underline{Y}_{t-1} + \underline{\epsilon}_t \tag{1.4}$$

$$\underline{I}_t = \nu(\underline{Y}_{t-1} - \underline{Y}_{t-2}) + \underline{\xi}_t \tag{1.5}$$

$$\underline{Y}_t = \underline{C}_t + \underline{I}_t + G_t \tag{1.6}$$

with $\underline{\epsilon}_t \sim N(0, \sigma_\epsilon^2)$ and $\underline{\xi}_t \sim N(0, \sigma_\xi^2)$, where the symbol $N(\mu, \sigma^2)$ represents a normal distribution with mean μ and variance σ^2, the symbol $\sim$ means 'distributed according to'; we underline stochastic variables. In Chapter 3 we shall show how to sample from a specific distribution; for the time being we suppose that lottery tickets are drawn for each period with the values for $\underline{\epsilon}_t$ and $\underline{\xi}_t$. Figure 1.3 gives one realization of the sample paths for the income Y_t, given the values of Figure 1.1 augmented with $\sigma_\epsilon^2 = \sigma_\xi^2 = 0.0625$.

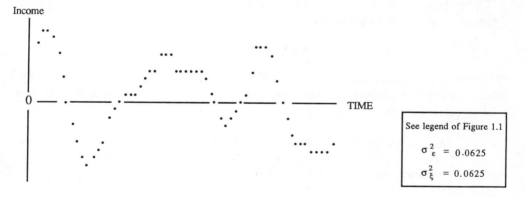

Figure 1.3   Macro-economic example, including noise

In Chapter 4 we shall discuss simultaneous equations. For example, suppose that consumption C_t depends on current income Y_t, not on previous income Y_{t-1}; see (1.1). At the same time, income Y_t depends on current consumption C_t as (1.3) showed. In Chapter 4 we shall also discuss micro-economic simulations; that is, individual consumers are simulated and the aggregation of their individual consumption values yields the macro-economic consumption C_t.

EXAMPLE 1.2: INVENTORY MODELS

Since the beginning of this century, inventory models have been applied to support managerial decision-making. For simple situations it is easy to derive the formula for the economic order quantity (EOQ):

$$\mathrm{EOQ} = \left[\frac{2 \times D \times k_3 \times (k_1 + k_2)}{k_1 \times k_2}\right]^{\frac{1}{2}},$$

(1.7)

where D denotes daily demand, k_1 denotes inventory costs per product unit per day, k_2 denotes stock-out costs per product unit, and k_3 denotes ordering costs per order. Simulation can be used to test if that formula also holds for more complex situations that have no analytic solution. In the flowchart of Figure 1.4 we assume random demand; more specifically $\underline{D} \sim N(\mu, \sigma^2)$. If the item is out of stock, the customer goes elsewhere (no backorders). The inventory level that triggers a new order is denoted by *ROP* (ReOrder Point). We assume that not more than one order can be in transit. The meaning of the other variables directly follows from the flowchart of Figure 1.4.

A 'run' of this simulation is a realization of the program from START to STOP in Figure 1.4. At the start of a run we should assign values to a number of variables; we set a number of variables to zero:

$$day := arrival\_day := stock := out\_of\_stock :=$$
$$inventory\_costs := order\_costs := 0.$$

We could also have started with a positive value for stock or with an order on its way. This initialization is not shown in Figure 1.4.

There are some more variables that must be initialized, because we wish to perform 'what-if' analysis and optimization. So we read:

$$\mu, \ \sigma, \ k_1, \ k_2, \ k_3, \ lead\_time, \ order, \ ROP, \ maxday.$$

We want to run the simulation model on a computer. Certain programming languages (such as Pascal) require that all variables be defined or 'declared' as being integer, real, and so on. So we define:

$k_1, k_2, k_3, stock, demand, order, ROP,$
$out\_of\_stock, inventory\_costs, order\_costs$: REAL
$maxday, day, lead\_time, arrival\_day$: INTEGER

Exercise 1.1: Why is *minus* $k_2 \times stock$ used in Figure 1.4 (after the question '*stock* > 0')?

Exercise 1.2: Why is stock made zero in Figure 1.4, after the out-of-stock costs have been booked?

Exercise 1.3: Does the variable *stock* in the upper part of Figure 1.4 represent physical or economic stock (= physical stock + order − backorder)?

Figure 1.5 displays one realization of the time path of physical inventory, given an expected demand of 80, a variance of 400, a fixed lead time of 4, an order size of 640 (8 days of expected demand), and a reorder point of 320.

We can simulate more complex inventory models. We can include, for example, quantity discounts and random lead times. We can also simulate more than one type of article, which results in joint or combined orders. Orders may not be purchased

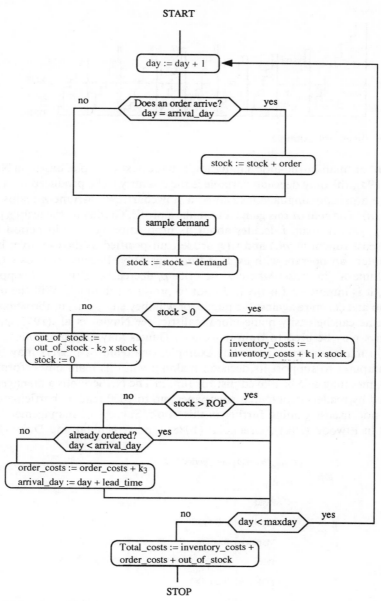

Figure 1.4 Inventory simulation

elsewhere but produced in the same organization, which leads to production planning and logistics systems. In Chapter 5 we shall return to inventory models.

EXAMPLE 1.3: MANAGEMENT GAMES

In a management game, players make decisions by assigning values to certain variables, whereupon the computer calculates the consequences of these decisions: 'man–machine

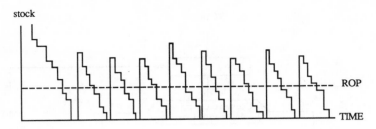

Figure 1.5 Inventory example

simulation' or 'man-in-the-loop simulation'. In the next example, based on Naylor et al. (1966, p. 199), the only decision variable is the quantity to be produced or X. In Figure 1.6 we use a pseudo-language instead of a flowchart. We assume n teams of players ($i = 1, \ldots, n$). The goal of this game is to make a profit. Guided by the team's past profits ($P_{it-1}, P_{it-2}, \ldots$), team i decides about its production volume in period t: X_{it}. The price and cost functions $p(.)$ and $C(.)$ are left unspecified in the example; in practice, the computer can operate with explicit functions only. Because the costs C_{it} increase as the volume X_{it} increases whereas the price p_t decreases as the total supply $\Sigma_{i=1}^{n} X_{it}$ increases, it is important for the team not to produce too much. Will the other teams see this too and conspire against the public, or will they engage in cut-throat competition?

This game can be easily made more realistic; see Naylor et al. (1966, pp. 205–15). Such games may be used to train managers. Games may also be applied to perform research in management science. For example, one team of players may be supplied with a computer to support its decision making: will this team outperform the other teams? Games may also be played just for fun: in The Netherlands a management game was played by readers of a Dutch newspaper; up to 5000 readers participated in 1985. We shall not discuss gaming further in this book. Surveys of management games can be found in Elwood (1981), Greenblat (1988), and Greenblat and Duke (1981).

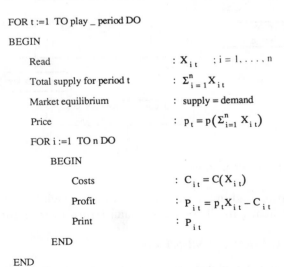

Figure 1.6 Management game

This type of gaming should not be confused with 'game theory' originated by Von Neumann and Morgenstern in the 1930s and further developed by mathematical economists. Their theory is mathematically advanced; it contains such concepts as 'zero-sum game', 'min–max strategy', 'core', and so on. We refer to Friedman (1986) and Owen (1982) for details.

EXAMPLE 1.4: MATHEMATICAL STATISTICS

To illustrate the application of simulation in statistical research, we consider the t statistic. First we assume that the variable $\underline{x}$ is distributed normally with mean μ and variance σ^2 and that there are $n > 1$ independent observations $\underline{x}_i$ $(i = 1, \ldots, n)$. Then it is well-known that the Student t statistic with $n - 1$ degrees of freedom is defined as follows:

$$\underline{t}_{n-1} = \frac{(\underline{\tilde{x}} - \mu)}{\underline{s}/\sqrt{n}} \quad \text{with} \quad \overline{x} = \frac{1}{n} \sum_{i=1}^{n} x_i \quad \text{and} \quad \underline{s}^2 = \frac{\sum_{1}^{n} (\underline{x}_i - \overline{x})^2}{(n-1)}. \tag{1.8}$$

Now we want to know what happens if $\underline{x}$ is distributed not normally but (say) *uniformly* on the interval from 0 to 1: $\underline{x} \sim U(0,1)$. We are especially interested in the tail behaviour for 'large samples':

> How large does n need to be so that $P(|\underline{t}_{n-1}| > t_{n-1}^{\alpha/2})$ is approximately equal to α, if $\underline{x} \sim U(0,1)$? $\hspace{2cm}$ (1.9)

To investigate this problem we execute the procedure of Figure 1.7. Note that in Figure 1.7 we do not save individual observations x_i: to calculate the variance estimate s^2, we use an elementary mathematical relationship:

$$s^2 = \left(\sum_{i=1}^{n} x_i^2 - n\overline{x}^2 \right) / (n-1). \tag{1.10}$$

The numerical accuracy of various expressions for s^2 is discussed in the appendix. We emphasize that we first estimate the mean $E(\underline{x})$ through $a\underline{x}$; next we use the true value 0.5 to calculate t_{n-1}. The variable 'count' shows how many times the variable $\underline{t}$ has a 'significant' value, that is $|\underline{t}_{n-1}| > t_{n-1}^{\alpha/2}$ where $t_{n-1}^{\alpha/2}$ is the $1 - \alpha/2$ quantile, which is tabulated and is the input of the computer program. If we may indeed use the t distribution, then (say) $\alpha = 0.05$ and $r = 1000$ 'macroreplications' should give a value for 'count' close to $0.05 \times 1000 = 50$.

Through the binomial distribution we can test if the realized value of 'count' is acceptable, as the next exercise demonstrates.

Exercise 1.4: Suppose that after 1000 macroreplications (each with n observations x_i) the count is 40. Should we reject $H_0 : E(\underline{\hat{\alpha}}) = \alpha = 0.05$? (Use the normal distribution to approximate the binomial distribution.)

Table 1.1 gives sampling results when Figure 1.7 is repeated for different sample sizes: $n = 2$, 6, and 12. Obviously as n increases, the t distribution holds better.

In Chapter 7 we shall return to statistical applications.

```
                BEGIN
                  count := 0 ;
                  α := 0.05;
                  DO r times
                     BEGIN
                       vx := 0; ax := 0;
                       DO n times
                         BEGIN
                           Sample x from U (0,1);
                           Calculate : ax := ax + x;
                                       vx : = vx +x*x
                         END;
                       Calculate: ax   := ax/n;
                              vx   := (vx-n*ax*ax) / (n-1);
                              t     := (ax-0.5) /sqrt (vx/n);
                               n-1
                       IF ABS (t    ) > t α    THEN count := count+1
                       END;        n-1    n-1
                  WRITELN ('Number of significant values ', count :8,' expected ' , α*r:8:0)
                END.
```

Figure 1.7 The *t*-test

Table 1.1 Effect of sample size *n* on fraction of significant *t* values ($\alpha = 0.10$)

n	Fraction
2	0.243*
6	0.148*
12	0.115

*Significant deviation from 0.10, since the 10% critical values are 0.08439 and 0.11561.

EXAMPLE 1.5: NUMERICAL INTEGRATION

The next example shows how the value of an integral can be estimated. We consider a circle with radius one. Of course we know that the area of such a circle equals the number π:

$$\iint\limits_{x_1^2 + x_2^2 \leqslant 1} dx_1 \, dx_2 = \pi. \tag{1.11}$$

But we can also estimate this double integral through the program of Figure 1.8. Each call of the function RANDOM yields an independent observation of a variable uniformly distributed between zero and one. It is simple to prove that $x = 2 \times \text{RANDOM} - 1$ is uniformly distributed between -1 and 1. So each pair (x_1, x_2) determines a point in the square of Figure 1.8; each point has the same probability. If that point falls within

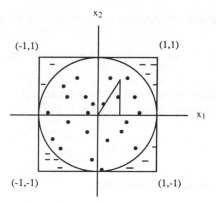

- pair (x_1, x_2) inside circle
- pair (x_1, x_2) outside circle

```
PROGRAM circle ;

VAR  x1, x2     : REAL ;
     count, r,i : INTEGER ;

BEGIN
  RANDOMIZE;
  count := 0; r := 1000;
  FOR i:=1 TO r DO
      BEGIN
        x1 := 2*RANDOM-1;
        x2 := 2*RANDOM-1;
        IF (sqrt(x1*x1+x2*x2) ≤ 1) THEN  count := count+1
      END;
  WRITELN ('The estimated area of the circle is',4*count/r:8:5);
  READLN
END
```

Figure 1.8 Numerical integration: estimate π

the unit circle (that is $x_1^2 + x_2^2 \leqslant 1$), we score a 'success' and augment the variable called *count*. To estimate the success probability p, this count is divided by the total number of times a point has been calculated. Because the area of the square equals four, the estimated area of the unit circle equals $4\hat{p}$. So the estimate of π is $4\hat{p}$.

Exercise 1.5: Make the algorithm more efficient by considering the first quadrant only.

In a similar way we can estimate the area of a lake on a map. The map forms a rectangle with a known area. We sample points within that rectangle such that each point has the same probability. We determine whether the sampled point falls within the lake (humans can do this easily, whereas computers cannot). After a number of replications, we estimate the probability of a point falling within the lake. The estimated area of the lake is then the product of this probability and the area of the total map.

   Obviously this approach can be extended to estimate the volume of an irregularly shaped three-dimensional body. The approach can be further extended to n dimensions. We do not always sample variables uniformly, as the next example illustrates.

In certain inventory problems the following integral must be computed:

$$\xi(\lambda, \sigma) = \int_{\nu}^{\infty} \frac{1}{x} \lambda e^{-\lambda x} dx \qquad \text{with } \lambda > 0, \quad \nu > 0. \tag{1.12}$$

In Chapter 3 we shall see that there is a subroutine for sampling from the exponential distribution with parameter λ, which is defined by

$$f(x) = \begin{cases} \lambda e^{-\lambda x} & \text{if } x > 0 \\ 0 & \text{if } x \leqslant 0. \end{cases} \tag{1.13}$$

The sampled value x is substituted into

$$g(x) = \begin{cases} 0 & \text{if } x < \nu \\ 1/x & \text{if } x \geqslant \nu. \end{cases} \tag{1.14}$$

Defining $g(x)$ this way means that its expected value is (1.12). After r samples from the exponential distribution (1.13) and substitution into (1.14), we compute the estimator

$$\hat{\xi}(\lambda, \nu) = \frac{\sum\limits_{i=1}^{r} g(\underline{x}_i)}{r}. \tag{1.15}$$

For further details we refer to Kleijnen (1968).

In the remainder of this book we shall not return to purely mathematical problems such as the estimation of multiple integrals. A classic reference is Hammersley and Handscomb (1964).

EXAMPLE 1.6: QUEUING MODELS

Because the simulation of queuing models is relatively difficult, we defer the discussion of the technique itself to Chapters 5 and 6. Here we only mention a few applications.

(1) Post-offices, gas stations and other service systems are often studied by simulation. The purpose of such studies is to balance the waiting times of customers and the idle times of resources (personnel and machines).
(2) Factories may have work centres with several machines that perform operations either successively or simultaneously. Such systems are investigated in job shop scheduling, flexible manufacturing systems (FMS) and logistics.
(3) The processing of jobs or tasks by the central processing unit (CPU) of a computer is often studied by simulation.
(4) Street intersections are simulated to investigate the effects of traffic lights on traffic flows.
(5) In project planning it is important to have the right materials in the right place at the right time. Simple planning can be done by techniques such as the program evaluation and review technique (PERT) and the critical path method (CPM). Simulation was used to plan the construction of a major storm surge barrier in The Netherlands (the so-called 'Delta Werken' project).

1.2 SOME DEFINITIONS

Next we shall describe a few concepts needed to define simulation and the Monte Carlo method. We do not intend to give rigorous definitions.

A *system* is a set of elements, which are also called objects or components. These elements are characterized by their attributes. Each attribute may have a logical or a numerical value. Among these elements there are relationships. But relationships do not have to be limited to elements within the system; they can also refer to the environment of a system. Another characteristic of systems is that, over time, they transform the input variables x_t into the output variables y_t. The input can also consist of the delayed output y_{t-1}; see Figure 1.9.

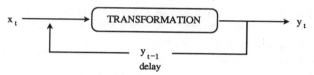

Figure 1.9 A system view

An example of a system is a factory. Its system elements are machines, employees, orders, and so on. The operation of a machine is an example of an internal relationship: that operation needs employees and orders. An example of an external relationship is provided by tax legislation that affects the results of the company. Examples of input variables x in Figure 1.9 are raw materials and components purchased outside the company. Examples of (delayed) output variables y are components that the company produces and that it processes itself, but also sells to other companies.

Each system can be viewed as part of a larger system. So the manufacturing company is part of the national economy, and this economy can again be regarded as a system. Conversely, each system can be split up into smaller systems. So a department of the manufacturing company can be considered as a system; in that case the rest of the company becomes the environment of the system. Thus the possibilities are countless. It is the researcher who determines the system boundary!

A second concept we shall use is that of a *model*. In principle, a model is anything that represents something else. This definition is so broad that statues and paintings are included. Therefore we introduce the concept of an abstract model. This is a model in the form of mathematical equations, a flowchart, or a computer program. Section 1.1 showed examples for each method of representation. Examples of non-abstract or physical models are a toy car and a plane in a wind tunnel. We will not consider physical simulators such as Link trainers for pilots. So in the following we restrict ourselves to abstract models.

For a complicated system we construct a model that describes only those aspects that seem relevant for the questions asked by the user; for example, we model only economic aspects. Next we study the response of the model to changes in the input. We can also analyse the sensitivity of the model to changes in the relationships among the model elements. Also see Examples 1 and 2 in Section 1.1.

Obviously a model should resemble the corresponding system. The elements of a system are represented by the so-called endogenous variables in the model. The inputs of the system are the exogenous variables or the delayed variables of the model. Relationships between variables may be represented by means of mathematical equations. A behavioural equation shows how the variables react to changes in other endogenous and exogenous variables; behavioural equations are characterized by parameters. A *parameter* is different from a variable in that a parameter is not directly observable. In practice the values for the parameters may be obtained by means of estimation, which requires statistical methods. In Example 1 the endogenous variables are Y_t, C_t and I_t; an exogenous variable is G_t; and the parameters are β_0, β_1 and ν. In Example 2 the reorder point ROP is a variable, and the inventory cost per product unit k_1 is a parameter. In queuing models the arrival rate is a parameter, and the time of arrival is a variable; the priority rule is a behavioural equation.

We further distinguish between stochastic or *random* models and *deterministic* models. For example, the inventory simulation in Figure 1.4 is random; the macro-economic model of (1.1) through (1.3) is deterministic. We will focus on random models, but will not entirely exclude deterministic models.

There are two types of solutions for models, namely *analytic* solutions, which use differential and integral calculus, and *numerical* solutions such as linear programming, the Gauss–Seidel and the Newton algorithms for systems of equations. Simulation is also a numerical technique. The numerical approach should be applied only if it is impossible to find an analytic solution. In practice, numerical solutions must often be used!

We speak of a *Monte Carlo* method whenever the solution makes use of random numbers, which are uniformly and independently distributed over the interval from zero to one. We speak of *simulation* whenever the model has a time dimension (the model is called dynamic), and it is solved numerically. The t test and the estimation of π in Examples 4 and 5 are Monte Carlo experiments; simulation examples are the macro-economic model, the inventory model, and the management game in Examples 1, 2 and 3 respectively. The stochastic macro-economic model in (1.4)–(1.6) and the inventory model in Example 2 combine both methods; such a combination may be called Monte Carlo or stochastic simulation.

A list of advantages and disadvantages of simulation and Monte Carlo methods can be found in Naylor et al. (1966, pp. 4–9). The most important *disadvantage* is characteristic for all numerical methods: these methods do not yield an explicit functional relationship among the output variables, the input variables, and the parameters. Therefore numerical methods require sensitivity or 'what-if' analysis. In simulation this analysis requires many runs of the computer program. An additional disadvantage of the Monte Carlo method is that its inherent sampling creates noise; therefore the experiment should be repeated many times. We shall return to sensitivity analysis, optimization, and sample-size determination. The most important *advantages* of simulation and Monte Carlo methods are: no advanced mathematics is required, and realistic models become possible.

APPENDIX: ALGORITHMS FOR THE COMPUTATION OF ESTIMATED MEANS, VARIANCES, AND CORRELATIONS

We discuss the numerical accuracy of different algorithms for the computation of estimated means, variances, and correlation coefficients. Double precision is always a simple and effective way to increase the accuracy. First we consider $\bar{x}$, the sample average, which estimates the population mean (say μ). Its computation is robust. If observations x_i become available sequentially (as they usually do in simulation), then a useful formula is

$$\bar{x}_i = \{\bar{x}_{i-1}(i-1)/i\} + x_i/i \qquad \text{with } i = 1, 2, \ldots, n \quad \text{and} \quad x_0 = 1. \tag{A.1}$$

The unbiased estimator of the variance (say) σ^2 is $SS/(n-1)$, and the maximum likelihood estimator is SS/n, where $SS = \Sigma_1^n(x_i - \bar{x}_n)^2$ is called the sum of squares about the mean. Inaccurate results tend to occur for the computational formula

$$SS = \sum_{1}^{n} x_i^2 - n\bar{x}_n\bar{x}_n,$$

unless double precision is used. Note that this formula is the one used in Figure 1.7. To obtain more accurate results, a two-pass algorithm can be used: first compute $\bar{x}_n$; next compute

$$SS_n = \sum_{i=1}^{n} (x_i - \bar{x}_n)^2. \tag{A.2}$$

The formula for updating SS is

$$SS_i = SS_{i-1} + (x_i - \bar{x}_{i-1})^2(i-1)/i \quad \text{and} \quad SS_0 = 0. \tag{A.3}$$

The correlation coefficient $\rho = \text{cov}(\underline{x}, \underline{y})/(\sigma_x \sigma_y)$ can be estimated by

$$\hat{\rho} = \frac{\displaystyle\sum_{i=1}^{n} (x_i - \bar{x}_n)(y_i - \bar{y}_n)}{(SS_x)(SS_y)}, \tag{A.4}$$

where SS_x equals SS_n computed by (A.2) or (A.3); SS_y is defined analogously. Inaccurate results tend to occur if the numerator of $\hat{\rho}$, say $\hat{\gamma}$, is computed as

$$\hat{\gamma} = \sum_{i=1}^{n} (x_i y_i) - \left(\sum_{i=1}^{n} x_i\right)\left(\sum_{i=1}^{n} y_i\right)\bigg/n, \tag{A.5}$$

unless double precision is used. The updating formula for the numerator of $\hat{\rho}$ is analogous to (A.3):

$$\hat{\gamma}_i = \hat{\gamma}_{i-1} + (x_i - \bar{x}_{i-1})(y_i - \bar{y}_{i-1})(i-1)/i \quad \text{and} \quad \gamma_0 = 0. \tag{A.6}$$

Note that $\underline{x}$ and $\underline{x} - c$ have the same variance. In Monte Carlo simulation $E(\underline{x})$ is often known, so $c = E(\underline{x})$ can be used. Obviously $\underline{x}$ and $\underline{y}$ have the same covariance and correlation as $\underline{x} + c_1$ and $\underline{y} + c_2$ have. Some alternative formulae and more discussion can be found in Cooke, Craven and Clarke (1985, p. 54) and Neely (1966).

REFERENCES

Cooke D., A. H. Craven and G. M. Clarke (1985) *Statistical Computing in PASCAL*, Edward Arnold, London.

Elwood C. (1981) *Handbook of Management Games* (2nd edn), Gower, Aldershot.

Friedman J. W. (1986) *Game Theory with Applications to Economics*, Oxford University Press, New York.

Greenblat C. S. (1988) *Designing Games and Simulations: an Illustrated Handbook*, Sage Publications, Newbury Park, California.

Greenblat C. S. and R. D. Duke (1981) *Principles and Practice of Gaming-simulation*, Sage Publications, Beverly Hills.

Hammersley J. M. and D. C. Handscomb (1964) *Monte Carlo Methods*, Wiley, New York.

Kleijnen J. P. C. (1968) Een toepassing van 'importance sampling' (An application of 'importance sampling'), *Statistica Neerlandica*, **22**(3), 179–98.

Ledbetter W. H. and J. F. Cox (1977) Operations research in production management: an investigation of past and present utilization, *Production and Inventory Management*, **18**(3), Third Quarter, 84–92.

Naylor T. H., J. L. Balintfy, D. S. Burdick, and Kong Chu (1966) *Computer Simulation Techniques*, Wiley, New York.

Neely P. M. (1966) Comparison of Several Algorithms for Computation of Means, Standard Deviations, and Correlations Coefficients, *Communications of the ACM*, **9**, 496–9.

Owen G. (1982) *Game Theory* (2nd edn), Academic Press, New York.

Random Numbers

Chapter 2 is organized as follows.

—2.1 Introduction
We give the mathematical definition of 'random numbers'.
—2.2 Techniques for generating random numbers
We survey practical techniques for random number generation: dice throwing and other physical devices, tables, and pseudorandom number generators.
—2.3 Pseudorandom numbers
Different mathematical techniques for pseudorandom number generation are discussed in separate subsections: midsquare method, congruential method, additive congruential method, Tausworthe generators, shuffling generators.
—2.4 Tests for pseudorandom numbers
We briefly discuss the lattice structure of certain generators. In separate subsections we present statistical procedures for testing whether the pseudorandom numbers are indeed uniformly distributed and do not have certain types of dependence.
—2.5 Practical computer subroutines
We examine NAG subroutines, and briefly discuss IMSL and personal computer generators.

2.1 INTRODUCTION

We assume that the reader has an intuitive idea of such concepts as chance, odds, luck, and law of nature. Exact definitions can lead to much controversy. For example, in probability theory chance or probability has been defined not only in an objective, frequentist way but also in a subjective, Bayesian way. And in physics, Einstein exclaimed that God does not throw dice, whereas advocates of quantum mechanics use probability to explain the behaviour of particles.

Let us illustrate the problems involved in the concept of chance. For an 'ideal' die the classical statistical model states that the probability that face i with $i = 1, \ldots, 6$ shows up equals $1/6$. However, when we take into account the angle at which the die is thrown, the surface on which it is thrown, and so on, then we get a whole range of possible models, besides the classical model: Zeigler (1976) developed ten different models for throwing a die! In the remainder of this book, however, all we need is the statistical concept of a random number.

A *random number* is a stochastic variable that meets certain conditions (all types of stochastic variables are often called random variables in the statistics literature; in simulation, however, we find such a terminology misleading). These conditions are: (1) the variable is uniformly distributed over the interval from zero to one, and (2) a sequence of these variables shows statistical independence. Let us consider these two conditions in detail.

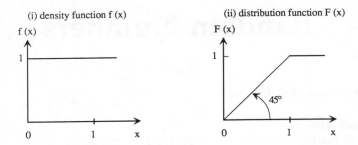

Figure 2.1 Random numbers x

(1) As Figure 2.1(i) illustrates, the random number x has a density function (say) $f(x)$ such that

$$f(x) = \begin{cases} 1 & \text{on the interval } [0,1) \\ 0 & \text{elsewhere.} \end{cases} \tag{2.1}$$

This density function corresponds with the (cumulative) distribution function $F(x)$ shown in Figure 2.1(ii). So

$$F(x) = \int_0^x f(z)\,dz = \int_0^x 1\,dz = x \qquad \text{if } 0 \leqslant x < 1, \tag{2.2a}$$

$$F(x) = 0 \qquad \text{if } x < 0, \tag{2.2b}$$

$$F(x) = 1 \qquad \text{if } x \geqslant 1. \tag{2.2c}$$

(2) The n elements of the sequence $x_1, x_2, \ldots, x_n$ with $n = 2, 3, \ldots$ are statistically independent. So their simultaneous or joint distribution F_n may be written as the product of their marginal distributions $F(x)$, which were given in (2.2a) through (2.2c). So $P(x_1 \leqslant x_1,\ x_2 \leqslant x_2, \ldots, x_n \leqslant x_n) = F_n(x_1, x_2, \ldots, x_n) = F(x_1) F(x_2) \cdots F(x_n)$, which yields

$$F_n(x_1, x_2, \ldots, x_n) = x_1 x_2 \cdots x_n \qquad \text{if } \forall\, x_i: 0 \leqslant x_i < 1 \tag{2.3a}$$

$$F_n(x_1, x_2, \ldots, x_n) = 0 \qquad \text{if } \exists\, x_i < 0 \tag{2.3b}$$

$$F_n(x_1, x_2, \ldots, x_n) = x_2 \cdots x_n \qquad \text{if } x_1 \geqslant 1, \tag{2.3c}$$

$$= x_1 x_3 \cdots x_n \qquad \text{if } x_2 \geqslant 1,$$

$$\vdots \qquad\qquad \vdots$$

$$= x_1 x_2 \cdots x_{n-1} \qquad \text{if } x_n \geqslant 1.$$

Statistical independence implies that knowledge about x_1 does not give any information about x_2. So the conditional distribution equals the marginal distribution: $P(\underline{x}_2 \leqslant x_2 | \underline{x}_1 \leqslant x_1) = P(\underline{x}_2 \leqslant x_2) = F(x_2)$.

We usually represent the stochastic variable that meets the conditions (1) and (2) by the symbol $\underline{r}$, which stands for random number. So random numbers are uniformly and independently distributed over the interval $[0, 1)$.

2.2 TECHNIQUES FOR GENERATING RANDOM NUMBERS

Equations (2.2) and (2.3) give a statistical model, that is, they define an ideal. But how are random numbers obtained in practice? We present five techniques.

2.2.1 The Ten-sided Die

By means of a ten-sided die with faces numbered $0, 1, \ldots, 9$ we can generate numbers with the desired accuracy; each decimal requires one throw.

2.2.2 Throwing a Coin

We assign the value 1 to (say) the head of a coin and the value 0 to the tail. Now we throw the coin n times, place the resulting n binary digits (bits) one after the other, and form a binary number of n bits. Dividing this number by $2^n - 1$ gives a decimal number between 0 and 1. In this way we can generate 2^n different random numbers. For example, for $n = 3$ the set of eight different binary numbers is

$$B = \{000, 001, 010, 011, 100, 101, 110, 111\}.$$

When we divide the elements of set B by the decimal number $2^3 - 1 = 7$ (its binary representation is 111), we get eight possible random numbers. All these numbers have equal probability, if the probability of heads is $1/2$.

2.2.3 Other Physical Devices

It is possible to construct more complicated mechanical devices (for example, wheels of fortune) and electronic devices; for example, Inoue et al. (1983, p. 115) utilize 'gamma rays emitted from radioactive nuclide'.

A disadvantage of these mechanical and electronic devices is that the resulting sequence of numbers is not *reproducible*. Reproducibility is important for debugging the simulation program: upon adjusting the computer program and feeding in the same numbers, the program should yield good results. Moreover reproducibility may be used to reduce the variance of the simulation output, as we shall see in a later chapter. Finally, reproducibility permits other researchers to repeat our simulation experiment. Physical devices can generate reproducible simulation output if their resulting random numbers are stored. This leads to the following technique.

2.2.4 Tables

The Rand Corporation (1955) published a table with one million random digits. Obviously the Rand Corporation had to apply one of the other techniques to construct this table. Such a table can be used to obtain random numbers: to form a number of (say) ten decimals, take ten digits from this table; to get the next number take the next ten digits. For simplicity's sake digits can be taken starting at the upper left corner and proceeding to the right; at the end of the first line the first digit on the second line is taken, and so on. Many other 'paths' through the table are permitted. Manual simulations indeed use tables with random digits. Such tables are found in books on mathematical statistics and operations research, especially older books. The examples in the preceding chapter, however, demonstrate that a simulation program needs many random numbers if accurate output is required. Therefore manual simulation has been replaced by computer simulation. Tables could then be replaced by their computerized version. For example, Inoue et al. (1983) can supply a magnetic tape with 100 million random digits generated by their 'radioactive' physical device. Magnetic tapes and disks, however, often create computer problems. For example, a particular computer may not be able to read this tape. Moreover, reading from secondary external memory is slow compared with reading from main memory. Storing the contents of a tape or disk in main memory takes too much space. Therefore, from the very beginning of computer simulation, the following technique has been used.

2.2.5 Pseudorandom Numbers

Digital computers gave rise to a number of techniques that use a recursive mathematical relation; that is, the number r_i is a function of the preceding numbers $r_{i-1}, r_{i-2}, \ldots$. Because the relation is deterministic, these numbers are not really random: they are called pseudorandom. However, if the mathematical relation is not known and is well chosen, then it is practically impossible to predict the next number. For example, can the reader guess what r_6 is, given $r_0 = 0.13$, $r_1 = 0.21$, $r_2 = 0.57$, $r_3 = 0.69$, $r_4 = 0.73$, and $r_5 = 0.41$? (The solution will be given in Section 2.3.2.) We now consider this technique in more detail.

2.3 PSEUDORANDOM NUMBERS

In this section we discuss several mathematical techniques for pseudorandom number generation. We give only short descriptions, as new techniques are invented virtually every day. For more extensive discussions we refer to surveys by James (1990), L'Ecuyer (1990), and Ripley (1990). We shall give additional references in each subsection.

2.3.1 Midsquare Method

The midsquare method was invented by the famous scientist John von Neumann in the 1940s. Assume a starting number x_0 that consists of m digits. When we square x_0, we get a number with up to $2m$ digits; if the squared number has fewer than $2m$ digits, we add zeros to the front. To obtain the next number x_1 we take the middle m digits of x_0^2. To get a number in the interval $[0, 1)$, we divide x_1 by 10^m. Repeating this procedure gives the sequence $(x_i: i = 0, 1, \ldots)$. Unfortunately not all 10^m numbers occur, as the next example illustrates.

EXAMPLE 2.1: MIDSQUARE METHOD

For simplicity's sake we take m as small as two. Hence the largest number is 99, so at most 100 different numbers can result. Let us take the starting number 23. Then we obtain the following results.

x	x^2	r
23	0529	0.52
52	2704	0.70
70	4900	0.90
90	8100	0.10
10	0100	0.10, and so on.

So the starting number 23 gets this method stuck on the 'random' number 0.10, after only four steps. Other starting numbers also give bad results. Therefore this method is no longer much applied, even though there are a number of variations that show better behaviour; see Landauer (1984) and Marsaglia (1985).

2.3.2 Congruential Method

Nowadays the congruential method is most popular. Let **N** represent the set of natural numbers (nonnegative integers). Let mod stand for modulo, so (x) mod m means that x is divided by m and the remainder is taken as result; for example, 13 mod 4 = 1. Now consider the relation

$$n_{i+1} = (an_i + b) \bmod m \qquad \text{with } n_0, a, b, m \in \mathbf{N}; \quad i = 0, 1, 2, \ldots, m-1. \quad (2.4)$$

The initial number n_0 is called the seed, 'a' the multiplier, b the additive constant, and m the modulo. The modulo operation in (2.4) means that at most m different numbers can be generated—namely the integers $0, 1, \ldots, m-1$. The actual maximum, say, $h(h \leqslant m)$ is called the *cycle length* or *period* of the generator.

EXAMPLE 2.2: CONGRUENTIAL METHOD

Selecting $a = 17$, $b = 0$, $m = 100$, $n_0 = 13$ in (2.4) gives a cycle length of 20:

i: 0 1 2 3 4 5 6 7 8 9 10 11 12 13 14 15 16 17 18 19 20

n_i: 13 21 57 69 73 41 97 49 33 61 37 29 93 81 77 9 53 1 17 89 13

The pseudorandom numbers r $(0 \leqslant r < 1)$ result from

$$r_i = \frac{n_i}{m}, \qquad (2.5)$$

Exercise 2.1: Why do equations (2.4) and (2.5) lead to the symbols $\leqslant$ and $<$ in $0 \leqslant r < 1$?

Exercise 2.2: Prove that the recursive relation in (2.4) implies that n_i is related to the seed n_0 as follows: $n_i = \left(a^i n_0 + \dfrac{b(a^i - 1)}{(a - 1)} \right) \bmod m$.

When the additive constant b is zero, the generator is called *multiplicative*; otherwise it is called a *mixed* generator.

A congruential generator produces all m different numbers (and thus has maximum cycle length), only if the constants a, b, m and n_0 meet a number of requirements. For example, the cycle length is m, independent of n_0, provided $a = 4d + 1$ with an arbitrary positive number d, b is odd, and $m = 2^k$. This example implies that a multiplicative generator ($b = 0$) never has a maximum cycle of length m. Actually, its maximum cycle length is $m/4$, provided $a = 3 \bmod 8$ or $5 \bmod 8$, n_0 is odd, and $m = 2^k \geqslant 16$. If m is a prime number (so $m \neq 2^k$), then a maximum cycle of $m - 1$ is possible. The selection of m is usually determined by the computer that the generator is implemented on. For a binary machine that operates on words of k bits, m is often chosen to be 2^k. An advantage of such a choice is that dividing by m in (2.5) reduces to subtraction in the exponent. Selecting m equal to $2^k - 1$ or $2^k + 1$ may yield a prime number m (which results in a longer cycle); its implementation is hardly more complicated than that of 2^k. For details we refer to Bratley, Fox and Schrage (1983), Fishman (1978), Park and Miller (1988), and Ripley (1987, p. 22).

So the constants a, b and m should meet certain mathematical conditions in order to realize a long cycle. There are several more requirements, which were explained in Section 2.2:

(1) Truly random numbers are uniformly distributed on the interval $[0, 1)$. Pseudorandom numbers should approximate this ideal. We shall return to this issue.
(2) Truly random numbers are statistically independent.
(3) The numbers must be reproducible.
(4) The generator must be fast, because the simulation program calls the generator very frequently.
(5) The memory size needed to implement the generator, must be small and independent of the simulation sample size.

The constants a, b and m have important effects on the independence of the pseudorandom numbers. For example, consider the correlation between $\underline{r}_i$ and $\underline{r}_{i+1}$, say ρ_1. It can be proved that

$$\rho_1 \approx (1/a) - (6b/am)(1 - b/m) \pm a/m, \tag{2.6}$$

where $\approx$ stands for 'approximately equal to'. So $a = 2^{34} + 1$, $b = 1$ and $m = 2^{35}$ yields $\rho_1 \approx 2^{-1}$, whereas $a = 2^{18} + 1$ gives $\rho_1 < 2^{-18}$; see Morgan (1984, p. 60). Notice that these two generators have full cycle lengths. We shall return to the independence issue.

A congruential generator implies sampling without replacement, since all h numbers within one cycle are different. Moreover, the continuous variable $\underline{r}$ has been made discrete: Figure 2.1(ii) becomes a step function with vertical steps of height $1/h$. For practical purposes these complications may be ignored.

The reader may skip the next two subsections, which discuss two special types of generators that are not essential for the remainder of this chapter. Optional subsections are denoted by an asterisk.

*2.3.3 Additive Congruential Method

The additive congruential method is defined by

$$n_{i+1} = (n_i + n_{i-k}) \bmod m. \tag{2.7}$$

This method can yield a cycle longer than m, because the pair (n_i, n_{i-k}) must be reproduced; it does not suffice that either n_i or n_{i-k} is reproduced. Furthermore, n_0 and n_{0-k} are not necessarily equal to n_m and n_{m-k}. For $k=1$ (2.7) is called the *Fibonacci method*. The additive congruential method has certain disadvantages. For example, the Fibonacci method yields an n_{i+1} that can never lie in the interval (n_{i-1}, n_i). Another disadvantage is that there may be simple relationships between the resulting numbers; for example, choosing $m = 2^{31}$, $k = 1$, $n_0 = 1$ and $n_{-1} = 2$ yields $3, 5, 8, 13, 21 \ldots$, or $n_i = n_{i-1} + n_{i-2}$. In practice, the Fibonacci method is no longer much applied. Nevertheless, applications of (2.7) have been developed that behave better; one example is the generator $n_{i+1} = (n_i + n_{i-97}) \bmod 2^{35}$; see Marsaglia (1985) and Oakenfull (1979).

*2.3.4 Tausworthe Generators

Tausworthe or shift-register generators are of a quite different type; see Tausworthe (1965). These generators operate on bits:

$$b_i = \left(\sum_{j=1}^{q} c_j b_{i-j} \right) \bmod 2, \tag{2.8}$$

with $c_q = 1$ and $c_j \in \{0, 1\}$ for $j = 1, 2, \ldots, q-1$, with at least one $c_j \neq 0$. In practice, Tausworthe generators are mostly of the simpler form

$$b_i = (b_{i-h} + b_{i-q}) \bmod 2, \tag{2.9}$$

with $0 < h < q$. The first q bits b_i must be specified, which is analogous to specifying the seed for other generators. The maximum period of the bits is $2^q - 1$. An important advantage of Tausworthe generators is that they are independent of the word size of the computer. Note that addition modulo 2 is equivalent to the 'exclusive or' (EOR) instruction, which is defined by 0 EOR 0 = 0, 0 EOR 1 = 1, 1 EOR 0 = 1, 1 EOR 1 = 0.

EXAMPLE 2.3: TAUSWORTHE GENERATOR

Suppose that in (2.9) we take $h = 3$, $q = 5$, and $b_1 = b_2 = b_3 = b_4 = b_5 = 1$. Then $b_6 = (b_3 + b_1) \bmod 2 = 2 \bmod 2 = 0$, and so on. The first 42 bits b_j are

$$111110001101110101000010010110011111000110.$$

The period of the bits is indeed $2^q - 1 = 31$.

To derive random numbers from such a sequence of bits, we may cut that sequence into adjacent strings of length (say) k with $0 < k < q$ to form a k-bit binary integer, and divide these integers by 2^k (see also the discussion on throwing a coin in Section 2.2). In the example, $k = 4$ yields $\frac{15}{16}$ (note $1111 = 15$), $\frac{8}{16}$ (as $1000 = 8$), $\frac{13}{16}$ (as $1101 = 13$), and so on. However, there are more sophisticated bit-selection procedures; see Fishman (1978, pp. 387–90) and Ripley (1987, pp. 26–33). The latter author lists combinations of h and q with $q \leqslant 36$ that give the maximum period $2^q - 1$.

2.3.5 Shuffling Generators

Many procedures have been invented to improve the statistical behaviour of a sequence of pseudorandom numbers. For example, a second generator can be used to *shuffle* the results of the first generator. So the first generator yields $r_1 \ldots r_{100}$; these results are stored. The second generator yields pseudorandom numbers (say) $u_1 \ldots u_{100}$ that determine which result of generator 1 is used as the next number. For example, if the integer part of $100u_1 + 1$ is 3, then r_3 is selected first. Fishman (1978, pp. 386–7) and Ripley (1987, pp. 42–3) give several forms of shuffling. A practical disadvantage is that the generation of pseudorandom numbers becomes slower. Another disadvantage is that the theoretical analysis of such generators becomes more difficult.

2.4 TESTS FOR PSEUDORANDOM NUMBERS

The most important reason for shuffling pseudorandom numbers (see Section 2.3.5) is the removal of possible dependencies. When r_i and r_j are indeed distributed uniformly and independently, then the pair (r_i, r_j) is distributed uniformly over the square $[0, 1) \times [0, 1)$. Figure 2.2 displays the pairs (r_0, r_1), (r_1, r_2), (r_2, r_3), $\ldots$, (r_{h-1}, r_h) for a simple generator. These pairs turn out to lie on only a few parallel lines. This is a serious deficiency of the generator. A necessary but not sufficient condition for acceptance of a generator is that its pairs lie on *many* parallel lines.

We may also form three-tuples: (r_0, r_1, r_2), (r_1, r_2, r_3), (r_2, r_3, r_4), $\ldots$. Then Figure 2.2 becomes three-dimensional, and the three-tuples turn out to lie on a few planes. And n-tuples with $n > 3$ lead to hyperplanes. The *lattice* and the *spectral tests* are sophisticated procedures to determine how dense the n-tuples lie within the unit hypercube $[0, 1)^n$. These two procedures evaluate the full cycle of pseudorandom numbers *ex ante*, using number theory, whereas the following statistical tests evaluate subsets of pseudorandom numbers after they have been generated (*ex post*). Many procedures have been devised to test whether a given sequence of pseudorandom numbers is indeed uniformly and independently distributed. Knuth (1981) gives a set of standard tests. Marsaglia (1985) gives more stringent tests, not discussed here. Also see L'Ecuyer (1990) and Ripley (1987).

2.4.1 Frequency Test

The interval $[0, 1)$ can be partitioned into k intervals of the same length, $1/k$ (this symbol k has nothing to do with the symbol k in the preceding sections). The null-hypothesis H_0 states that the n pseudorandom numbers are uniformly distributed. So the expected

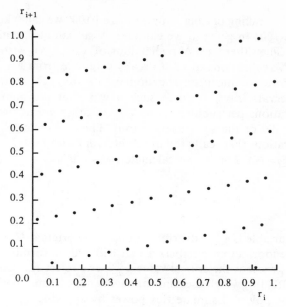

Figure 2.2   The pairs (r_i, r_{i+1}) of the generator $n_{i+1} = (13n_i + 1) \bmod 64$ with $n_0 = 17$

number of pseudorandom numbers per interval is n/k. Let f_i represent the actual number of pseudorandom numbers in interval i with $i = 1, \ldots, k$. Then the following statistic is approximately χ^2-distributed with $k-1$ degrees of freedom (the χ^2 or chi-square distribution holds only approximately since it is an asymptotic test; a rule of thumb requires $n \geqslant 5k$):

$$\underline{\chi}^2_{k-1} = \frac{k}{n} \sum_{i=1}^{k} \left(\underline{f}_i - \frac{n}{k} \right)^2. \tag{2.10}$$

So the null-hypothesis is rejected if the actual value of the statistic is 'significant', that is, χ^2_{k-1} exceeds the $(1-\alpha)$ quantile $\chi^{2(\alpha)}_{k-1}$ (that quantile is defined by $P(\underline{\chi}^2_{k-1} < \chi^{2(\alpha)}_{k-1}) = 1 - \alpha$).

EXAMPLE 2.4

To illustrate this test, we apply (2.10) not to $\underline{r} \sim U(0,1)$ but to the following non-uniform distribution:

$$\begin{aligned} f(r) &= 1.25 - 0.5r && \text{if } 0 \leqslant r \leqslant 1, \\ &= 0 && \text{elsewhere.} \end{aligned} \tag{2.11}$$

We choose $k = 10$ and $n = 100$ in (2.10). This yields one realization of χ^2_9. We repeat this procedure 100 times, and find that 12 of the 100 χ^2_9 values are significant at $\alpha = 0.05$ (the critical value is 16.919). Next we choose $n = 10\,000$ in (2.10). Then all 100 χ^2_9 values turn out to be significant; that is, a bigger sample size n yields a more powerful test (smaller β or type II error).

Exercise 2.3: Instead of taking one big sample of size $10\,000$ we can take 100 subsamples of size 100. In general, we can take N subsamples, and apply (2.10) N times. Then there are N realizations of χ^2_{k-1}. We wish to test whether these N realizations of (2.10) really originate from a χ^2_{k-1} distribution. Therefore we partition the domain of the χ^2_{k-1} distribution into p subintervals, say $p = 10$, in such a way that the number of expected observations per subinterval is N/p (in other words, we use the $100/p$-percentiles of the χ^2_{k-1} distribution). Then we count $\underline{F}_j$, the number of observations that really fall in subinterval j with $j = 1, 2, \ldots, p$ (obviously $\sum_{j=1}^{p} \underline{F}_j = N$). Finally we calculate the statistic

$$\underline{\chi}^2_{p-1} = \frac{p}{N} \sum_{j=1}^{p} \left(\underline{F}_j - \frac{N}{p} \right)^2.$$

This variable is χ^2_{p-1} distributed under the original H_0 (which states that the pseudorandom numbers are distributed uniformly); in other words, if $\underline{\chi}^2_{p-1}$ exceeds the critical value $\chi^{2(\alpha)}_{p-1}$, we reject H_0. Compared with the test of (2.10), which uses only one sequence of n numbers, the second test has less power. Estimate this power by applying $\underline{\chi}^2_{k-1}$ and $\underline{\chi}^2_{p-1}$ to the non-uniform distribution in (2.11). Repeat this procedure for a more uniform distribution: $f(r) = 1.125 - 0.25r$ for $0 \leqslant r \leqslant 1$.

Besides the χ^2 statistic there are many more *goodness of fit* statistics for testing whether a stochastic variable follows a specific marginal distribution; see Kleijnen (1987, pp. 94–5). Next we shall discuss a more difficult problem, namely statistical independence. Unfortunately there are many types of dependence.

2.4.2 Test on Pairs of Pseudorandom Numbers

We consider the $n-1$ pairs $(\underline{r}_1, \underline{r}_2), (\underline{r}_2, \underline{r}_3), \ldots, (\underline{r}_{n-1}, \underline{r}_n)$; also see again Figure 2.2. We partition both the x-axis and the y-axis into k equal intervals. Hence there are k^2 squares of the same size. The expected number of pairs per square is $(n-1)/k^2$. Let $\underline{f}_{jh}$ denote the actual number of pairs in square (j, h) with $j, h = 1, 2, \ldots, k$. We compute the following statistic:

$$\underline{\psi}^2 = \frac{k^2}{n-1} \sum_{j=1}^{k} \sum_{h=1}^{k} \left(\underline{f}_{jh} - \frac{n-1}{k^2} \right)^2. \tag{2.12}$$

This statistic does not have a χ^2 distribution, as the $\underline{f}_{jh}$ are dependent.

Exercise 2.4: Why are the $\underline{f}_{jh}$ in (2.12) dependent?

It can be proved, however, that the difference $\underline{\psi}^2 - \underline{\chi}^2_{k-1}$ (the statistic of (2.12) minus that of (2.10)) is distributed approximately as a χ^2 statistic with $k(k-1)$ degrees of freedom; see Fishman (1973, p. 189). Notice that this method can also be applied to n-tuples with $n \geqslant 3$; see Marsaglia (1985).

Next we consider only $n/2$ pairs, namely (r_1, r_2), (r_3, r_4), . . ., (r_{n-3}, r_{n-2}), (r_{n-1}, r_n), where n is supposed to be even. The statistic (2.12) is then replaced by

$$\chi^2_{k^2-1} = \frac{k^2}{n/2} \sum_{j=1}^{k} \sum_{h=1}^{k} \left(\underline{f}_{jh} - \frac{n/2}{k^2} \right)^2. \tag{2.13}$$

According to Fishman (1973, p. 189) it is better to use the $n/2$ independent pairs of (2.13) than the dependent pairs of (2.12). This procedure can again be extended to three-tuples distributed over three-dimensional subcubes with equal volume, but the necessary number of observations n becomes very large.

2.4.3 Correlation Test

The correlation coefficient for two stochastic variables (say) $\underline{x}$ and $\underline{y}$ is usually denoted by ρ. The well-known relation between the correlation coefficient and the covariance is

$$\rho = \frac{\text{cov}(\underline{x}, \underline{y})}{\sigma_x \sigma_y}, \tag{2.14}$$

where $\text{cov}(\underline{x}, \underline{y}) = E[\{\underline{x} - E(\underline{x})\}\{\underline{y} - E(\underline{y})\}]$ and $\sigma_x^2 = E\{\underline{x} - E(\underline{x})\}^2$. We use the symbol γ for the covariance. If the ith and the $(i+j)$th pseudorandom numbers in the sequence $(\underline{r}_i)$ are distributed independently, then

$$\gamma_j = E\{(\underline{r}_i - 0.5)(\underline{r}_{i+j} - 0.5)\} = 0 \qquad \text{for } j > 0, \tag{2.15}$$

where $E(\underline{r}_i) = 0.5$ and $E(\underline{r}_{i+j}) = 0.5$ because $\underline{r}_i$ and $\underline{r}_{i+j}$ are assumed to be uniformly distributed on $[0, 1)$. The 'lag j' covariance γ_j can be estimated through

$$\hat{\underline{\gamma}}_j = \frac{1}{(n-j)} \sum_{i=1}^{n-j} \{(\underline{r}_i - 0.5)(\underline{r}_{i+j} - 0.5)\}. \tag{2.16}$$

Note that for $j = 0$ this expression reduces to the maximum likelihood estimator of the variance. Because of (2.15) we have $E(\hat{\underline{\gamma}}_j) = 0$ for $j > 0$. Moreover it can be proved that $\hat{\underline{\gamma}}_j$ is asymptotically normal with var $(\hat{\underline{\gamma}}_j) = 1/(144(n-j))$; see Fishman (1978, p. 384). So the normal distribution can be used to test $H_0: \rho_j = 0$ with $j = 1, 2, \ldots, J$ and $n \gg J$ (where the symbol $\gg$ stands for 'much larger than'). Unfortunately, $H_0: \rho_{j'} = 0$ may be accepted for some j' and $H_0: \rho_{j'+1} = 0$ may be rejected; see Fishman (1973, p. 192).

If a specific generator passes a number of statistical tests, there is no guarantee that it is a good generator. For example, the generator that yields Figure 2.2 satisfies many tests for independence, yet it is a bad generator. Constructing a good generator is hard, as Park and Miller (1988) show in detail. The use of a wrong generator might lead to serious errors in the simulation, though we personally have never experienced such an event in practice! (Usually a simulation program is rejected because it contained bugs or unrealistic modules; see Chapter 11.) Yet Ripley (1988, p. 58) mentions two cases that gave wrong results because of an inferior generator.

In the following subsections we shall present some more tests that may be skipped; so the reader may proceed to Section 2.5.

*2.4.4 Run Tests

Some tests check whether a relatively large pseudorandom number r_i results in a next number r_{i+1} that is also large. We present two tests.

Runs Up and Down

Consider a sequence of n pseudorandom numbers $(\underline{r}_1, \underline{r}_2, \ldots, \underline{r}_n)$. This sequence yields a sequence of $n-1$ binary variables defined by

$$\underline{s}_i = \begin{cases} 1 & \text{if } \underline{r}_i \leqslant \underline{r}_{i+1} \\ 0 & \text{if } \underline{r}_i > \underline{r}_{i+1} \end{cases} \quad (i = 1, 2, \ldots, n-1). \tag{2.17}$$

If k consecutive values of $\underline{s}$ are equal to one, then we have a 'run up of length k'; a sequence of k consecutive zeros is a 'run down of length k'. Figure 2.3 gives an example with $k = 1, 2, 2, \ldots, 2, 2, 1, 1$, which corresponds with Figure 2.2.

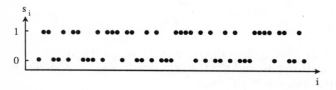

Figure 2.3 Runs up and down for $n_{i+1} = (13n_i + 1) \bmod 64$; $n_0 = 17$

Bad generators tend to give too many long runs (high k values); see Naylor et al. (1966, p. 60). Let the total number of runs up (U) and down (D) of length k be denoted by $\underline{RU}_k$ and $\underline{RD}_k$ respectively. For a sequence of n truly random numbers with large n, the following can be proved:

$$E(\text{total number of runs}) = \frac{(2n-1)}{3};$$

$$E(\underline{RU}_k + \underline{RD}_k) = \frac{2\{(k^2 + 3k + 1)n - (k^3 + 3k^2 - k - 4)\}}{(k+3)!} \quad \text{with } k \leqslant n-2;$$

$$\tag{2.18}$$

$$E(\underline{RU}_{n-1} + \underline{RD}_{n-1}) = \frac{2}{n!}.$$

For a few specific k values these equations imply

$$E(\underline{RU}_k + \underline{RD}_k) = \begin{cases} 0.4167n + 0.0833 & \text{for } k = 1 \\ 0.1833n - 0.2333 & \text{for } k = 2 \\ 0.0528n - 0.1306 & \text{for } k = 3 \\ 0.0115n - 0.0413 & \text{for } k = 4 \\ 0.0020n - 0.0095 & \text{for } k = 5. \end{cases}$$

For $k \geqslant 6$ we can combine runs. We again use a χ^2 statistic to test whether the generator is acceptable. The standard χ^2 test, however, does not apply because of the dependence between the successive $\underline{RU}_k$ (and $\underline{RD}_k$), and the dependence between $\underline{RU}_k$ and $\underline{RD}_k$, with $k, k' = 1, 2, \ldots, n-1$. It is also possible to test only $\underline{RU}_k$ or $\underline{RD}_k$; see Fishman (1978, pp. 373–6) and Morgan (1984, pp. 143–5).

Runs Above and Below the Average

We again define a sequence of binary variables, but now we replace (2.17) by

$$\underline{s}_i = \begin{cases} 0 & \text{if } \underline{r}_i \leqslant 0.5 \\ 1 & \text{if } \underline{r}_i > 0.5. \end{cases} \tag{2.19}$$

An illustration is given in Figure 2.4.

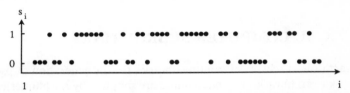

Figure 2.4 Runs above and below the average for $n_{i+1} = (13n_i + 1) \bmod 64$; $n_0 = 17$

It can be proved that for a sequence of n truly random numbers the following formulae apply:

$$E(\text{total number of runs}) = 0.5(n + 1)$$
$$E(\text{number of runs of length } k) = (n - k + 3) \times 2^{-(k+1)}. \tag{2.20}$$

*2.4.5 Gap Test

Consider a subinterval $[\alpha, \beta)$ within the unit interval $[0, 1)$. If both r_i and r_{i+k} fall in the interval $[\alpha, \beta)$ but the intermediate numbers $r_{i+1}, r_{i+2}, \ldots, r_{i+k-1}$ do not, we speak of a gap of length k. If $\underline{r}$ is uniformly distributed over $[0, 1]$, then $P(\alpha \leqslant \underline{r} < \beta) = \beta - \alpha$. If, moreover, the observations on $\underline{r}$ are independent, then

$$P(\text{gap length} = k) = (\beta - \alpha)(1 - \beta + \alpha)^{k-1}. \tag{2.21}$$

Mitrani (1982, p. 81) formulates a χ^2 test. This test can be used not only for the pseudorandom numbers (reals on the unit interval), but also for the individual digits 0 through 9.

*2.4.6 Poker Test

In the poker test we transform the reals $\underline{r}_i$ into integers: we multiply $\underline{r}_i$ by an integer (say) k such that $\underline{x}_i = \lfloor k\underline{r}_i \rfloor$ is distributed uniformly on $\{0, 1, \ldots, k-1\}$ where $\lfloor y \rfloor$

denotes the integer part of y; for example, $\lfloor 3.2 \rfloor = \lfloor 3.9 \rfloor = 3$. The value $k = 5$ yields five-tuples that look like the seven combinations in the game of poker:

—all five numbers are different;
—two numbers are the same;
—three numbers are the same;
—there are two (different) pairs;
—there is a combination of two and three identical numbers;
—four numbers are identical;
—all numbers are the same.

We count the number of times each five-tuple occurs. We compare these numbers with their expected values, by means of a χ^2 test. This test can also be applied for $k \neq 5$, and for the individual digits $0, 1, \ldots, 9$ of the pseudorandom numbers $\underline{r}$. Also see Mitrani (1982).

2.5 PRACTICAL COMPUTER SUBROUTINES

Simulation practitioners rely on subroutine libraries for the generation of pseudorandom numbers. Well-known libraries for mainframes are supplied by the Numerical Algorithm Group (NAG) in the United Kingdom, and by IMSL Inc. in the United States. First we shall discuss NAG routines in some detail; next we shall briefly present IMSL routines for mainframes and subroutines for personal computers.

The NAG library contains a number of FORTRAN subroutines for pseudorandom number generation; the names of all these subroutines start with GO5. The subroutines can be called in a Pascal program as follows.

—FUNCTION GO5CAF(x: DOUBLE): DOUBLE; EXTERNAL;
The generator GO5CAF uses words that are double the length of a REAL; its output is stored in x; see the parameter list. This generator is based on the multiplicative congruential method: $b = 0$ in (2.4). Furthermore, $a = 13^{13}$, $m = 2^{59}$ and $n_0 = 123456789$ $(2^{32} + 1)$. The following procedures can be used to control this generator.
—PROCEDURE GO5CBF(i: INTEGER); EXTERNAL;
This subroutine makes the generator GO5CAF start with a fixed number, namely $n_0 = 2i + 1$ where i is an integer parameter that must be read; see the parameter list.
—PROCEDURE GO5CCF; EXTERNAL;
This subroutine generates a starting value for GO5CAF that depends on the internal clock of the computer.

The following two procedures make it possible to store information about the current state of the generator GO5CAF and to retrieve this information later on.

—PROCEDURE GO5CFF(VAR *ia*: IVEC; *ni*: INTEGER; VAR *xa*: VEC; *nx,ifail*: INTEGER): EXTERNAL;
—PROCEDURE GO5CGF(VAR *ia*: IVEC; *ni*: INTEGER; VAR *xa*: VEC; *nx,ifail*: INTEGER); EXTERNAL;

Procedure GO5CFF stores the state of the generator GO5CAF. This information is stored in two arrays with lengths ni and nx respectively. IVEC is an ARRAY $[1 .. ni]$ OF INTEGERS and VEC is an ARRAY $[1 .. nx]$ OF DOUBLE. The optimum value for ni and nx is 9. The results can be written to disk, so that the simulation can be restarted in a new session exactly where it ended in a previous session. To start GO5CAF again, the procedure GO5CGF is called. Printing (on screen or paper) of the initial and the final numbers of GO5CAF is not accurate enough; so we do need GO5CFF and GO5CGF. Our advice is *always write the first and last numbers of the pseudorandom generator in a simulation experiment to disk*!

IMSL uses the congruential method with $m = 2^{31} - 1$, $b = 0$, and three different multipliers, namely $a = 16807$ or 397204094 or 950706376. It has very simple subroutines for retrieving the current value of the seed so that the simulation can be restarted (namely RNGET), to initialize with a fixed seed or with a clock generated seed (RNSET), and to shuffle the numbers (RNOPT).

With *personal computers* (PCs) it is often unknown which generator has been implemented. This may lead to incorrect simulation results. And when the generator is known, the user should still be careful because the cycle length is often limited. For instance, one BASIC generator on the IBM PC has a cycle length of only 65 535; see Modianos et al. (1987). The cycle length can be increased considerably by combining various generators (Wichmann and Hill, 1987). Because of the popularity of Turbo Pascal, we give the parameters for Turbo Pascal Rev. 3: in the congruential method of (2.4) $a = 129$, $b = 907\,633\,385$ and $m = 2^{32}$; Knuth (1981, p. 38) discusses this particular multiplier value. Newer versions of Turbo Pascal have better generators. Implementing various generators on PCs is discussed by several authors: L'Ecuyer (1990), Marsaglia, Zaman and Tsang (1990), Park and Miller (1988), and Ripley (1990).

The procedures for selecting random number seeds become relevant in the following situation. Assume that we have executed a number of runs with a simulation model; for example, we have simulated a number of days for an inventory system. When we want to add one more run (for example, one more simulated day), there are three possibilities:

(1) We use the internal clock to pick a seed. If the new seed happens to be a number used in one of the preceding runs, then these two runs use partly the same pseudorandom numbers and become dependent. This dependence violates the assumptions of the statistical analysis techniques for simulation (as we shall see in later chapters). The chance of overlap between different runs might be ignored, if the generator's cycle length is large compared with the number of pseudorandom numbers of a simulation run. Note that GPSS/H provides a report that enables the detection of overlap, but it does so for option (2), not (1).

(2) We use starting numbers that are 100 000 apart. For a multiplicative generator the first two seeds s_0 and s_1 are related by the expression $s_1 = (a^{100\,000} s_0) \bmod m$; see Exercise 2.2. Fishman (1978, pp. 482–487) gives tables with such seeds, and Schriber (1991, p. 316) describes how GPSS/H implements this idea. One disadvantage is that these seeds are readily available for certain generators only. The computer centre may generate a table of seeds for its generator, and make that table available on

disk. A second, more serious, disadvantage is that splitting the full cycle into parts may generate strong autocorrelations. For example, splitting a multiplicative generator's output into two equal parts (of length $h/2$) means that these two parts show a strong negative correlation; see Kleijnen and Annink (1992). So we reject probability (2).

(3) We continue with the new run where we stopped the previous run. We must then have stored the generator's state in computer memory, unless we finish the whole study in a single session. Schriber (1991, p. 319) explains how GPSS/H implements this option.

REFERENCES

Bratley P., B. L. Fox, and L. E. Schrage (1983) *A Guide to Simulation*, Springer-Verlag, New York.

Fishman G. S. (1973) *Concepts and Methods in Discrete Event Digital Simulation*, Wiley, New York.

Fishman G. S. (1978) *Principles of Discrete Event Simulation*, Wiley, New York.

Inoue H., H. Kumahore, Y. Yoshizawa, M. Ichimura, and O. Miyatake (1983) Random numbers generated by a physical device, *Applied Statistics*, 32(2), 115-20.

James F. (1990) A review of pseudorandom number generators, *Computer Physics Communications*, 60, 329-44.

Kleijnen J. P. C. (1987) *Statistical Tools for Simulation Practitioners*, Marcel Dekker, New York and Basel.

Kleijnen J. P. C. and B. Annink (1992) Multiplicative generators for supercomputers and other computers, *European Journal of Operational Research* (in press).

Knuth D. E. (1981) *The Art of Computer Programming, Vol. 2: Seminumerical Algorithms*, Addison-Wesley, Reading, Massachusetts.

Landauer E. G. (1984) The effect of random number generators on an application, *Computer & Industrial Engineering*, 8, 65-72.

L'Ecuyer P. (1990) Random numbers for simulation, *Communications of the ACM*, 33(10), 85-97.

Marsaglia G. (1985) A current view of random number generators. In L. Billard (ed.), *Computer Science and Statistics: Proceedings of the Sixteenth Symposium on the Interface*, Elsevier Science Publishers (North-Holland), pp. 3-10.

Marsaglia G., A. Zaman, and W. Tsang (1990) Toward a universal random number generator, *Statistics & Probability Letters*, 8, 35-9.

Mitrani I. (1982) *Simulation Techniques for Discrete Event Systems*, Cambridge University Press, London.

Modianos D. T., R. C. Scott, and L. W. Cornwell (1987) Testing intrinsic random-number generators, *Byte*, 12, 175-8.

Morgan B. J. T. (1984) *Elements of Simulation*, Chapman and Hall, London.

Naylor T. H., J. L. Balintfy, D. S. Burdick, and Kong Chu (1966) *Computer Simulation Techniques*, Wiley, New York.

Oakenfull E. (1979) Uniform random number generators and the spectral test. In D. McNeil (ed.), *Interactive Statistics*, North-Holland, Amsterdam, pp. 17-37.

Park S. K. and K. W. Miller (1988) Random number generators: good ones are hard to find. *Communications of the ACM*, 31(10), 1192-1201.

Rand Corporation (1955) *A Million Random Digits with 100,000 Normal Deviates*, The Free Press, Glencoe, Ill.

Ripley B. D. (1987) *Stochastic Simulation*, Wiley, New York.

Ripley B. D. (1988) Uses and abuses of statistical simulation, *Mathematical Programming*, 42, 53-68.

Ripley B. D. (1990) Thoughts on pseudorandom number generators, *Journal of Computational and Applied Mathematics*, 31, 153-63.

Schriber T. J. (1991) *An Introduction to Simulation Using GPSS/H*, Wiley, New York.

Tausworthe R. C. (1965) Random numbers generated by linear recurrence modulo two, *Mathematics of Computation*, 201–9.

Wichmann B. and D. Hill (1987) Building a random-number generator, *Byte*, **12**, 127–8.

Zeigler B. (1976) *Theory of Modelling and Simulation*, Wiley Interscience, New York.

Chapter 3

Sampling from Non-uniform Distributions

Chapter 3 is organized as follows.

—3.1 Table look-up for discrete distributions
Starting with an example we discuss the table look-up method for discrete distributions. For some discrete distributions this method can be simplified; the geometric distribution provides an example.
—3.2 Simulating the statistical process
We show how to simulate the processes that lead to the binomial and hypergeometric distributions respectively.
—3.3 Inverse transformation
The table look-up for discrete distributions leads to the inverse transformation method for continuous distributions. The latter method is illustrated by the exponential and uniform distributions.
—3.4 Distributions related to the exponential distribution
Some continuous variables have no explicit distribution function, so the inverse transformation method cannot be applied. We can then utilize relationships between certain variables; that is, the exponential distribution is used to sample from the gamma, Erlang, chi-square, beta, and Poisson distributions.
—3.5 Normal distribution
Because the normal distribution function cannot be represented explicitly, we may decide to use the central limit theorem to generate approximately normal variables. The Box–Muller method is an exact sampling procedure.
—3.6 Rejection method
The rejection method is a very general sampling procedure, which we demonstrate by applying it to normal variables.
—3.7 Distributions related to the normal distribution
We discuss four types of distributions: lognormal, chi-square, Student's t, and F.
—3.8 Multivariate distributions
In the discussion of multivariate distributions we emphasize multivariate normal distributions.
—3.9 Time series
We concentrate on stationary time series, especially time series with linear and exponential autocorrelation functions respectively.

—3.10 Epilogue
    If the pseudorandom numbers are not truly random, then problems may arise.
—Appendix: NAG routines

    Note that definitions of various distributions, formulae for their means and variances, applications, and much more information can be found in a set of four books; see Johnson and Kotz (1972). In this chapter we emphasize the derivation of subroutines for sampling from those distributions.

3.1 TABLE LOOK-UP FOR DISCRETE DISTRIBUTIONS

We start with an *example* of a discrete distribution that has only three possible outcomes, each with a certain probability (also see Figure 3.1a):

$$P(\underline{x}=5)=0.1, \qquad P(\underline{x}=6)=0.6, \qquad P(\underline{x}=7)=0.3. \tag{3.1}$$

By definition, the sum of all probabilities is one. Now consider a ten-sided die with faces numbered from 0 through 9. The sampling procedure for (3.1) could be (see Figure 3.1b):

$\underline{x}=5$ if 0 is thrown,
$\underline{x}=6$ if 1 or 2 or ... or 6 is thrown,
$\underline{x}=7$ if 7 or 8 or 9 is thrown.

    In practice, a die is not used but a pseudorandom number generator (as we saw in the preceding chapter). To start our explanation we consider only the first digit after the decimal point of the pseudorandom number r (with $0 \leqslant r < 1$). This yields 10 possible outcomes $(0.0, 0.1, \ldots, 0.9)$, which we can assign as we did for the ten-sided die: $\underline{x}=5$ if $r=0.0, \ldots, \underline{x}=7$ if $r=0.9$.

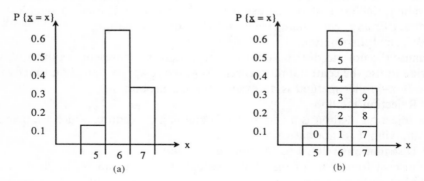

Figure 3.1 Sampling from discrete distributions: an example: (a) density function; (b) relation with a ten-sided die

    We shall see that it is convenient to interpret $\underline{r}$ as a *continuous* variate. So the actual sampling procedure is

$$x = 5 \quad \text{if } 0.0 \leqslant \underline{r} < 0.1,$$
$$x = 6 \quad \text{if } 0.1 \leqslant \underline{r} < 0.7,$$
$$x = 7 \quad \text{if } 0.7 \leqslant \underline{r} < 1.0.$$

Why is this procedure correct? Let us consider (say) the event $\underline{x} = 6$. The procedure implies

$$P(\underline{x} = 6) = P(0.1 \leqslant \underline{r} < 0.7) = \int_{0.1}^{0.7} 1 \, dr = [r]_{0.1}^{0.7} = 0.6,$$

which indeed agrees with the density function specified in (3.1).

Exercise 3.1: Calculate $P(\underline{x} = 5)$ in the same way.

Now we consider the general class of discrete density functions

$$P(\underline{x} = x_i) = p_i \quad \text{with } i = 0, 1, \ldots, n \quad \text{and} \quad n \in \mathbf{N}, \tag{3.2}$$

which yields the distribution function

$$F(x_i) = P(\underline{x} \leqslant x_i) = \sum_{j=0}^{i} p_j. \tag{3.3}$$

This general discrete distribution function is illustrated in Figure 3.2.

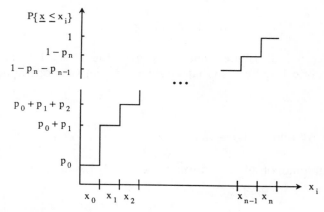

Figure 3.2 General discrete distribution function

The sampling procedure for (3.3) becomes

$$\underline{x} = x_i \quad \text{if } \sum_{j=0}^{i-1} p_j \leqslant \underline{r} < \sum_{j=0}^{i} p_j \quad \text{with } i = 0, 1, \ldots, n, \tag{3.4}$$

where by definition $\sum_0^{-1} p_j = 0$ and $\sum_0^n p_j = 1$. This method is known as the 'table look-up method', since the elements $\sum_0^i p_j$ are stored in a table. Searching in a table can be done efficiently by means of certain computer science techniques; see Ripley (1987, pp. 71–2). The general formula (3.4) can result in simpler formulae for special discrete distributions so it is not necessary to use a table, as we shall see next.

3.1.1 Geometric Distribution

Let the probability of 'success' be p with $0 \leqslant p \leqslant 1$, and the probability of 'failure' be $q = 1 - p$; for example, p denotes the probability of drawing a white ball from an urn. Let x be the number of failures before there is a success; for example, x denotes the number of non-white balls drawn before the first white ball. Then x has the geometric distribution $G(p)$. It can be proved that the density function of x is

$$P(\underline{x} = i) = pq^i \qquad \text{with } i = 0, 1, \ldots , \tag{3.5}$$

and that the distribution function is

$$F(\underline{x} = i) = \sum_{j=0}^{i} pq^j = 1 - q^{i+1}. \tag{3.6}$$

The general sampling procedure of (3.4) gives

$$\underline{x} = i \quad \text{if} \quad 1 - q^i \leqslant \underline{r} < 1 - q^{i+1}. \tag{3.7}$$

This procedure, however, can be simplified. First we rewrite (3.7) as

$$\underline{x} = i \quad \text{if} \quad q^i \geqslant 1 - \underline{r} > q^{i+1}.$$

Both $\underline{r}$ and $1 - \underline{r}$ are distributed uniformly over the interval from zero to one. Therefore we replace $1 - \underline{r}$ by $\underline{r}$, so that we save one computer operation, namely one subtraction.

Exercise 3.2: Prove that $P(\underline{r} \leqslant r) = P(1 - \underline{r} \leqslant r) = r$.

Now we perform a monotonic transformation, namely the logarithm transformation, which yields

$$\underline{x} = i \quad \text{if} \quad i \ln(q) \geqslant \ln(\underline{r}) > (i + 1) \ln(q).$$

Because $q < 1$ we know that $\ln(q) < 0$, which yields

$$\underline{x} = i \quad \text{if} \quad i \leqslant \ln(\underline{r}) / \ln(q) < i + 1.$$

So the sampling procedure for the geometric distribution reduces from (3.7) to

$$\underline{x} = \lfloor \ln(\underline{r}) / \tilde{q} \rfloor , \tag{3.8}$$

where $\lfloor y \rfloor$ denotes the integer part of y, and $\tilde{q} = \ln q$ is a constant.

3.2 SIMULATING THE STATISTICAL PROCESS

The table look-up method can sometimes be replaced by a simulation of the process that leads to a specific statistical distribution. As an example we take the *binomial* distribution. Consider a population of N elements, say, an urn with N balls. Of these, M elements have a certain property, for example, M balls are white. We take a sample of n elements with $n < N$. Before taking a ball, we put the previous ball back: sampling *with* replacement. Consequently the urn contains N balls every time we start taking a ball; we may take the same ball we sampled before. Let p denote the probability of 'success' (a white ball); so $p = M/N$. Under these assumptions the number of successes in the sample, denoted by $\underline{x}$, follows the binomial distribution denoted by $B(n,p)$:

$$P(\underline{x}=k) = \binom{n}{k} p^k (1-p)^{n-k} \qquad \text{with } k=0,1,\ldots,n, \quad n\in\mathbf{N} \quad \text{and} \quad 0\leqslant p \leqslant 1, \quad (3.9)$$

where $\binom{n}{k} = n!/\{k!(n-k)!\}$ with $n! = n(n-1)\ldots 2.1$. It can be shown that

$$\left.\begin{array}{l} E(\underline{x}) = np \\ \mathrm{var}(\underline{x}) = np(1-p). \end{array}\right\} \qquad (3.10)$$

Figure 3.3 shows how to simulate this process.

In the next subsection we shall consider a slightly more complicated simulation. In later sections we shall present more examples of simulating the statistical process (Poisson process, central limit theorem).

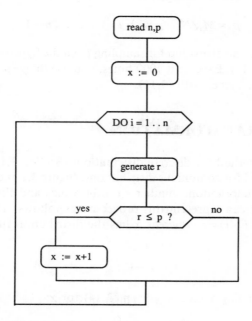

Figure 3.3   Simulation of binomial process

3.2.1 Hypergeometric Distribution

We assume a population similar to the binomial case, but now we take a sample *without replacement* (in the urn example we do not put back the ball drawn before; such a situation often exists in quality control). It can be proved that the number of 'successes' in the sample now follows the hypergeometric distribution $H(n, M, N)$:

$$P(\underline{x}=k) = \frac{\binom{M}{k}\binom{N-M}{n-k}}{\binom{N}{n}} \quad \text{with } k \leqslant n, \ k \leqslant M \text{ and } n-k \leqslant N-M. \tag{3.11}$$

This distribution has

$$\left.\begin{array}{l} E(\underline{x}) = np \\ \text{var}(\underline{x}) = np(1-p)(N-n)/(N-1) \end{array}\right\} \tag{3.12}$$

(so its variance is smaller than the binomial variance). To simulate the hypergeometric distribution we must change the probability of success after each draw. So we define p_i as the probability of success *after* the ith draw with $i = 0, 1, \ldots, n-1$ and $p_0 = M/N$ as in the binomial distribution. Furthermore, N_i is the number of elements after the ith draw. The following recursive relation holds: $N_0 = N$ and $N_i = N_{i-1} - 1$ with $i = 1, 2, \ldots, n-1$. Analogously we define $\underline{M}_i$ as the number of 'good' elements after the ith draw. So we have the following recursive relation: $\underline{M}_0 = M$ and $\underline{M}_i = \underline{M}_{i-1} - \underline{\delta}_i$ where $\underline{\delta}_i = 1$ if sample i yields a success and $\underline{\delta}_i = 0$ if sample i does not yield a success, with $i = 1, 2, \ldots, n-1$. Finally this yields

$$\underline{p}_i = \underline{M}_i / N_i \quad \text{with } i = 0, 1, \ldots, n-1. \tag{3.13}$$

Exercise 3.3: Construct an algorithm for sampling from the hypergeometric distribution, using (3.13). Execute it 1000 times, and use the χ^2 statistic to check if the outcome agrees with (3.11)

3.3 INVERSE TRANSFORMATION

The 'table look-up' method for discrete distributions (Section 3.1) leads to the inverse transformation method for continuous distributions. Figure 3.2 and equation (3.4) mean that we place the pseudorandom number r on the y-axis and find the corresponding x. Mathematically we can represent this procedure as follows. The variable $\underline{r}$ has the distribution function $F_1(r) = r$, whereas $\underline{x}$ has the distribution function F_2. Placing r on the y-axis means

$$r = F_2(x). \tag{3.14}$$

Finding the corresponding x means solving (3.14) for x:

$$x = F_2^{-1}(r) = \min\{x \mid F_2(x) \geqslant r\}, \tag{3.15}$$

where F_2^{-1} denotes the inverse of F_2. This procedure is correct indeed, because (3.15) implies

$$P(\underline{x} \leqslant x) = P(F_2^{-1}(\underline{r}) \leqslant x) = P(\underline{r} \leqslant F_2(x)) = F_2(x). \tag{3.16}$$

In the following examples we shall omit the index 2 in $F_2(x)$. (In Section 3.4 we shall see what to do if no explicit inverse F_2^{-1} is known.)

3.3.1 Exponential Distribution

The exponential distribution, denoted by $Ne(\alpha)$, is given by

$$F(x) = \int_0^x \alpha e^{-\alpha z} \, dz = 1 - e^{-\alpha x} \quad \text{with } \alpha > 0 \quad \text{and} \quad x \geqslant 0. \tag{3.17}$$

Applying (3.14), in combination with Exercise 3.2 (r and $1 - r$ have the same distribution), gives

$$r = 1 - e^{-\alpha x} \Rightarrow x = \frac{\ln(1-r)}{-\alpha} \Rightarrow x = \frac{\ln(r)}{-\alpha}. \tag{3.18}$$

It is always prudent to check which values of x correspond with the extreme values of r (namely 0 and 1): is the 'range' of x correct? For example, (3.18) gives $x = \infty$ for $r = 0$, and $x = 0$ for $r = 1$, which does not conflict with (3.17).

As the information about $\underline{x}$ usually concerns its expectation and variance, we give the relations between these two moments and the parameter α of the exponential distribution:

$$\left. \begin{array}{l} E(\underline{x}) = \int_0^\infty x\alpha e^{-\alpha x} \, dx = \dfrac{1}{\alpha} \\[3mm] \text{var}(\underline{x}) = \int_0^\infty (x - (1/\alpha))^2 \, \alpha e^{-\alpha x} \, dx = \dfrac{1}{\alpha^2}. \end{array} \right\} \tag{3.19}$$

So the mean and standard deviation have the same value, namely $1/\alpha$.

3.3.2 Uniform Distribution

The distribution function of a variable that is distributed uniformly on the interval $[a, b]$ is

$$F(x) = \int_a^x \frac{1}{(b-a)} \, dt = \frac{(x-a)}{(b-a)} \quad \text{with } a \leqslant x \leqslant b. \tag{3.20}$$

This distribution is denoted by $U(a, b)$. Note that for a continuous variable it does not make any difference whether we include the extreme points of the interval from a to b: $P(\underline{x} < b) = P(\underline{x} \leqslant b)$ and $P(\underline{x} \geqslant a) = P(\underline{x} > a)$.

The inverse transformation gives

$$\underline{x} = a + (b-a)\underline{r} \qquad \text{with } \underline{r} \sim U(0,1). \tag{3.21}$$

The resulting range is correct indeed, since $r=0$ yields $x=a$ and $r=1$ gives $x=b$. The expectation and variance of $\underline{x} \sim U(a,b)$ are

$$\left. \begin{array}{l} E(\underline{x}) = \displaystyle\int_a^b \frac{x}{(b-a)}\, dx = \frac{(b+a)}{2} \\[4mm] \text{var}(\underline{x}) = \displaystyle\int_a^b \frac{(x-E(\underline{x}))^2}{(b-a)}\, dx = \frac{(b-a)^2}{12}. \end{array} \right\} \tag{3.22}$$

So the parameters a and b of the uniform distribution are related to the mean and variance, as follows:

$$\left. \begin{array}{l} a = E(\underline{x}) - \sqrt{(3\,\text{var}(\underline{x}))} \\[2mm] b = E(\underline{x}) + \sqrt{(3\,\text{var}(\underline{x}))}. \end{array} \right\} \tag{3.23}$$

3.4 DISTRIBUTIONS RELATED TO THE EXPONENTIAL DISTRIBUTION

If the distribution function F_2 in (3.14) is not explicitly known, the inverse transformation method cannot be applied. There are several alternatives to the inverse transformation. One alternative uses the relationships that exist between distributions. For example, many distributions can be related to the exponential distribution, as we shall see in the next two subsections. Other distributions are related to the normal distribution, which will be discussed later on.

Exercise 3.4: Name a few stochastic variables that have no explicit distribution functions.

3.4.1 Gamma, Erlang, Chi-square, and Beta Distributions

We discuss a class of distributions often applied in models that assume continuous, non-negative variables with unimodal density functions. The *gamma* density function is

$$p(x) = \frac{\alpha^k x^{(k-1)} e^{-\alpha x}}{(k-1)!} \qquad \text{with } \alpha>0,\ k>0 \text{ and } x \geqslant 0. \tag{3.24}$$

A variable x with this density is denoted by $x \sim \Gamma(k,\alpha)$. The corresponding distribution function is not known explicitly; so the inverse transformation method does not apply. However, consider the subclass of gamma variables with *integer* parameter k, which are known as *Erlang* variables. It can be proved that an Erlang variable with parameters k and α has the same distribution as the sum of k exponentially distributed variables y_i with constant parameter α. To sample from the exponential distribution with parameter α we can use (3.18). So to sample from the Erlang distribution with parameters α and k we use

$$\underline{x} = \sum_{i=1}^{k} \underline{y}_i(\alpha) = \sum_{i=1}^{k} -(\alpha)^{-1}\ln(\underline{r}_i) = -(\alpha)^{-1}\ln\left(\prod_{i=1}^{k} \underline{r}_i\right). \tag{3.25}$$

Exercise 3.5: Why do we replace $\Sigma_{i=1}^{k} \ln(\underline{r}_i)$ by $\ln(\Pi_{i=1}^{k} \underline{r}_i)$ in (3.25)?

It can be proved that the expectation and variance of the gamma variable are

$$\left. \begin{aligned} E(\underline{x}) &= \frac{k}{\alpha} \\[2em] \text{var}(\underline{x}) &= \frac{k}{\alpha^2}. \end{aligned} \right\} \tag{3.26}$$

For the sampling of gamma variables with non-integer k we refer to Devroye (1986, p. 825) and Ripley (1987, pp. 88–90).

The *chi-square* variable with n degrees of freedom, denoted by χ_n^2, can be proved to be a gamma variable with parameters $k = n/2$ and $\alpha = 0.5$. If n is even, then $n/2$ is an integer and (3.25) applies. If n is odd, we can use the fact that by definition χ_n^2 equals the sum of n squared independent standard normal variables. This yields

$$\chi_n^2 = \underline{y} + \underline{z}^2 \quad \text{with } \underline{y} \sim \Gamma((n-1)/2, 0.5) \quad \text{and} \quad \underline{z} \sim N(0,1), \tag{3.27}$$

where $n-1$ is even so (3.25) applies. How to sample $\underline{z}$ will be shown later.

The *beta* variable, $x \sim \text{Be}(n,m)$, is defined by

$$\underline{x} = \frac{\underline{y}_1}{(\underline{y}_1 + \underline{y}_2)}, \tag{3.28}$$

where $\underline{y}_1$ and $\underline{y}_2$ are gamma variables with the same α parameter: $\underline{y}_1 \sim \Gamma(n,\alpha)$ and $\underline{y}_2 \sim \Gamma(m,\alpha)$. So once we know how to sample from gamma distributions, we can simply compute the ratio (3.28). The mean and the variance of the beta variable are

$$\left. \begin{aligned} E(\underline{x}) &= \frac{n}{(n+m)} \\[2em] \text{var}(\underline{x}) &= \frac{mn}{(n+m+1)(n+m)^2}. \end{aligned} \right\} \tag{3.29}$$

We do not give the formula for the density function of the beta variable, since this formula is complicated and does not give useful information.

3.4.2 Poisson Distribution

The Poisson process is often used in queuing studies. It can be proved that a Poisson process can be characterized in the following two ways.

(1) The number of 'successes' (a success can be a customer arrival) per period has a Poisson distribution:

$$P(\underline{x}=k)=\frac{\alpha^k}{k!}e^{-\alpha} \quad \text{with } \alpha>0 \quad \text{and} \quad k=0,1,\ldots \tag{3.30}$$

The Poisson variable $\underline{x} \sim P(\alpha)$ has a mean and variance equal to the parameter α:

$$E(\underline{x}) = \text{var}(\underline{x}) = \alpha. \tag{3.31}$$

(2) The time $\underline{t}$ between two successive 'successes' has an exponential distribution with parameter α; see (3.17) with x replaced by t. Note that $E(\underline{t})=1/\alpha$ according to (3.19).

Figure 3.4 illustrates the relationship between the Poisson variable $\underline{x}$ and the exponentially distributed interarrival time $\underline{t}$. Note that all variables are expressed in some basic time unit (for example, minutes).

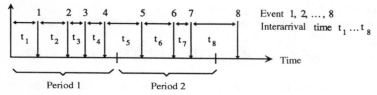

Period 1   Period 2

Figure 3.4 Poisson process

Exercise 3.6: Consider Figure 3.4: which realization does $\underline{k}$ have in the first and second period respectively?

To sample $\underline{x}$ from the Poisson distribution with parameter α (see equation 3.30), we can use a sequence of exponentially distributed independent variables with constant parameter α. Let these exponential variables be denoted by $\underline{t}_i(\alpha)$. Then $\underline{x}$ is the highest value of $\underline{k}$ for which the sum of $\underline{k}$ interarrival times still falls within one period:

$$\underline{x}=k \quad \text{if} \quad \sum_{i=1}^{k} \underline{t}_i(\alpha) \leqslant 1 < \sum_{i=1}^{k+1} \underline{t}_i(\alpha). \tag{3.32}$$

Note that $\underline{x}=0$ if the first interarrival time, $\underline{t}_1(\alpha)$, exceeds the value one (by definition $\Sigma_1^0=0$). We program (3.32) as follows. We combine the latter equation with (3.25), the equation for sampling a sum of exponentials:

$$\underline{x}=k \quad \text{if} \quad -(\alpha)^{-1}\ln\left(\prod_{i=1}^{k} r_i\right) \leqslant 1 < -(\alpha)^{-1}\ln\left(\prod_{i=1}^{k+1} r_i\right)$$

or

$$\ln\left(\prod_{i=1}^{k} r_i\right) \geqslant -\alpha > \ln\left(\prod_{i=1}^{k+1} r_i\right).$$

In other words

$$x = k \quad \text{if} \quad \prod_{i=1}^{k} r_i \geqslant e^{-\alpha} > \prod_{i=1}^{k+1} r_i. \tag{3.33}$$

The product $\prod_{i=1}^{k} r_i$ decreases as k increases (since $0 \leqslant r < 1$). So k is the largest number of pseudorandom numbers multiplied with each other, such that their product is larger than or equal to the constant $e^{-\alpha}$. The following Pascal function generates samples from a Poisson distribution.

```
FUNCTION Poisson (a: REAL): INTEGER;
VAR b,r: REAL;
    k  : INTEGER;
BEGIN
  k := 0;
  b := EXP(- a);
  r := RANDOM;
  WHILE r >= b DO
  BEGIN
    k := k + 1;
    r := r*RANDOM
  END;
  Poisson := k
END;
```

For more efficient algorithms we refer to Devroye (1986, p. 835). He also gives algorithms for Poisson processes with a parameter α that varies over time: *non-homogeneous Poisson processes*.

3.5 NORMAL DISTRIBUTION

The *standard* normal or Gaussian density function is defined by

$$p(x) = \frac{1}{\sqrt{(2\pi)}} e^{-x^2/2} \quad \text{with} \quad -\infty < x < \infty. \tag{3.34}$$

This variable has mean zero and variance 1, and is denoted by $x \sim N(0,1)$. The corresponding distribution function cannot be represented explicitly (the table for the normal distribution is computed numerically). There are many procedures for sampling from the normal distribution, as we shall see next.

3.5.1 Central Limit Theorem

The simplest (but obsolete) procedure is based on the central limit theorem, which can be formulated as follows. Let $y_1, y_2, \ldots, y_n$ be a sequence of independently and identically distributed (i.i.d.) variables with mean $E(y_i) = \mu_y$ and variance $\text{var}(y_i) = \sigma_y^2 < \infty$; denote their average by $\bar{y}_n = (1/n) \sum_{i=1}^{n} y_i$. Then the variable

$$x = \frac{(\bar{y} - \mu_y)}{\sigma_y / \sqrt{n}} \qquad (3.35)$$

converges in distribution to the standard normal distribution; in other words, for large n the difference between x and the standard normal variable can be ignored for practical purposes. So to generate a sample from the standard normal distribution, we may take n independent random numbers $r_i \sim U(0, 1)$. Equations (3.35) and the equations for the mean and variance of a uniform variable (see equation 3.22) result in

$$z = \frac{\sum_{i=1}^{n} r_i - \frac{n}{2}}{\sqrt{(n/12)}}. \qquad (3.36)$$

Figure 3.5 displays sampling results for (3.36) if $n = 2$, 3, and 12. The figure summarizes 400 realizations of z per n-value. The tails of the histogram are cut off at -2.20 and $+2.20$ with $P(x > 2.20) = 0.0139$. The histogram has 13 classes. When we fit a normal distribution to the histogram in this figure, we do not estimate its mean and variance since these two parameters are specified by the hypothesis: $E(z) = 0$ and $\text{var}(z) = 1$. So to test whether the results are from a standard normal distribution, we use a χ_{12}^2 statistic. The significance level $\alpha = 0.05$ gives the critical value $(\chi_{12}^2)^{0.95} = 21.0$. For $n = 2$ we reject this sampling procedure since $\chi_{12}^2 = 24.6$; for $n = 3$ we do not. By chance, $n = 12$ gives a higher χ_{12}^2 value than $n = 3$ does, but neither value is significant.

Exercise 3.7: Simulate (3.36) for $n = 1, 2, 3, \ldots$.

It can be proved that a linear transformation $x_2 = ax_1 + b$ of a normally distributed variable x_1 remains normally distributed. Obviously if $E(x_1) = \mu_1$ and variance $\text{var}(x_1) = \sigma_1^2$ then $x_2 = ax_1 + b$ has mean $a\mu_1 + b$ and variance $a^2\sigma_1^2$. Hence, to sample from the distribution of a normal variable x with mean μ and variance σ^2, we transform (3.36) as follows:

$$x = \sigma z + \mu. \qquad (3.37)$$

The distribution of this x is often denoted by $N(\mu, \sigma^2)$, but some software uses the notation $N(\mu, \sigma)$. So the user should be careful not to confuse the variance and the standard deviation.

When we choose $n = 12$ in (3.36), the denominator reduces to the value one. This choice saves one square root operation. But then (3.37) gives values within the interval $(-6\sigma, +6\sigma)$ (corresponding to $r_1 = \cdots = r_{12} = 0$ and $r_1 = \cdots = r_{12} = 1$). This is a disadvantage if the extreme tails of the distribution are important (the interval $(-6\sigma, +6\sigma)$ covers nearly 100% of the standard normal distribution). Therefore we give two more techniques.

3.5.2 Box–Muller Method

The Box–Muller method is an exact method that uses two independent (pseudo)random variables r_1 and r_2 to sample two *independent* standard normal variables x_1 and x_2:

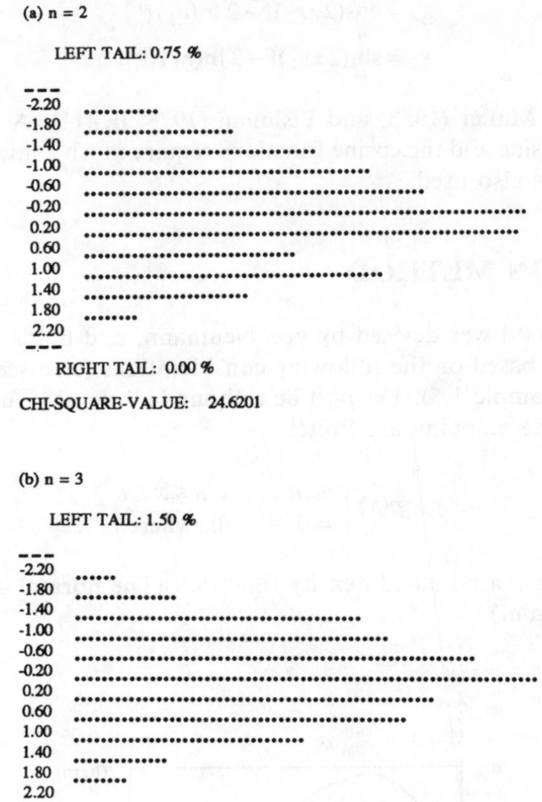

(a) n = 2

LEFT TAIL: 0.75 %

```
---
-2.20    ..........
-1.80    .....................
-1.40    ..........................................
-1.00    ..................................................
-0.60    ..........................................
-0.20    ...............................................................
 0.20    ..............................................................
 0.60    .........................................
 1.00    ......................
 1.40    ......................
 1.80    ........
 2.20
---
```

RIGHT TAIL: 0.00 %

CHI-SQUARE-VALUE: 24.6201

(b) n = 3

LEFT TAIL: 1.50 %

```
---
-2.20    ......
-1.80    ..............
-1.40    .......................................
-1.00    ..............................................
-0.60    ...............................................................
-0.20    ...................................................................
 0.20    ...........................................................
 0.60    ......................................
 1.00    ...........................
 1.40    ...............
 1.80    ........
 2.20
---
```

RIGHT TAIL: 0.50 %

CHI-SQUARE-VALUE: 9.4575

(c) n = 12

LEFT TAIL: 1.75 %

```
---
-2.20    ........
-1.80    ..................
-1.40    .........................
-1.00    ...............................
-0.60    ...................................
-0.20    .........................................
 0.20    .......................................................
 0.60    ...............................................
 1.00    .......................................
 1.40    ...........................
 1.80    ....................
 2.20
---
```

RIGHT TAIL: 1.00 %

CHI-SQUARE-VALUE: 13.5310

Figure 3.5   Central limit theorem; simulation 400 realizations $> P(\underline{x} > 0.20) = 0.0139$; $(\chi^2_{12})^{0.95} =$ 21.0.

$$\left.\begin{array}{l} \underline{x}_1 = \cos(2\pi\underline{r}_2)\{-2\ln(\underline{r}_1)\}^{0.5} \\ \underline{x}_2 = \sin(2\pi\underline{r}_2)\{-2\ln(\underline{r}_1)\}^{0.5}. \end{array}\right\} \tag{3.38}$$

Also see Box and Muller (1958) and Fishman (1978, p. 411). A disadvantage of this method is that the sine and the cosine functions require much computer time. Therefore the next method is also used.

3.6 REJECTION METHOD

The rejection method was devised by von Neumann, and holds not only for normal distributions. It is based on the following considerations (also see the estimation of π in Section 1.1, Example 1.5). Let $p(x)$ be a 'bounded' density function, that is, both the domain and the mapping are finite:

$$p(x)\begin{cases} \leqslant m & \text{if } a \leqslant x \leqslant b \\ = 0 & \text{elsewhere.} \end{cases} \tag{3.39}$$

Figure 3.6 illustrates a bounded density function. (The normal distribution does not have a finite domain.)

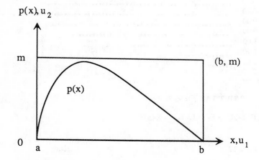

Figure 3.6   Rejection method

Now consider the independent uniform variables $\underline{u}_1 \sim U(a,b)$ and $\underline{u}_2 \sim U(0,m)$. It is easy to sample such variables, as we saw in Section 3.3.2. Obviously the point (u_1, u_2) is a point in the rectangle of Figure 3.6. If that point lies above the curve $p(x)$, it is rejected; otherwise u_1 is used as a sample for $\underline{x}$. It can be proved that this procedure is correct indeed. Intuitively we see that as $p(x)$ increases, the probability of accepting $x = u_1$ increases. Obviously the rejection method becomes more efficient as the ratio of the area under $p(x)$ and the area of the total rectangle increases.

It is not necessary to use a rectangle in Figure 3.6. It can be proved that any method for sampling a given variable can be used to sample another variable, provided the ratio of their density functions is limited. So simple density functions can be used to simulate complicated density functions. See Devroye (1986, p. 837), Fishman (1978, pp. 399–401), Ripley (1987, pp. 60–3), and Ross (1985, pp. 438–42).

3.6.1 Normal Distribution

It can be proved that the following rejection procedure gives two independent standard *normal* variables x_1 and x_2.

PROCEDURE 3.1
(1) generate $r_1, r_2 \sim U(0,1)$.
(2) calculate $w_1 = 2r_1 - 1$ and $w_2 = 2r_2 - 1$.
(3) if $w = w_1^2 + w_2^2 > 1$ go to (1).
(4) calculate $c = \sqrt{(-2\ln(w)/w)}$, $x_1 = cw_1$ and $x_2 = cw_2$.

This procedure is expected to be faster than the Box–Muller method.

3.7 DISTRIBUTIONS RELATED TO THE NORMAL DISTRIBUTION

In this section we shall discuss lognormal, chi-square, Student, and F distributions, using the fact that these distributions are related to the normal distribution.

3.7.1 Lognormal Distribution

If $x \sim N(\mu_x, \sigma_x^2)$ then $y = e^x$ is distributed lognormally, since $\ln(y)$ equals x and x is distributed normally. The notation is $y \sim LN(\mu_y, \sigma_y^2)$ with

$$\left. \begin{array}{l} E(y) = \mu_y = e^{\mu_x + \sigma_x^2/2} \\[2mm] \mathrm{var}(y) = \sigma_y^2 = \mu_y^2(e^{\sigma_x^2} - 1). \end{array} \right\} \tag{3.40a}$$

or

$$\left. \begin{array}{l} E(x) = \mu_x = \log(\mu_y) - 0.5\ln[\,(\sigma_y^2/\mu_y^2) + 1\,] \\[2mm] \mathrm{var}(x) = \sigma_x^2 = \log[\,(\sigma_y^2/\mu_y^2) + 1\,]. \end{array} \right\} \tag{3.40b}$$

This leads to the following procedure for sampling the lognormally distributed variable y.

PROCEDURE 3.2
(1) generate $z \sim N(0,1)$.
(2) $x := \mu_x + \sigma_x z$.
(3) $y := \exp(x)$.

Note that if the parameters μ_y and σ_y^2 are given, then (3.40b) gives the parameters μ_x and σ_x^2, which are used in step (2) of the procedure.

3.7.2 Chi-square Distribution

A chi-square variable with n degrees of freedom is defined by

$$\chi_n^2 = \sum_{i=1}^{n} z_i^2 \qquad \text{with } z_i \sim NID(0,1), \tag{3.41}$$

where NID stands for normally and independently distributed. So to sample χ_n^2 we can take n independent samples from $N(0,1)$. An alternative procedure uses the gamma distribution, as (3.25) and (3.27) showed. But there are more techniques; see Fishman (1978, pp. 410–17) and Ripley (1987, pp. 82–7).

It is well-known that n independent samples $\underline{x}_i$ from $N(\mu, \sigma^2)$ give the unbiased estimator of σ^2

$$\underline{s}^2 = \frac{\sum_{i=1}^{n} (\underline{x}_i - \bar{\underline{x}})^2}{(n-1)}, \tag{3.42}$$

and that

$$\frac{(n-1)\underline{s}^2}{\sigma^2} = \underline{\chi}_{(n-1)}^2. \tag{3.43}$$

Note that one degree of freedom is lost in the latter equation because of the constraint $\sum_{i=1}^{n} \underline{x}_i/n = \bar{\underline{x}}$. So instead of going through the traditional computation of s^2 in (3.42), we can sample χ_{n-1}^2 and compute $\frac{\sigma^2}{(n-1)} \chi_{n-1}^2$ (the example with the t distribution in Chapter 1 used the traditional approach).

3.7.3 Student's t Distribution

In Chapter 1, equation (1.8), we saw the well-known definition of Student's t statistic with $n-1$ degrees of freedom:

$$\underline{t}_{n-1} = \frac{\bar{\underline{x}} - \mu}{\underline{s}/\sqrt{n}}, \tag{3.44}$$

where $\underline{s}^2$ was defined in (3.42); $\bar{\underline{x}}$ and $\underline{s}$ are mutually independent if (and only if) $\underline{x}_i$ is normally distributed. Obviously

$$\underline{z} = \frac{\bar{\underline{x}} - \mu}{\sigma/\sqrt{n}} \sim N(0,1). \tag{3.45}$$

Substitution of (3.43) and (3.45) into (3.44) gives

$$\underline{t}_{n-1} = \frac{\underline{z}}{\sqrt{(\underline{\chi}_{n-1}^2/(n-1))}}, \tag{3.46}$$

where $\underline{z}$ and $\underline{\chi}_{n-1}^2$ are independent. It is well-known that

$$\left. \begin{array}{l} E(\underline{t}_{n-1}) = 0 \\[2mm] \mathrm{var}(\underline{t}_{n-1}) = (n-1)/(n-3), \end{array} \right\} \tag{3.47}$$

provided $n \geqslant 4$. Equation (3.46) shows that to sample $\underline{t}_{n-1}$ we can combine the algorithms for sampling normal variables and χ^2 variables. For $n > 30$, however, $\underline{t}_{n-1}$ may be approximated through the standard normal distribution.

3.7.4 F Distribution

The F statistic is often used to test the equality of two estimated variances:

$$\underline{F}_{n-1,m-1} = \frac{\underline{s}_x^2}{\underline{s}_y^2}, \tag{3.48}$$

where $\underline{s}_x^2$ is given by (3.42) and where

$$\underline{s}_y^2 = \frac{\sum\limits_{j=1}^{m} (\underline{y}_j - \underline{\bar{y}})^2}{m-1} \tag{3.49}$$

with $\underline{y}_j \sim \mathrm{NID}(\mu_y, \sigma_y^2)$ where $\sigma_y^2 = \sigma_x^2 = \sigma^2$; moreover $\underline{y}_j$ is independent of $\underline{x}_i$. Substitution of (3.43) into (3.48) and assuming n and m degrees of freedom (for ease of representation) gives the following expression for the F statistic with n and m degrees of freedom:

$$\underline{F}_{n,m} = \frac{\underline{\chi}_n^2/n}{\underline{\chi}_m^2/m}, \tag{3.50}$$

where $\underline{\chi}_n^2$ and $\underline{\chi}_m^2$ are independent. So to sample the F variable we generate two independent χ^2 variables with the appropriate degrees of freedom (see Section 3.7.2). It can further be proved that

$$\begin{aligned} E(\underline{F}_{n,m}) &= m/(m-2) \\ \mathrm{var}(\underline{F}_{n,m}) &= \{2m^2(m+n-2)\}/\{n(m-2)^2(m-4)\} \quad \text{with } m > 4. \end{aligned} \left.\begin{aligned} \\ \\ \end{aligned}\right\} \tag{3.51}$$

3.8 MULTIVARIATE DISTRIBUTIONS

First we will describe multivariate distributions in general; then we will focus on multivariate normal distributions. For an extensive treatment of sampling from multivariate distributions we refer to Johnson (1987) and Devroye (1986, pp. 554–610).

If $\mathbf{y} = (\underline{y}_1, \underline{y}_2, \ldots, \underline{y}_n)'$ were a vector of *independent* variables, then the simultaneous distribution function of $\mathbf{y}$ would be

$$F(y) = \prod_{i=1}^{n} F_i(y_i), \tag{3.52}$$

where $F_i(y_i)$ represents the marginal distribution function of $\underline{y}_i$. So to sample the vector $(\underline{y}_1, \underline{y}_2, \ldots, \underline{y}_n)'$ we sample the component $\underline{y}_i$ from its distribution F_i independently.

The problem becomes more complex when the variables are *dependent*. Then the joint distribution function can be expressed through the conditional distributions:

$$F(\mathbf{y}) = F_1(y_1) F_2(y_2 | \underline{y}_1 = y_1) \cdots F_n(y_n | \underline{y}_1 = y_1, \ldots, \underline{y}_{n-1} = y_{n-1}). \quad (3.53)$$

To sample the vector $\mathbf{y}$, we may generate n independent random numbers $\underline{r}_1, \ldots, \underline{r}_n$, and solve the following set of recursive non-linear equations:

$$\left. \begin{array}{l} F_1(y_1) = r_1 \\ F_2(y_2 | \underline{y}_1 = y_1) = r_2 \\ \phantom{F_2(y_2 | \underline{y}_1 = y_1) = r_2} \vdots \\ F_n(y_n | \underline{y}_1 = y_1, \ldots, \underline{y}_{n-1} = y_{n-1}) = r_n. \end{array} \right\} \quad (3.54)$$

Since the indices $1, 2, \ldots, n$ can be permuted, it is not known in advance which solution sequence is most efficient; there are $n!$ possibilities.

3.8.1 Multivariate Normal Distribution

The density function of the n-variate normal vector $\underline{\mathbf{y}} = (\underline{y}_1, \ldots, \underline{y}_n)'$ is

$$p(\mathbf{y}) = ((2\pi)^n |\Omega|)^{-1/2} \exp\{-\tfrac{1}{2}(\mathbf{y} - \boldsymbol{\mu})' \, \Omega^{-1} \, (\mathbf{y} - \boldsymbol{\mu})\}, \quad (3.55)$$

where the vector of n means is $\boldsymbol{\mu} = (\mu_1, \ldots, \mu_i, \ldots, \mu_n)'$ with $\mu_i = E(\underline{y}_i)$, and Ω denotes the $n \times n$ covariance matrix. For example, $n = 2$ gives

$$\boldsymbol{\mu} = \begin{bmatrix} \mu_1 \\ \mu_2 \end{bmatrix} \quad \text{and} \quad \Omega = \begin{bmatrix} \sigma_1^2 & \sigma_{12} \\ \sigma_{12} & \sigma_2^2 \end{bmatrix} = \begin{bmatrix} \sigma_1^2 & \rho\sigma_1\sigma_2 \\ \rho\sigma_1\sigma_2 & \sigma_2^2 \end{bmatrix}.$$

Obviously $n = 1$ gives $\boldsymbol{\mu} = \mu_1$ and $\Omega = \sigma_1^2$; see Section 3.5. The n-variate normal distribution with the vector of means $\boldsymbol{\mu}$ and the covariance matrix Ω is denoted by $N_n(\boldsymbol{\mu}, \Omega)$. Obviously we have $\Omega = (\text{cov}(\underline{y}_i, \underline{y}_j)) = (\sigma_{ij})$ with $i, j = 1, \ldots, n$; if $i = j$, then $\text{cov}(\underline{y}_i, \underline{y}_i) = \text{var}(\underline{\mathbf{y}}) = \sigma_i^2$. The matrix Ω must be symmetric and 'positive definite'; that is, $\mathbf{y}' \Omega \mathbf{y} > 0$ for all $\mathbf{y} \neq 0$.

To sample $\underline{\mathbf{y}}$ we use the fact that Ω can be written as

$$\Omega = \mathbf{A}\mathbf{A}'. \quad (3.56)$$

The matrix $\mathbf{A}$ is not unique. One choice is the unique $n \times n$ lower triangular matrix

$$\mathbf{A} = \begin{bmatrix} a_{11} & 0 & \ldots & 0 \\ a_{21} & a_{22} & \ldots & 0 \\ \vdots & \vdots & & \vdots \\ a_{n1} & a_{n2} & \ldots & a_{nn} \end{bmatrix}, \quad (3.57)$$

which is computed through Choleski's technique: see Johnson (1987, p. 53) and Naylor et al. (1966, pp. 97–9) and standard software libraries such as IMSL and NAG. For example, $n=2$ gives

$$\begin{bmatrix} \sigma_1^2 & \rho\sigma_1\sigma_2 \\ \rho\sigma_1\sigma_2 & \sigma_2^2 \end{bmatrix} = \begin{bmatrix} \sigma_1 & 0 \\ \sigma_2\rho & \sigma_2(1-\rho^2)^{\frac{1}{2}} \end{bmatrix} \begin{bmatrix} \sigma_1 & \sigma_2\rho \\ 0 & \sigma_2(1-\rho^2)^{\frac{1}{2}} \end{bmatrix}.$$

To sample $\underline{y}$ we consider linear transformations of multivariate normal variables:

$$\underline{y} = \mathbf{L}\underline{z} + \boldsymbol{\mu}, \tag{3.58}$$

where $\underline{z} \sim N_m(\boldsymbol{\mu}_z, \boldsymbol{\Omega}_z)$, $\mathbf{L}$ is an $n \times m$ matrix with $n \leqslant m$, and $\boldsymbol{\mu}$ is a vector with n elements. Then obviously $\underline{y}$ is a vector of n stochastic variables. It can be proved that $\underline{y}$ remains multivariate normal (linear transformations of univariate normal variables were discussed in the text leading to equation (3.37)). Its means vector $\boldsymbol{\mu}_y$ and its covariance matrix $\boldsymbol{\Omega}_y$ follow from

$$\left. \begin{array}{l} E(\underline{y}) = \mathbf{L}\ E(z) + \boldsymbol{\mu} \\ \boldsymbol{\Omega}_y \ = \mathbf{L}\boldsymbol{\Omega}_z\mathbf{L}', \end{array} \right\} \tag{3.59}$$

which hold not only for multivariate normally distributed variables but for all multivariate variables.

Exercise 3.8: Suppose $\underline{z}_1$ and $\underline{z}_2$ have variance σ_1^2 and σ_2^2 respectively, and covariance σ_{12}. Use (3.59) to derive the formula for $\mathrm{var}(\underline{y})$ with $\underline{y} = \underline{z}_1 + \underline{z}_2$.

If in (3.58) we take $\mathbf{L} = \mathbf{A}$, where $\mathbf{A}$ is the lower triangular matrix of (3.57), then we get

$$\left. \begin{array}{l} y_1 = a_{11}z_1 + \mu_1 \\ y_2 = a_{21}z_1 + a_{22}z_2 + \mu_2 \\ \quad\vdots \\ y_n = a_{n1}z_1 + a_{n2}z_2 + \cdots + a_{nn}z_n + \mu_n. \end{array} \right\} \tag{3.60}$$

Before we can apply this set of equations, we must express $\mathbf{A}$ in terms of $\boldsymbol{\Omega}$, since $\boldsymbol{\Omega}$ is a given parameter of the multivariate normal distribution $N_n(\boldsymbol{\mu},\boldsymbol{\Omega})$. It can be proved that (3.56) yields the following set of recursive equations:

$$\left. \begin{array}{ll} a_{i1} = \sigma_{i1}/\sigma_{11}^{1/2} & \text{with } 1 \leqslant i \leqslant n \\ a_{ii} = (\sigma_{ii} - \Sigma_{k=1}^{i-1}\ a_{ik}^2)^{1/2} & \\ a_{ij} = (\sigma_{ij} - \Sigma_{k=1}^{j-1}\ a_{ik}a_{jk})/a_{jj} & \text{with } 1 < j < i \leqslant n. \end{array} \right\} \tag{3.61}$$

The final result is Procedure 3.3.

PROCEDURE 3.3

(1) read μ and $\Omega = (\sigma_{ij})$.
(2) calculate $\mathbf{A} = (a_{ij})$ from Ω, using (3.61).
(3) generate $\mathbf{z} = (z_1, \ldots, z_n)'$ from $N_n(\mathbf{0}, \mathbf{I})$, using a procedure for independent standard normal variables (see Section 3.5).
(4) calculate $\mathbf{y} = \mathbf{A}\mathbf{z} + \mu$.

For example, $n = 2$ yields

$$\left. \begin{aligned} y_1 &= \sigma_1 z_1 + \mu_1 \\ y_2 &= \sigma_2 \{\rho z_1 + (1 - \rho^2)^{1/2} z_2\} + \mu_2. \end{aligned} \right\}$$

3.9 TIME SERIES

In many applications it is unrealistic to assume that the stochastic variables are independent over time. For example, waiting times are positively correlated, that is, a long waiting time for a customer increases the probability of a long waiting time for the next customer. We use the following symbols for a time series: $\{x_t : t = \ldots, -1, 0, 1, \ldots\}$, $E(x_t) = \mu_t$, $\mathrm{var}(x_t) = \sigma_t^2$ and $\mathrm{cov}(x_t, x_{t'}) = \sigma_{tt'}$. We are particularly interested in *wide-sense stationary* time series, that is, the expectations and the variances are independent of time, and the covariances depend only on the distance or 'lag' (say) k between the points in time t and t', with $k = |t - t'|$. In other words, we have $E(x_t) = \mu$, $\mathrm{cov}(x_t, x_{t'}) = \sigma_{|t-t'|}$, and $\mathrm{var}(x_t) = \sigma_{|0|} = \sigma^2$. Its autocorrelation with lag k is

$$\rho(k) = \frac{\mathrm{cov}(x_t, x_{t+k})}{\sigma_t \sigma_{t+k}} = \frac{\mathrm{cov}(x_t, x_{t+k})}{\sigma^2}. \tag{3.62}$$

Next we shall focus on special types of autocorrelation functions, namely linearly and exponentially decreasing ones. Boender and Romeijn (1989) give a solution for arbitrary autocorrelation functions. We concentrate on normal time series. For more literature on time series we refer to Devroye (1986, p. 571).

3.9.1 Linear Autocorrelation Function

A linearly decreasing autocorrelation function is defined as

$$\rho(k) = \begin{cases} 1 - \alpha k & \text{if } k = 1, 2, \ldots, m \quad \text{and} \quad m \leqslant 1/\alpha < m + 1 \\ 0 & \text{if } k = m + 1, m + 2, \ldots. \end{cases} \tag{3.63}$$

Let z be uniformly distributed on the interval $[-a, a]$. So its variance is $\sigma_z^2 = a^2/3$; see (3.22). Now we define the initial element of the time series:

$$x_0 = \sum_{j=1}^{n} z_j. \tag{3.64}$$

Because of the central limit theorem this variable $\underline{x}_0$ approximates a Gaussian distribution. Its expectation is 0 and its variance is $n\sigma_z^2 = na^2/3$. To generate the next variable of the time series, we drop p old variables $\underline{z}$ and draw p new ones. In general the tth variable is

$$\underline{x}_t = \sum_{j=tp+1}^{tp+n} \underline{z}_j. \qquad (3.65)$$

Because $\underline{x}_t$ and $\underline{x}_{t+1}$ have a number of variables in common (namely $n-p$ variables $\underline{z}$), they are correlated. The exact correlation is calculated as follows. As the variables $\underline{z}$ are independent, we have

$$E(\underline{x}_t \, \underline{x}_{t+k}) = E\left\{ \left(\sum_{i=tp+1}^{tp+n} \underline{z}_i \right) \left(\sum_{j=(t+k)p+1}^{(t+k)p+n} \underline{z}_j \right) \right\}$$

$$= \begin{cases} (n-pk)\sigma_z^2 & \text{if } pk < n \\ 0 & \text{otherwise.} \end{cases} \qquad (3.66)$$

The definition of the autocorrelation in (3.62) and $E(\underline{x}_t) = 0$ give

$$\rho(k) = \frac{(n-pk)\sigma_z^2}{n\sigma_z^2} = 1 - k\frac{p}{n}. \qquad (3.67)$$

Comparing (3.63) and (3.67) shows that the desired autocorrelation function (3.63) with given α is obtained by $p = \alpha n$ (the real number α is approximated by the rational number p/n). For example, $\alpha = \frac{1}{4}$ and $n = 12$ gives $p = 3$; however, given $\alpha = \frac{1}{4}$ a solution is also $n = 20$ and $p = 5$. The latter solution takes more computer time but better approximates a normal distribution.

Exercise 3.9: Implement the procedure of this section; sample 500 observations and estimate $\rho(1)$.

3.9.2 Exponential Autocorrelation Function

Exponentially decreasing autocorrelation functions are often used in economic models, for example, in so-called exponential smoothing and in adaptive expectations. Waiting times also show this type of autocorrelation function. This function is defined by

$$\rho(k) = \lambda^k \qquad \text{with } 0 < \lambda < 1 \quad \text{and} \quad k = 1, 2, \ldots . \qquad (3.68)$$

This function can be generated by taking a Gaussian 'noise' $\underline{y}_t$ that is a linear combination of the previous noise $\underline{y}_{t-1}$ and independent 'white noise' $\underline{x}_t$:

$$\underline{y}_t = \lambda \underline{y}_{t-1} + \underline{x}_t \qquad \text{with} \quad t = 1, 2, \ldots$$

$$\underline{x}_t \sim \text{NID}(0, \sigma_x^2). \qquad (3.69)$$

To initialize the process we sample $\underline{y}_0 \sim N(0, \sigma_x^2/(1-\lambda^2))$. This initialization implies $\text{var}(\underline{y}_t) = \lambda^2 \sigma_x^2/(1-\lambda^2) + \sigma_x^2 = \sigma_x^2/(1-\lambda^2)$, $t = 0, 1, 2, \ldots$ so the variance is constant over time.

Exercise 3.10: Prove that $\text{cov}(\underline{y}_t, \underline{y}_{t+k}) = \lambda^k \sigma_x^2/(1 - \lambda^2)$ with $k = 0, 1, \ldots$.

3.10 EPILOGUE

All methods discussed in this chapter assume that the random numbers $\underline{r}$ are truly uniformly distributed: $\underline{r} \sim U(0, 1)$. Chapter 2 showed that most pseudorandom number generators show a lattice structure. In general, this lattice structure is transformed to a structure in the variates generated, so the results must be treated with caution. See Ripley (1987, pp. 56–68).

APPENDIX: NAG ROUTINES

There is much software available for mainframes to sample all kinds of variables. These subroutines call the pseudorandom generator. The user may treat the subroutines as 'black boxes'. For example, the NAG library has subroutines for all distributions discussed in this chapter. Some examples are the following Pascal versions of these NAG routines.

FUNCTION GO5DDF(m,s: DOUBLE): DOUBLE; EXTERNAL;
This function gives samples from a normal distribution with mean m and standard deviation s. Note that s does not denote the variance.

FUNCTION GO5DBF(a: DOUBLE): DOUBLE; EXTERNAL;
This function samples from the exponential distribution with mean a. Remember that the mean equals the inverse of the parameter α in the distribution function (3.17); see (3.19).

For the following procedures we define VEC as an ARRAY [1..nx] OF DOUBLE as in Section 2.5.

PROCEDURE GO5ECF(a: DOUBLE; VAR x: VEC; nx,ifail: INTEGER);
EXTERNAL;
This procedure samples from a Poisson distribution with mean a. It gives a reference vector x of length nx, which is used in the following function, called, GO5EYF.

FUNCTION GO5EYF(x: VEC; nx: INTEGER): INTEGER; EXTERNAL;
This function samples from a discrete distribution that has probabilities given by the vector x; see the table look-up method in Section 3.1.

Exercise 3.11: (a) Use a subroutine to sample $\underline{x}$ 25 times from the exponential distribution with parameter $\alpha = 2$. Test if $E(\underline{x}) = 2$ and $E(\underline{x}) = \frac{1}{2}$ respectively, using a t statistic.
           (b) Sample $\underline{x}$ 25 times from $N(0, 2)$ and compute s^2. Test if $E(\underline{s}^2) = 2$ and $E(\underline{s}^2) = 4$ respectively, using a χ^2 statistic.

REFERENCES

Boender C. G. E. and H. C. Romeijn (1989) *Simulating the Future Behavior of Inflation and Interest Rates.* Erasmus University Rotterdam, H2–24, P.O. Box 1738, Rotterdam.

Box G. E. P. and M. E. Muller (1958) A note on the generation of random normal deviates. *Annals of Mathematical Statistics*, **29**, 610–11.

Devroye L. (1986) *Non-uniform Random Variate Generation*, Springer-Verlag, New York.

Fishman G. S. (1978) *Principles of Discrete Event Simulation*, Wiley, New York.

Johnson M. E. (1987) *Multivariate Statistical Simulation*, Wiley, New York.

Johnson N. L. and S. Kotz (1972) *Distributions in Statistics: Continuous Multivariate Distributions*, Wiley, New York.

Naylor T. H., J. L. Balintfy, D. S. Burdick, and Kong Chu (1966) *Computer Simulation Techniques*, Wiley, New York.

Ripley B. D. (1987) *Stochastic Simulation*, Wiley, New York.

Ross S. M. (1985) *Introduction to Probability Models*, Academic Press, Orlando, Florida.

REFERENCES

_____ Chapter 4

Economic and Corporate Models

In this chapter we consider the use of simulation in the scientific disciplines of economics and business administration. Readers not interested in one or more topics of this chapter, can skip the corresponding sections, since the following chapters do not build on this chapter.

Chapter 4 is organized as follows.

—4.1 Macro-economic models
  First we give a simple example, namely a model developed by Klein (1950). Next we discuss general macro-economic models including simultaneous equations, which can be solved by the Gauss–Seidel algorithm. Finally, we augment these models with stochastic noise, which may or may not be additive.
—4.2 Meso-economic models
  Some models describe sectors of the national economy, such as the hide–leather–shoe industry. The theoretical background of many sectorial models is a simple demand and delayed supply model, which leads to 'cobweb' or 'hog cycle' behaviour.
—4.3 Micro-economic models
  We briefly discuss classical optimizing models versus behavioural, bounded rationality, satisficing models.
—4.4 Micro-simulation
  A sample of individuals may be simulated in order to quantify the aggregate effects of, say, tax reforms. We briefly discuss different types of micro-simulation.
—4.5 Corporate models
  Corporate models are very practical models, which have become popular with the introduction of spreadsheet software on microcomputers. An example of an older model, run on a mainframe, is the Anheuser–Busch beer model.
—4.6 Risk analysis
  To quantify the risks of an investment project, stochastic cash flows may be simulated.
—4.7 System dynamics
  Forrester's industrial dynamics was inspired by optimal control theory, which emphasizes concepts like feedback and exponential delay. We discuss various concepts in system dynamics and include graphical and mathematical examples.

4.1 MACRO-ECONOMIC MODELS

A simple model has already been presented in Chapter 1, equations (1.1)–(1.3). In practice, more complicated models are used to evaluate economic scenarios. The Dutch Central Planning Bureau (CPB), for example, uses simulation to examine the consequences of different governmental policies. In most developed countries, similar models are used by governments and large financial institutions. Moreover, private companies develop their own models to forecast economic developments, and sell these forecasts to other corporations, which use these predictions for their own policy making (as we shall see in Section 5 of this chapter). Most governments publish the results of their simulation studies in quarterly and annual economic surveys and policy evaluations. In the Netherlands the models of the Central Planning Bureau are also used during election time to quantify the consequences of economic reforms proposed in the election programs of the various political parties.

The economic simulations mentioned above are deterministic. So the model builders assume that stochastic noise may be ignored. They ignore disturbance terms, as it would be hard to distinguish between the effects of the disturbance terms and the effects of economic policies. Moreover it would take extra computer time to sample disturbance terms (to account for noise) and to replicate simulation runs (to get statistically reliable results; see Chapter 10).

We first give an example of a simple econometric model, and then discuss general econometric models, including simultaneous equations and noise respectively.

4.1.1 Klein's Model

Klein's (1950) model consists of three behavioural equations: one for total real consumption C, one for real 'net' investment I (which excludes depreciation), and one for the real total wage bill in the private sector W_1. In addition, the model has three definitional equations: one for total profits P, one for capital K, and one for real national income Y. The policy variables are: business taxes TX, wages paid by the government W_2, and governmental plus net foreign demand G. The total model is as follows:

$$\underline{C}_t = \beta_0 + \beta_1(\underline{W}_{1t} + W_{2t}) + \beta_2\underline{P}_t + \beta_3\underline{P}_{t-1} + \underline{\epsilon}_t \tag{4.1}$$

$$\underline{I}_t = \gamma_0 + \gamma_1\underline{P}_t + \gamma_2\underline{P}_{t-1} - \gamma_3\underline{K}_{t-1} + \underline{\xi}_t \tag{4.2}$$

$$\underline{W}_{1t} = \alpha_0 + \alpha_1(\underline{Y}_t + TX_t - W_{2t}) + \alpha_2(\underline{Y}_{t-1} + TX_{t-1} - W_{2t-1}) + \alpha_3 t + \underline{\eta}_t \tag{4.3}$$

$$\underline{P}_t = \underline{Y}_t - (\underline{W}_{1t} + W_{2t}) \tag{4.4}$$

$$\underline{K}_t = \underline{K}_{t-1} + \underline{I}_t \tag{4.5}$$

$$\underline{Y}_t = \underline{C}_t + \underline{I}_t + G_t - TX_t \tag{4.6}$$

This set of equations forms a linear model, without constraints. The lack of explicit constraints means implicitly that C, W_1, K and Y are assumed to remain positive; I and P may be negative. Hence the disturbance terms ($\underline{\epsilon}$, $\underline{\xi}$, $\underline{\eta}$) must have such a joint distribution that C, W_1, K and Y remain positive. For a further analysis of this model we refer to Theil (1971, pp. 434–8).

*4.1.2 Simultaneous Equations

It is well-known that econometric models can be represented by a system of *non-linear* equations with $p+1$ vectors of (possibly delayed) endogenous variables $\mathbf{y}_t, \mathbf{y}_{t-1}, \ldots, \mathbf{y}_{t-p} \in \mathbb{R}^n$, $q+1$ vectors of (possibly delayed) exogenous and policy variables $\mathbf{x}_t, \mathbf{x}_{t-1}, \ldots, \mathbf{x}_{t-q} \in \mathbb{R}^m$, a vector of coefficients related to the endogenous variables $\mathbf{a} \in \mathbb{R}^{n(p+1)}$, and a vector of coefficients related to the exogenous and policy variables $\mathbf{b} \in \mathbb{R}^{m(q+1)}$:

$$y_{it} = f_i(\mathbf{y}_t, \mathbf{y}_{t-1}, \ldots, \mathbf{y}_{t-p}, \mathbf{x}_t, \mathbf{x}_{t-1}, \ldots, \mathbf{x}_{t-q}; \mathbf{a}, \mathbf{b})$$

$$\text{with } i = 1, 2, \ldots, n \quad \text{and } t = 0, \ldots, T. \tag{4.7}$$

We assume that the model is 'normalized', that is, $a_i = 0$ in the ith equation. We call the computation of (4.7) 'deterministic simulation'. This type of simulation is simple: given the starting values for the delayed endogenous vectors $\mathbf{y}_{-1}, \mathbf{y}_{-2}, \ldots, \mathbf{y}_{-p}$ and the values for the vectors of exogenous and policy variables for the past and the future $\mathbf{x}_t$ with $t = -q, -q+1, \ldots, 0, 1, \ldots, T$, it is straightforward to compute $\mathbf{y}_0, \mathbf{y}_1, \ldots, \mathbf{y}_T$.

If the system of equations in (4.7) contains *simultaneous* equations, then the *Gauss–Seidel* algorithm can be applied to compute the vector $\mathbf{y}$ for each period t. This is an iterative algorithm. We demonstrate this algorithm through the (linear) Klein model, which was presented in (4.1)–(4.6), excluding noise. We begin by picking an initial value for Y_t, say $Y_t^{(1)}$ (often we take the most recent known value Y_{t-1}). Then we can calculate $W_{1t}^{(1)}$ by means of (4.3). Next we compute $P_t^{(1)}$ through (4.4). Using these $W_{1t}^{(1)}$ and $P_t^{(1)}$ values, we calculate $C_t^{(1)}$ from (4.1) and $I_t^{(1)}$ from (4.2). We determine $K_t^{(1)}$ by means of (4.5). Substitution of $I_t^{(1)}$ and $C_t^{(1)}$ (besides the values of the exogenous variables G_t and TX_t) into (4.6) gives a new value for Y_t, namely $Y_t^{(2)}$, which very probably deviates from the original value $Y_t^{(1)}$. So the second iteration begins. Now we substitute the new value $Y_t^{(2)}$ into (4.3) and calculate $W_{1t}^{(2)}$, and so on. After a number of iterations the new iteration yields results that hardly deviate from the results of the previous iteration, and we stop. In general we stop the computation for period t, as soon as the following condition holds for all n endogenous variables y_{it} ($i = 1, \ldots, n$):

$$|y_{it}^{(j+1)} - y_{it}^{(j)}| < \epsilon, \tag{4.8}$$

where ϵ is a small predetermined value, for example, $\epsilon = 0.01$. The Gauss–Seidel algorithm is applied for all periods $t = 1, \ldots, T$. Note that the Gauss–Seidel algorithm does not always converge.

In Klein's model we began by picking a value for a certain variable, namely Y_t, and substituted this value into (4.3). A bad choice would have been C_t, because in that case we would also have to fix I_t in order to compute Y_t through (4.6). In general we can simplify the Gauss–Seidel solution if we make the system of equations *recursive*, as much as possible. So in the example we first move all endogenous variables in (4.1) through (4.6) to the left of the equality signs. Then the left-hand side of the model becomes, in matrix notation,

$$
\begin{bmatrix}
1 & 0 & -\beta_1 & -\beta_2 & 0 & 0 \\
0 & 1 & 0 & -\gamma_1 & 0 & 0 \\
0 & 0 & 1 & 0 & 0 & -\alpha_1 \\
0 & 0 & 1 & 1 & 0 & -1 \\
0 & -1 & 0 & 0 & 1 & 0 \\
-1 & -1 & 0 & 0 & 0 & 1
\end{bmatrix}
\begin{bmatrix}
\underline{C}_t \\
\underline{I}_t \\
\underline{W}_{1t} \\
\underline{P}_t \\
\underline{K}_t \\
\underline{Y}_t
\end{bmatrix} .
$$

Next we rearrange the order of the equations:

$$
\begin{bmatrix}
1 & 0 & 0 & 0 & -\alpha_1 & 0 \\
1 & 1 & 0 & 0 & -1 & 0 \\
-\beta_1 & -\beta_2 & 1 & 0 & 0 & 0 \\
0 & -\gamma_1 & 0 & 1 & 0 & 0 \\
0 & 0 & -1 & -1 & 1 & 0 \\
0 & 0 & 0 & -1 & 0 & 1
\end{bmatrix}
\begin{bmatrix}
\underline{W}_{1t} \\
\underline{P}_t \\
\underline{C}_t \\
\underline{I}_t \\
\underline{Y}_t \\
\underline{K}_t
\end{bmatrix} .
$$

This rearrangement yields a nearly lower triangular matrix: there are only two non-zero elements above the main diagonal. Linear models are recursive if the matrix of the coefficients of the endogenous variables is lower triangular. So we start with the equation for $\underline{W}_{1t}$, which requires a value for $\underline{Y}_t$ (see the coefficient $-\alpha_1$). Figure 4.1 gives example output for Klein's model, ignoring noise. The stopping criterion (4.8) is (arbitrarily) replaced by

$$
|C^{(j)} - C^{(j-1)}| + |I^{(j)} - I^{(j-1)}| \leqslant 0.02.
$$

Note that a linear model such as Klein's model can also be solved by inversion of the matrix of coefficients. We used Klein's model only for a simple demonstration of the Gauss–Seidel algorithm. For non-linear equations we refer to Van der Giessen (1970).

4.1.3 Noise

Macro-economic models can be augmented with *noise*. Then the simulation becomes stochastic. Should that noise be *additive* or *multiplicative*? Often models are transformed such that they become linear with additive noise. For example, economists frequently use the Cobb–Douglas production function

$$
y = \alpha x_1^\beta \, x_2^\gamma, \tag{4.9a}
$$

where y denotes output, x_1 and x_2 refer to input of type 1 and 2 respectively, α is a scaling constant, β and γ denote 'production elasticities', which measure the relative change in output in response to a relative change in one input: $\beta = (\partial y / y)/(\partial x_1 / x_1)$ and $\gamma = (\partial y / y)/(\partial x_2 / x_2)$. In practice, it is simple to estimate β and γ (besides α), when a *linear* regression model is used. Therefore a logarithmic transformation is applied to (4.9a):

$$\ln(y) = \ln(\alpha) + \beta \ln(x_1) + \gamma \ln(x_2). \tag{4.9b}$$

Upon defining $y^* = \ln(y)$, $\alpha^* = \ln(\alpha)$, $x_1^* = \ln(x_1)$, and $x_2^* = \ln(x_2)$, this equation is equivalent to

$$y^* = \alpha^* + \beta x_1^* + \gamma x_2^*. \tag{4.9c}$$

Specifying additive noise $\underline{\epsilon}^*$ yields

$$\underline{y}^* = \alpha^* + \beta x_1^* + \gamma x_2^* + \underline{\epsilon}^*. \tag{4.10a}$$

So (4.10a) is a linear regression model (we shall further discuss linear regression in other chapters). Note that the additive noise $\underline{\epsilon}^*$ in (4.10a) implies multiplicative noise $\underline{\epsilon}$ with $\underline{\epsilon}^* = \ln \underline{\epsilon}$ in the original model (4.9a):

$$\underline{y} = \alpha x_1^\beta \, x_2^\gamma \, \underline{\epsilon}. \tag{4.10b}$$

Next $\underline{\epsilon}^*$ in (4.10a) is assumed to be normally and independently distributed with zero mean and constant variance σ^2 (so $\underline{\epsilon}$ is lognormally distributed; see Section 3.7.1). The unknown σ^2 is estimated from the mean squared residuals (MSR)

$$\hat{\sigma}^2 = \frac{\sum\limits_{t=1}^{T} (\underline{y}_t^* - \hat{\underline{y}}_t^*)^2}{T - 3}, \tag{4.11}$$

where the predictor $\hat{\underline{y}}_t^*$ follows from (4.10a):

$$\hat{\underline{y}}_t^* = \hat{\underline{\alpha}}^* + \hat{\underline{\beta}} x_{1t}^* + \hat{\underline{\gamma}} x_{2t}^*, \tag{4.12}$$

where $\hat{\underline{\alpha}}^*$, $\hat{\underline{\beta}}$ and $\hat{\underline{\gamma}}$ are ordinary least squares estimators. The denominator in (4.11) is explained by the fact that three regression parameters are estimated from T observations.

Klein's model in (4.1)–(4.6) also has additive noise ($\underline{\epsilon}_t$, $\underline{\xi}_t$, $\underline{\eta}_t$). Now the distribution of these disturbance terms must be specified. Practitioners use normally independently distributed (NID) disturbances with zero expectations and variances that are constant over time but different for each endogenous variable; for example, in Klein's model we have

$$\left. \begin{array}{l} \underline{\epsilon}_t \sim \mathrm{NID}(0, \sigma_\epsilon^2) \\[2mm] \underline{\xi}_t \sim \mathrm{NID}(0, \sigma_\xi^2) \\[2mm] \underline{\eta}_t \sim \mathrm{NID}(0, \sigma_\eta^2) \end{array} \right\} \quad \text{with} \quad t = 0, \ldots, T. \tag{4.13}$$

It may be more realistic to assume cross-correlations, that is, the endogenous variables are dependent within period t; for example, $\mathrm{cov}(\underline{\epsilon}_t, \underline{\xi}_t) \neq 0$. Autocorrelations may also be important; for example $\mathrm{cov}(\underline{\epsilon}_t, \underline{\epsilon}_{t'}) \neq 0$ with $t' = 0, \ldots, T$. Nevertheless, correlated noise is hardly used in economic models.

Noise implies that disturbance terms are sampled for each period, which yields one time path for each endogenous variable. By repeating this sampling, it becomes possible to give probability statements about the behaviour of the model, such as 'in five years employment will have increased by 100 000 jobs, with a *probability* of 75%'. Figure 4.2 gives example output for Klein's model including noise. This figure gives single time paths, so probability statements are not possible! Comparison with Figure 4.1 shows that noise gives time paths that are more erratic.

When forecasting a single period ahead, actual observations can be used for the delayed endogenous variables; for the non-delayed endogenous variables simulated values are used. When forcasting several periods ahead, simulated observations must be used for all future periods.

$$
\begin{aligned}
C_t &= 16.79 + 0.80(W_{1t} + W_{2t}) \\
&\quad + 0.22P_t + 0.02P_{t-1} \\
I_t &= 17.78 + 0.23P_t + 0.55P_{t-1} \\
&\quad - 0.15K_{t-1} \\
W_{1t} &= 1.60 + 0.42(Y_t + TX_t - W_{2t}) \\
&\quad + 0.16(Y_{t-1} + TX_{t-1} - W_{2(t-1)}) + 0.00t \\
P_t &= Y_t - (W_{1t} + W_{2t}) \\
K_t &= K_{t-1} + I_t \\
Y_t &= C_t + I_t + G_t - TX_t
\end{aligned}
$$

The development of CONSUMPTION over 60 periods.
Maximum : 43.689

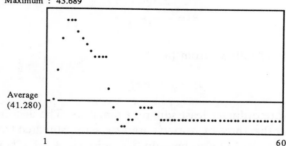

Average (41.280)

1   60

The development of INVESTMENTS over 60 periods.
Maximum : 2.696

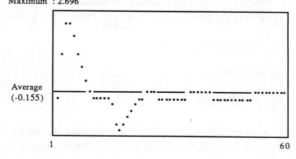

Average (-0.155)

1   60

Figure 4.1 Klein model

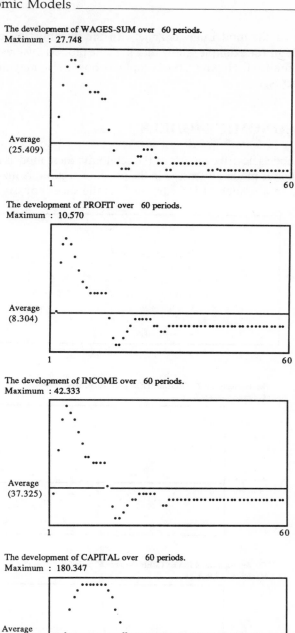

Figure 4.1 *(continued)*

The behaviour of the model may change with the introduction of noise. Adelman and Adelman (1959), for example, show that in some models business cycles occur only when noise is introduced. Howrey (1966) explains how noise may nullify the effect of a stabilizing policy.

4.2 MESO-ECONOMIC MODELS

Meso-economic models describe sectors of the economy; these models are disaggregations of the macro-economic models discussed in the previous section. A meso-economic model may be restricted to a branch of industry such as the shoe industry, or may comprise

$$
\begin{aligned}
C_t &= 16.79 + 0.80(W_{1t} + W_{2t}) \\
    &\quad + 0.22P_t + 0.02P_{t-1} + ec_t \\
I_t &= 17.78 + 0.23P_t + 0.55P_{t-1} \\
    &\quad - 0.15K_{t-1} + ei_t \\
W_{1t} &= 1.60 + 0.42(Y_t + TX_t - W_{2t}) \\
    &\quad + 0.16(Y_{t-1} + TX_{t-1} - W_{2(t-1)}) + 0.00t + ew_{1t} \\
P_t &= Y_t - (W_{1t} + W_{2t}) \\
K_t &= K_{t-1} + I_t \\
Y_t &= C_t + I_t + G_t - TX_t
\end{aligned}
$$

The development of CONSUMPTION over 60 periods.
Maximum : 44.630

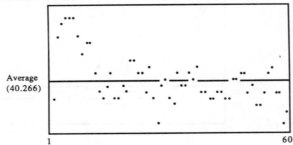

Average
(40.266)

1   60

The development of INVESTMENTS over 60 periods.
Maximum : 2.944

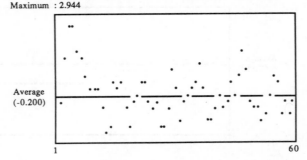

Average
(-0.200)

1   60

Figure 4.2   Stochastic Klein model ($\sigma_c = 1.1$; $\sigma_\xi = 0.05$; $\sigma_\eta = 1.1$)

The development of WAGES-SUM over 60 periods.
Maximum : 27.745

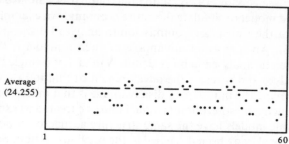

Average
(24.255)

1   60

The development of PROFIT over 60 periods.
Maximum : 10.919

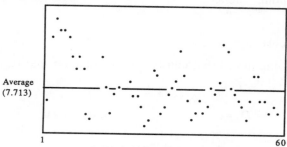

Average
(7.713)

1   60

The development of INCOME over 60 periods.
Maximum : 43.494

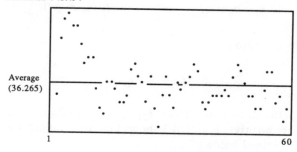

Average
(36.265)

1   60

The development of CAPITAL over 60 periods.
Maximum : 180.356

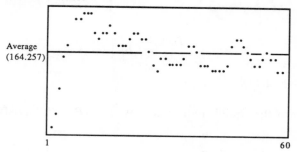

Average
(164.257)

1   60

Figure 4.2   *(continued)*

(say) the whole hide–leather–shoe industry (hides are transformed into leather, which is made into shoes); see Naylor (1979). Individual industries can also be combined into a large disaggregated model to simulate the entire economy. An example is the HERMES model developed for the European Commission to analyse European energy scenarios (see Italianer, 1986). An important advantage of such a model is that the effects of economic policies can be analysed in more detail. A model of a single branch of industry may be used to analyse and forecast the development of that industry, and to evaluate proposals for improving the industry. A disadvantage is that macro-economic variables that are needed in such a meso-economic model must be treated as exogenous variables. Many meso-economic models have the same structure as macro-economic models have; the latter models have already been discussed in the previous section. So in the remainder of this section we shall focus on cobweb models, which form the theoretical background of many meso-economic models.

4.2.1 Cobweb Models

Consider the following model that consists of an equation that relates demand D_t to the current price P_t

$$\underline{D}_t = a_0 - a_1 \underline{P}_t + \underline{\varepsilon}_t \qquad \text{with } a_0,\ a_1 \geqslant 0, \qquad (4.14)$$

an equation that relates supply S_t to the previous price P_{t-1}

$$\underline{S}_t = b_0 + b_1 \underline{P}_{t-1} + \underline{\xi}_t \qquad \text{with } b_0,\ b_1 \geqslant 0, \qquad (4.15)$$

and an equilibrium condition

$$\underline{D}_t = \underline{S}_t + \underline{\eta}_t. \qquad (4.16)$$

The distribution of the disturbance terms ($\underline{\varepsilon}_t, \underline{\xi}_t, \underline{\eta}_t$) should be defined such that the physical variables are positive. Figure 4.3 shows how to simulate this model (the name 'cobweb' will be explained below).

For this simple model the following analytical results can be derived. The equilibrium or long run price P_e is

$$P_e = \frac{a_0 - b_0}{a_1 + b_1}. \qquad (4.17)$$

Exercise 4.1: Prove (4.17).

The deviations from the equilibrium price (say) $\underline{p}_t = (\underline{P}_t - P_e)$ satisfy

$$\underline{p}_t = \frac{1}{a_1} \sum_{j=0}^{\infty} \left(\frac{b_1}{a_1} \right)^j (\underline{\varepsilon}_{t-j} - \underline{\xi}_{t-j} - \underline{\eta}_{t-j}). \qquad (4.18)$$

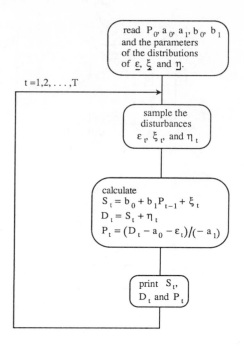

Figure 4.3 Simulation of cobweb model

Exercise 4.2: Prove (4.18).

Obviously p_t and $\underline{P}_t$ have the same variance. If all disturbance terms are independent (neither cross-correlations nor autocorrelations), the variance of $\underline{p}_t$ is

$$\text{var}(\underline{p}_t) = \left(\frac{1}{a_1^2 - b_1^2}\right)(\sigma_\varepsilon^2 + \sigma_\xi^2 + \sigma_\eta^2) \qquad \text{if } b_1 < a_1. \tag{4.19}$$

Exercise 4.3: Prove (4.19).

For more complicated models it is not possible to derive such mathematical relationships, so we resort to simulation. Such simulations are used in welfare theory, and in the analysis of the effects of export quotas and buffer inventories for raw material markets. Because these models were first applied to the hog market, they are called hog cycle models. The models are also called cobweb models, which is explained by Figure 4.4. In that figure, certain circumstances (for example, governmental regulations) lead to a price P_0 higher than the equilibrium price P_e. Then (4.14) means that demand responds immediately and drops to Q_0. Supply, however, responds to price changes one period later, and increases to Q_1; see (4.15). When Q_1 is offered, consumers pay only P_1. This price leads to supply Q_2 in the next period; and so on. After 'many' periods the equilibrium situation is restored: $P = P_e$, $Q = Q_e$. The other situations in Figure 4.4 can be explained in the same way: combination (b) of supply and demand leads to oscillations with a constant amplitude; situation (c) gives oscillations that

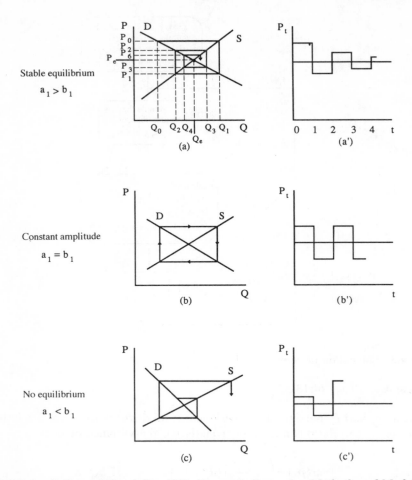

Stable equilibrium

$a_1 > b_1$

Constant amplitude

$a_1 = b_1$

No equilibrium

$a_1 < b_1$

Figure 4.4 Cobweb (Source: Gandolfo, 1980, *Economic Dynamics: Methods and Models*, 2nd edn, Fig. 3.1, p. 26. Reproduced by permission of Elsevier Science Publishers B.V.)

increase, so the system 'explodes'. The model can be augmented with an equation for inventories (Naylor et al., 1966, pp. 192–7) and with price expectations (Turnovsky, 1979).

4.3 MICRO-ECONOMIC MODELS

There are two schools in micro-economic theory. The classical micro-economics school concentrates on the optimal behaviour of individual households and firms. The behavioural school uses the principle of 'bounded rationality', introduced by Simon, and applies the technique of simulation. We now discuss these two schools briefly.

Classical economists derive models for the behaviour of individual producers and consumers, assuming that firms want to maximize profits and consumers want to maximize utility. Such models should provide insight into the actual actions of companies and people. Micro-economic results are also used to justify macro-economic relationships (using the assumption of a 'representative' producer or consumer). A well-known example is the 'theory of the firm', which describes the results of rational 'actors', given a market relationship such as monopoly, oligopoly, or perfect competition.

In the 1960s, however, behavioural models of the firm were introduced. These models include not only economic factors but also institutional, psychological, sociological, and organizational factors. There is no longer a single objective (such as profit) that guides a firm's decisions. Instead, the firm is modelled as an organization with a number of 'agents', each with several objectives; decisions may be taken independently of each other. So decisions are based on the multiple objectives of individual decision-makers, which may collide with the overall goals of the firm. But even if all decision-makers were to strive after the same goal, it would not be feasible to choose an optimal alternative, because in practice not all alternatives are known. Usually the agents stop their search for alternatives as soon as the goals meet a number of prespecified conditions, such as a minimum profit and a certain turnover. In the literature this behaviour is known as 'satisficing' behaviour; it is based on 'bounded rationality' and 'imperfect knowledge'. The first applications of this theory are Bonini (1963), and Cyert and March (1963); a review is Simon (1982).

These micro-economic models have nothing new to offer with respect to the *technique* of simulation. Nowadays the next group of models receive more attention.

4.4 MICRO-SIMULATION

Macro-economic questions (such as 'what are the consequences for the governmental budget of this tax measure?') might be answered by simulating at the level of the individual. A representative sample of the population of individuals is then taken, and the consequences that are computed for the individuals are aggregated (added up). In this way, insight is gained into both the macro-economic effects and the consequences for the individuals. This information is much more detailed than is the information acquired by simulating macro-economic models (see Section 4.1). An important characteristic of this so-called micro-simulation is that it takes into account non-economic factors such as the changes in the total population and in the age composition. Orcutt was the first one to apply micro-simulation; see Orcutt et al. (1961). Let us consider some technical details.

Micro-simulation is always *stochastic*. In a demographic model, for example, each individual in a certain group has a chance to die, marry, get a divorce, bear a child, become disabled, and so on. These probabilities are based on data obtained through censuses and other investigations. The probabilities differ over the various groups; for example, eighty-year old persons have a higher chance of dying than those in their thirties. Technically, we sample in micro-simulation as follows. We generate a random number r_{ij} to check if an event of type i (for example, death) happens to individual j. Let p_i denote the probability of event i for the subpopulation to which this individual belongs (for example, p_i denotes the probability of death in age group i, say the group between eighty and ninety). When $r_{ij} < p_i$, the event does occur (individual j dies). Of course the simulation must remain consistent: an individual who died must remain dead; an individual who is not married cannot get a divorce, and so on.

The total micro-simulation model may consist of a number of submodels that represent demographic developments, labour supply, labour demand, 'factor income' (the rewards for the production factors, labour and capital), taxes and social security payments, consumption and savings, and so on. In most cases these submodels form a (nearly) 'block-recursive system', that is, a submodel is influenced by preceding submodels but not by succeeding submodels. Figure 4.5 shows that first the demographic developments are simulated. Once the demographic developments are computed, the consequences for the supply of labour are computed through the next submodel. The results of these two submodels are inputs for the labour demand model. And so the simulation goes on. Note that in micro-simulation a representative sample comprises between 5000 and 100 000 individuals. In the Netherlands, micro-data are collected by the Census Bureau (CBS); moreover, the developments in 4000 households are measured by means of half-yearly interviews.

In recent years there has been a revival of the models introduced by Orcutt et al. (1961). These models are used to determine the effects of tax legislation; see Orcutt, Merz and Quinke (1986) and, for the Netherlands, De Kam, Wiebrens and Van Herwaarden (1987) and Van Fulpen et al. (1985).

Fishman (1978, pp. 326–44) also discusses micro-simulation of population dynamics. He illustrates these models through a population of female elephants. In Figure 4.6, K_{ij} denotes the number of female elephants of age i and state j with $j = 0$ (immature), $j = 1$ (pregnant), and $j = 2$ (mature, non-pregnant). For example, part (a) shows how some of the K_{i0} elephants survive (chance mechanism), of which some mature, of which some become pregnant (so they have changed to state 1 after they have aged one period). Elephants who have become pregnant may give birth to young calves; see part (b). Of course these calves are of age 1 and are immature (state 0).

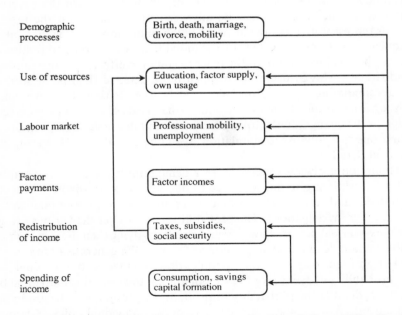

Figure 4.5 Micro-simulation: economics example (Source: Galler, 1980, *Handbuch zum Mikrosimulationsmodel des Sfb 3*, p. I.2.2. Reproduced by permission of J.W. Goethe Universität, Frankfurt)

(a)

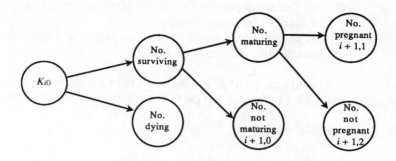

(b)

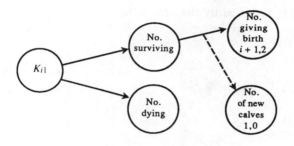

(c)

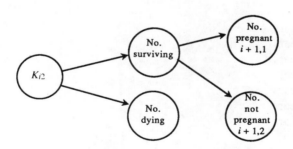

Figure 4.6 Micro-simulation: elephant example: (a) disposition of immature elephants of age i; (b) disposition of pregnant elephants of age i; (c) disposition of mature nonpregnant elephants of age i. (Source: Fishman, 1978, *Principles of Discrete Event Simulation*, Fig. 7.6, p. 329. Reproduced by permission)

Exercise 4.4: In the magic country Amazonia there are 40 girls. Their ages are uniformly distributed between 25 and 40 years. We wish to know how this population will develop over the next 80 years. We repeat the simulation run 100 times (100 macro-replications), and compute the averages of the following response variables.

(1) the number of females at the end of each year;
(2) the 'female population pyramid' after 80 years, that is, the number of females per age group;
(3) the probability of extinction, which happens if there are no females younger than 45 years of age.

The probability of giving birth to a baby equals factor 1 (previous child) multiplied by factor 2 (age). Factor 1 is given by the following table:

No children yet	0.15
Last child born last year	0.20
Last child born two or three years ago	0.40
Last child born four or five years ago	0.20
Last child born more than five years ago	0.00

Factor 2 is specified by the next table:

0–19 years of age	0.00
20–24	1.00
25–29	0.70
30–34	0.50
35–39	0.25
40–44	0.05
$\geqslant 45$	0.00

Of the newborn babies, 50% are female. The probability of death depends on age only:

0 year	0.010
1–39 years	0.001
40–49 years	0.005
50–59 years	0.010
60–69 years	0.020
70–74 years	0.050
75–79 years	0.100
80–89 years	0.200
90–99 years	0.400
100 years	1.000

*4.4.1 Typology of Micro-simulation

Different types of micro-simulation are distinguished. A first distinction depends on the type of data. If empirical data are available (as assumed above), this is called *empirical* simulation. In *standard* simulation there are only hypothetical micro-units (for example, a representative household), and for these micro-units, standard data are used (for instance, representative income). A second distinction is between static and dynamic simulations. In *static* simulation, only the immediate, first-order effects of a measure are computed; no possible feedbacks in time are simulated. Within dynamic simulation two types are distinguished, namely longitudinal and cross-sectional simulations. In *longitudinal* simulation, dynamics are taken into account (so the life history of each micro-unit is simulated during a run), but interactions among micro-units are not considered. For example, if production households form a micro-unit, the first unit is simulated until a stop criterion is reached (bankruptcy occurs or the end of the simulation period is reached); next a second unit is simulated, and so on. Because interactions among micro-units and the effects of economic development are largely ignored, the results of this type of simulation are only tentative. In *cross-sectional* simulations, the interactions among micro-units are considered. So within each time unit, all micro-units are processed, and at the end of each period interactions do occur. This yields the development per period and a hypothetical sample, which is used in the following period. It is advisable to compare the results of this simulation with (predictions of) aggregated data, and—if necessary—to adjust the cross-sectional simulation. Computationally, cross-sectional simulations are the most demanding type in the realm of micro-simulation.

4.5 CORPORATE MODELS

Corporate models are very realistic, empirical models, which should be distinguished from the theoretical, abstract 'models of the firm' discussed in Section 4.3. Corporate models describe and explain the activities of real firms. Submodels for individual departments such as production, marketing, finance, and research and development may be linked, so that a model for the total company results. The data of a corporate model may consist of objective and subjective data. The objective data may refer to historical sales, inventories, and production, to forecasts of economic activities (see Section 4.1), and so on. The subjective data reflect judgements and opinions of managers. So corporate models are not based on a complete and consistent theory, whereas classical micro-economic models and—to a certain degree—behavioural models are (see Section 4.3). The mathematical formulation of a corporate model corresponds with that of macro-economic models in Section 4.1, that is, these models are sets of difference equations. Simple corporate models are programmed for microcomputers by means of *spreadsheet* programs, such as Lotus 1-2-3; more complex models run on mainframes under software like FCS, IFPS, and System-W; see Chapter 6. These models are used to support decision-making; they may be part of a so-called *Decision Support System* (DSS). A DSS consists of a collection of models (modelbank), data (accessible through a Data Base Management System), and a user-friendly interface; see Turban (1990).

Corporate models are used for *what-if* analysis: the model is simulated for a set of alternative decisions or 'scenarios', and results are compared. This analysis has the following advantages, in comparison with optimization:

(1) No explicit information about the managers' preferences is needed.
(2) It offers the kind of information that managers desire when making decisions.
(3) The functional form of the models is not restricted by the requirements of mathematical analysis; yet their solution remains simple.

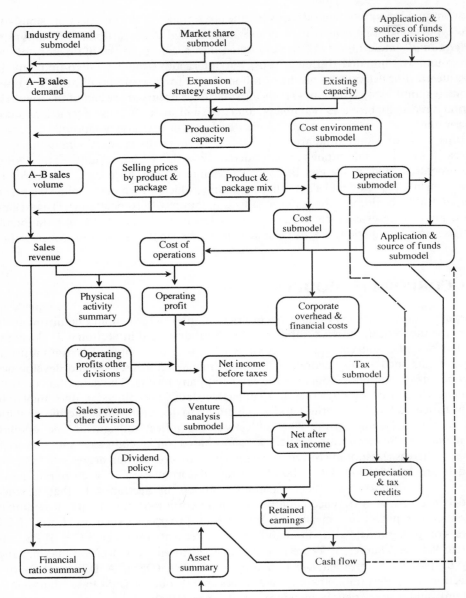

Figure 4.7 Anheuser–Busch model (Source: Naylor, 1971, *Computer Simulation Experiments with Models of Economic Systems*, Fig. 3.12, p. 69. Reproduced by permission)

A major disadvantage is that no general solutions are found. On the other hand, an optimizing model may give the exact solution for the wrong problem. Simulation can give a 'satisficing' solution for the real problem. We also refer to Chapters 1 and 8, and Naylor (1979).

4.5.1 Example: Anheuser–Busch Model

The general structure of the Anheuser–Busch model is given in Figure 4.7. The model consists of a number of submodels or modules; each module describes a part of the system. The model refers to the production and sales of beer by the American brewery Anheuser–Busch, abbreviated to A–B in Figure 4.7. The arrows show the structure of the model; a relatively simple scheme may easily result in a complex model. The advantage of this model is that nearly all arrows point in one direction; that is, the model is almost 'block recursive' (see Section 4.4). One of the submodels, namely the industry demand for beer (see the block at the top left of Figure 4.7), is further specified in Figure 4.8.

Exercise 4.5: The balance sheet for our new company looks as follows (numbers represent millions of dollars).

Fixed assets	10	Bank loans	3
Inventories	6	Accounts payable	2
Accounts receivable	5	Bonds	10
		Reserves	2
		Equity	3
	21		20

Last year, sales amounted to 20 million dollars. Profit before tax is 10% of sales. Interest amounts to 10% of bank loans and bonds, and is to be paid at the beginning of the year. Fixed assets have a lifespan of ten years; the fixed assets on the balance sheet are brand new. Bonds must be paid back within 10 years. Taxes are 40% of profits.

The company expects a sales increase of 5–10%, with any percentage in between equally likely. Inventories will remain 30% of sales, accounts receivable 20%, and accounts payable 10%. Machine utilization is now 60%. When utilization exceeds 90%, new machines must be bought. It costs 2.5 million dollars to expand current capacity by 25%. Dividends equal half of profit after taxes. Bank loans cannot exceed half of accounts receivable plus inventories; otherwise bonds are issued, which must be paid back within 10 years. The total amount of a new bond issue must be an integer multiple of one million dollars.

Simulate the company's growth over the next 10 years; repeat this simulation 1000 times. Compute the average reserves, bonds, and bank loans in each year.

4.6 RISK ANALYSIS

Risk analysis is used to quantify the risk of an investment project, and was originally developed by Hertz (1964). Consider the cash flow CF in year t, up to the 'planning horizon' T, with $t = 0, 1, \ldots, T$. The cash flows of an investment are non-linear functions of n input variables x_i, such as production costs, product price, and market share:

$$CF_t = f(x_{1t}, x_{2t}, \ldots, x_{it}, \ldots, x_{nt}) \qquad \text{with } t = 0, 1, \ldots, T. \qquad (4.20)$$

Often the function $f(\ )$ has such a form that it can be easily programmed in a spreadsheet; for example, x_{1t} is multiplied by x_{2t} per period t (price times sales volume gives sales revenues). Typically, for the first few years the cash flows are negative; in later years

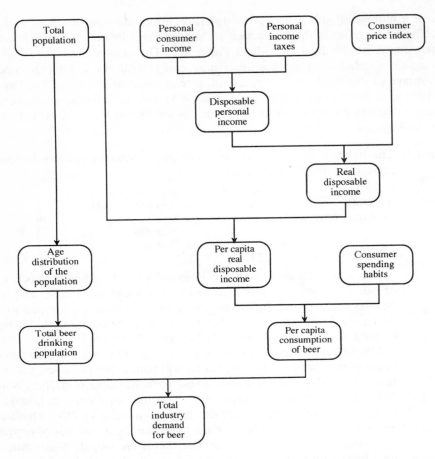

Figure 4.8 Industry demand for beer submodel (Source: Naylor, 1971, *Computer Simulation Experiments with Models of Economic Systems*, Fig. 3.7, p. 60. Reproduced by permission)

positive cash flows follow. The net present value (*NPV*) accounts for this time pattern: given an interest rate *r*, the *NPV* of the investment is

$$NPV = \sum_{t=0}^{T} \frac{CF_t}{(1+r)^t} \,. \tag{4.21}$$

Note that financial software has a subroutine for computing *NPV* through (4.21).

The latter two equations imply *known* values for the input variables x_{it}. In practice, an investment generates cash flows in the future, and the future is uncertain. Consequently, the inputs are stochastic variables $\underline{x}_{it}$, which have distributions (say) F_{it}. Stochastic inputs create stochastic cash flows $\underline{CF}_t$ and a stochastic $\underline{NPV}$. Assuming specific distributions for $\underline{x}_{it}$ and specific functional relationships (4.20), it is simple to simulate the distribution of $\underline{NPV}$. Figure 4.9 gives an outline of this simulation. Note that the amount to invest (CF_0) is treated separately in Figure 4.9; it would be more efficient to calculate *NPV* within the *t* loop: increase *NPV* with $CF_t/(1+r)^t$.

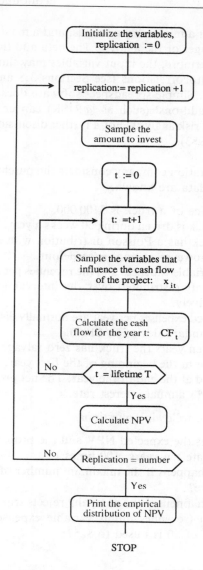

Figure 4.9 General outline of risk analysis

Management must decide whether to go on with the investment project or not. To make that decision, they may consider

$$P(\underline{NPV} \leqslant 0) = p_0, \tag{4.22}$$

where p_0 is estimated through simulation. It is up to management to decide whether the estimated value (say) $\hat{p}_0$ is acceptable. So the basic idea of risk analysis is simple.

A practical problem is how to determine the distribution of the inputs $\underline{x}_{it}$. Usually Gaussian, beta, or triangular distributions are assumed. The Gaussian and the beta distributions were discussed in Chapter 3 (Sections 3.5 and 3.4.1 respectively). The triangular distribution has a minimum, a modus, and a maximum value for x_{it}, which are specified by the manager or the analyst. The beta and the triangular distributions have finite ranges. Furthermore, the input variables may show statistical dependence: cross-correlations and autocorrelations (see Sections 3.8 and 3.9). In practice, such dependencies are ignored. Simple spreadsheet software does not provide risk analysis facilities, but so-called 'add-ons' (such as @RISK) can be purchased to extend the spreadsheet software with risk analysis. For a further discussion of risk analysis we refer to Hertz and Thomas (1983).

Exercise 4.6: A transportation company considers the purchase of an extra truck. The following data are known.

(1) The price of a truck is $100 000.
(2) The truck is driven during 50 weeks a year. The mean number of trips per week has a Poisson distribution with mean two; the number of trips, however, cannot exceed four.
(3) The variable expenses and the revenues per trip are independently and uniformly distributed over the interval [550,850] and [750,1250] respectively.
(4) The fixed expenses per year are normally distributed with mean $16 000 and standard deviation $1000.
(5) After ten years the truck has zero salvage value. The truck must be paid for at the beginning of the first year. All expenses and revenues are paid at the end of the year. The net present value (NPV) is based on a 5% annual interest rate.

Answer the following questions.

(a) What is the expected NPV and the probability of a negative NPV? (Simulate ten years, 100 times.)
(b) What happens if the maximum number of trips per week is not four but five?
(c) What happens if the company rejects trips that give a negative gross margin (revenues minus variable expenses)? What happens if the hurdle of $0 is raised to $25?

4.7 SYSTEM DYNAMICS

System dynamics is also known as Forrester's industrial dynamics and Meadows's world dynamics. It studies the dynamic behaviour of systems; the systems range from private companies to the world's ecology. System dynamics uses the technique of simulation, but it is certainly more than a technique: it is a world view.

Like the other models of this chapter, system dynamics evaluates the state of a system at equidistant points of time, say $t = 0, \ldots, T$ (see the macro-economic model of equation (4.7) and the risk analysis model of equation (4.20)). Mathematically such a modelling approach means that difference equations are used. System dynamics views the world as a system of vessels or storage tanks connected by pipes with faucets or valves that control the flows into and out of the vessels. The system's state is characterized by the *levels* of the fluids in the vessels. Examples of levels are the stock of consumer goods, the number of females of a certain age group, the size of a bank account, the items on a balance sheet (also see the models of the preceding sections). The valves control the rates at which the levels change. Examples of flow quantities are provided by the items on the profit-and-loss account (sales revenues per period, material costs per period).

Note that in some disciplines, for example physics, time is modelled as a continuous variable and differential equations are used. If the 'true' model has continuous time, then its approximation through discrete time becomes a challenging numerical problem. Different methods have been proposed. The simplest solution is provided by 'Euler's' method, which assumes that rates remain constant within the time interval between two successive points in time; Runge–Kutta methods are more complicated; see Richmond, Vescuso and Peterson (1987). Economic and business models, however, do not assume continuous time. For example, net present value (*NPV*) is computed using discrete time; see (4.21). Mortgage banks follow this convention when computing annuity payments. Engineers sometimes use continuous time when computing *NPV*; see Gordon (1978, p. 83). So continuous models are most realistic when modelling storage levels in chemical tanks or when modelling the bouncing of balls. For economic systems, however, difference equations are used.

The following notation is standard in system dynamics. Three equidistant, successive points in time (say $t-1, t, t+1$) are denoted by J, K and L respectively. So K denotes the present, J the preceding, and L the successive points in time. The 'basic time period' is the time between two successive points of time; it is denoted by DT. This yields the identities $K = J + DT$ and $L = K + DT$. In economics the basic time period DT is (usually) determined by the data available; for example, if data are collected quarterly, then DT is a quarter. In other applications DT has to be chosen carefully; see Wolstenholme (1990, p. 232). Now consider the identity

$$y_t = y_{t-1} + \Delta y. \tag{4.23}$$

If the rate of change between $t-1$ and t is constant, we have

$$\frac{\Delta y}{\Delta t} = c(t-1, t). \tag{4.24}$$

Combining these two equations gives

$$y_t = y_{t-1} + \Delta t \times c(t-1, t). \tag{4.25a}$$

Translation of (4.25a) into the symbols of system dynamics yields

$$LEVEL.K = LEVEL.J + (DT)(RATE.JK). \tag{4.25b}$$

If the 'vessel' has both input and output, then by definition the rate of change over time is the difference between the input and the output rates:

$$RATE.JK = IN.JK - OUT.JK. \tag{4.26}$$

For example, inventory increases with production and decreases with sales, so (4.25b) and (4.26) give

$$INVENTORY.K = INVENTORY.J + DT(PRODRATE.JK - SALESRATE.JK).$$

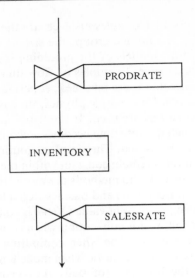

Figure 4.10 Levels, rates and flows

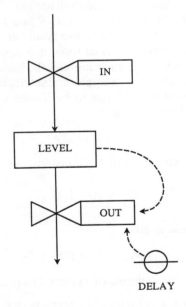

Figure 4.11 Exponential delay

This equation is represented by Figure 4.10, which uses system dynamics symbols to represent levels, rates and flows of physical goods, namely rectangles, 'yo-yos', and solid arrows respectively (more symbols will follow).

If a valve is opened, it may take some time before the fluid flows out of the vessel. In general, commodities and information require time to 'flow' from one place to another; for example, it takes time to convert raw materials into final products. Consider the example of Table 4.1 and Figure 4.11, where information flows are denoted by dashed

Table 4.1 Example of exponential delay: pulse input

Period	Level	In	Out = Level/10
1	0	0	0
2	0	10	0
3	10	0	1
4	9	0	0.9
5	8.1	0	0.81
6	7.29	0	0.729
7	6.561	0	0.6561

Table 4.2 Example of exponential delay: step input

Period	Level	In	Out = Level/10
1	0	0	0
2	0	10	0
3	10	10	1
4	19	10	1.9
5	27.1	10	2.71
6	34.39	10	3.439
7	40.951	10	4.0951

arrows and constants by 'sliced' circles. Suppose that in period 2 the input rate increases from zero to ten, and in period 3 it drops back to zero and remains zero: an *input pulse*. Suppose further that the output rate is 10% of the preceding level:

$$OUT.JK = \frac{LEVEL.J}{10}.$$

So the input rate is exogenous in this example, whereas the output rate is endogenous. This example yields Table 4.1, which corresponds with the upper part of Figure 4.12. The example demonstrates how the effect of the input pulse fades away exponentially. A related example is displayed in Table 4.2 and the lower part of Figure 4.12. Now the input increases permanently to a new value: *input step*. Figure 4.12 shows that the output responds with steps that have heights decreasing exponentially over time; after infinitely many periods the output reaches its final value (which is not displayed). We see that successive output values in Table 4.2 are equal to the successive sum of the output values in Table 4.1: an input step equals an input pulse that occurs in every period. Note that in Keynesian macro-economics the multiplier model can give the same behaviour as Figure 4.12 demonstrates.

If the delay factor 10 in Table 4.1 decreases, then the output rate increases and the total level reaches its final value faster; see Table 4.3 and Figure 4.13.

These examples illustrate the first order exponential delay, which results from a rate equation of the form

$$OUT.JK = \frac{LEVEL.J}{DELAY}. \tag{4.27}$$

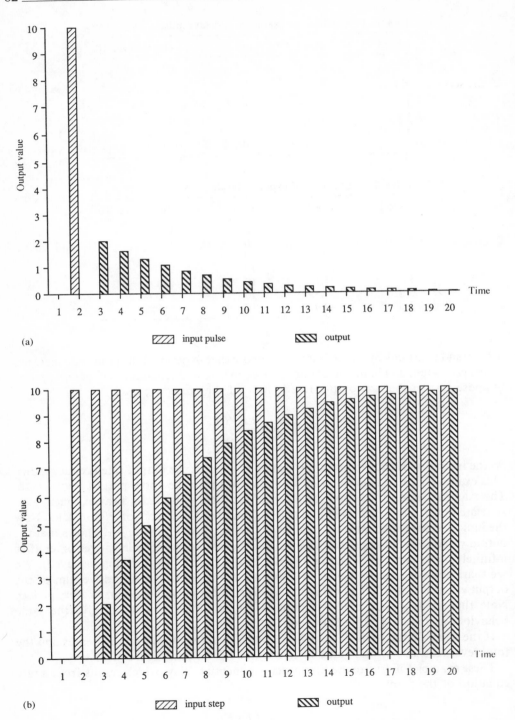

Figure 4.12 First-order exponential delay

The factor *DELAY* may be interpreted as an average delay. Note the dimensions in (4.27): the rate is in units per time unit, the level is in units, and the delay is in time units.

There are also higher-order exponential delays. For example, a third-order delay is obtained by applying a series of three first-order delays; see Figure 4.14. The inputs of the second and third levels are the outputs of the preceding levels. DELAY/3 is used as the delay factor, which leads to the same average delay for delays of different orders. The levels 1, 2 and 3 in Figure 4.14 are auxiliary variables that are introduced to obtain a desired output pattern of the delay; within the model they have no real meaning. Conceptually there is a single black box system; its input is INPUT and its output is OUTPUT 3. The total quantity in the delay is obtained by adding up the levels 1, 2 and 3; see Table 4.4. Comparison of Figures 4.12 and 4.15 shows that the effect of a first-order delay starts earlier and has decreasing effects, whereas the effect of a third-order delay starts only after three periods, and first increases before it decreases.

Exercise 4.7: Give the system dynamics equations for a third-order delay and for the quantity in delay.

Besides exponential delays (of different orders) there are other types such as discrete or pipeline delays. (It can be proved that discrete delays are an infinite series of exponential delays.) The correct modelling of the delay structure is one of the most important steps in system dynamics modelling, since it determines the behaviour of the model. Selecting the delay structure requires sensitivity analysis.

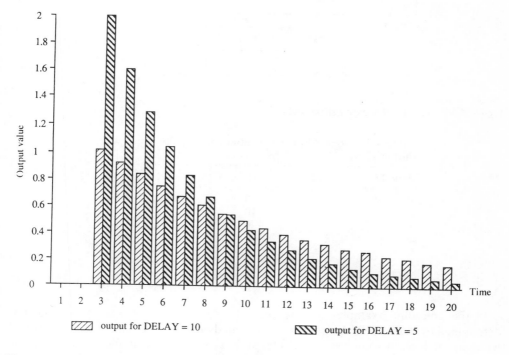

Figure 4.13 First-order exponential delay (delays of different length)

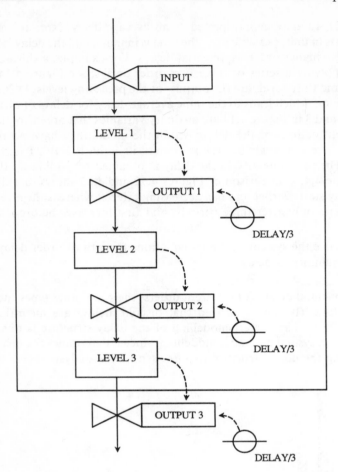

Figure 4.14 Third-order exponential delay

Table 4.3 Example of exponential delay: pulse input with shorter delay

Period	Level	In	Out = Level/5
1	0	0	0
2	0	10	0
3	10	0	2
4	8	0	1.6
5	6.4	0	1.28
6	5.12	0	1.024
7	4.096	0	0.8192

In the preceding examples we supposed that the input rate was exogenous (not determined by the model). Actually in the system dynamics view, valves may be opened wider as the level of some vessel indicates such a move. For example, to speed up the decrease of the inventory level, we can decrease the production rate and/or increase

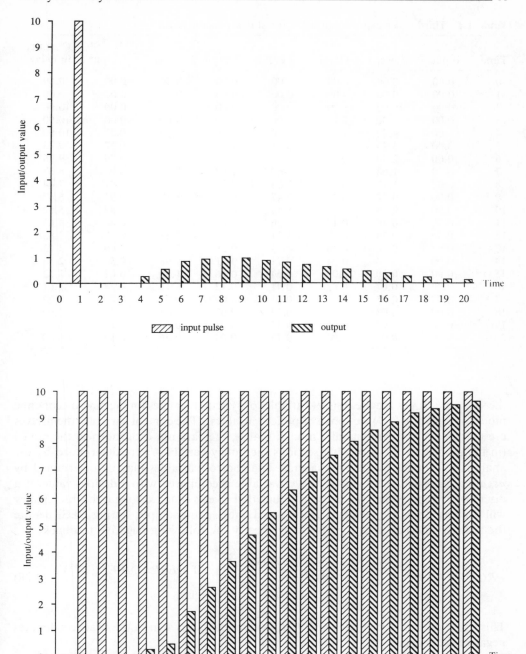

Figure 4.15 Third-order exponential delay

Table 4.4 Third-order exponential delay (total delay factor is 10)

Time	Input	Level 1	Output 1	Level 2	Output 2	Level 3	Output 3	Quantity in delay
0	0.00	0.00	0.00	0.00	0.00	0.00	0.00	0.00
1	10.00	0.00	0.00	0.00	0.00	0.00	0.00	0.00
2	0.00	10.00	3.00	0.00	0.00	0.00	0.00	10.00
3	0.00	7.00	2.10	3.00	0.90	0.00	0.00	10.00
4	0.00	4.90	1.47	4.20	1.26	0.90	0.27	10.00
5	0.00	3.43	1.03	4.41	1.32	1.89	0.57	9.73
6	0.00	2.40	0.72	4.12	1.23	2.65	0.79	9.16
7	0.00	1.68	0.50	3.60	1.08	3.09	0.93	8.37
8	0.00	1.18	0.35	3.03	0.91	3.24	0.97	7.44
9	0.00	0.82	0.25	2.47	0.74	3.18	0.95	6.47
10	0.00	0.58	0.17	1.98	0.59	2.96	0.89	5.52
11	0.00	0.40	0.12	1.56	0.47	2.67	0.80	4.63
12	0.00	0.28	0.08	1.21	0.36	2.33	0.70	3.83
13	0.00	0.20	0.06	0.93	0.28	2.00	0.60	3.13
14	0.00	0.14	0.04	0.71	0.21	1.68	0.50	2.53
15	0.00	0.10	0.03	0.54	0.16	1.39	0.42	2.02
16	0.00	0.07	0.02	0.41	0.12	1.13	0.34	1.61
17	0.00	0.05	0.01	0.31	0.09	0.92	0.27	1.27
18	0.00	0.03	0.01	0.23	0.07	0.73	0.22	0.99
19	0.00	0.02	0.01	0.17	0.05	0.58	0.17	0.77
20	0.00	0.02	0.00	0.13	0.04	0.46	0.14	0.60

the sales rate. Rates are the control variables of system dynamics (in the macro-economic model of equation (4.7) we spoke of policy variables). The control variables themselves are part of the system dynamics model; that is, they are not exogenous to the model (in the models of the preceding sections the policy variables were determined by the analysts and policy-makers/managers). The control variables may be determined by *negative feedback*: the value of a level variable is compared with a desired value; if a discrepancy occurs, then the rate controlling that level is changed so that the discrepancy will decrease (positive feedback is discussed later). For example, letting DESI denote the desired value of inventory, we may specify the following negative feedback:

$$PRODRATE.JK = \begin{cases} \dfrac{(DESI.J - INVENTORY.J)}{DELAY} & \text{if } DESI > INVENTORY. \\ 0 & \text{else.} \end{cases} \quad (4.28)$$

This equation is pictured in Figure 4.16, where the minus sign in the brackets denotes negative feedback.

So to change the level of a vessel faster, the faucets can be further opened or closed; that is, the input and output rates can be changed.

Besides negative feedback there is *positive feedback*. For example, net present value (*NPV*), defined in (4.21), is related to 'compound interest': an amount of money or capital (*CAP*) earns interest (*INT*), given a constant percentage of interest (*PERCENT*) and that interest is added to the capital to earn more interest. In system dynamics we write

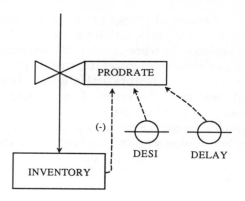

Figure 4.16 Negative feedback

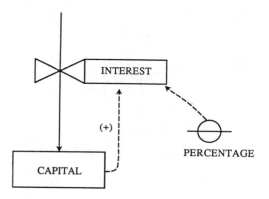

Figure 4.17 Positive feedback

$$INT.JK = (CAP.J)(PERCENT) \qquad (4.29)$$

$$CAP.K = CAP.J + DT(INT.JK). \qquad (4.30)$$

See also Figure 4.17. Positive feedback yields exponential growth, which means that the level 'explodes quickly'. Such behaviour was found in the world dynamics models (see Forrester, 1971, and Meadows, Meadows and Randers, 1991).

So exponential growth means that a level is multiplied by a constant; see (4.29) and (4.30). Exponential delay means that the level decreases at a rate determined by dividing that level by a constant larger than one; that constant denotes the average delay before the level has vanished, as (4.25)–(4.27) show.

As we saw in the preceding chapters, a model usually consists of more than a single equation (see Klein's model in equations (4.1)–(4.6), the cobweb model in equations (4.14)–(4.16), the micro-simulation models in Figures 4.5 and 4.6, the corporate models in Figures 4.7 and 4.8). In the system dynamics view of the world, a fluid may flow from vessel to vessel; moreover there may be different fluids flowing through the system. Actually system dynamics distinguishes six interrelated networks of flows: capital goods, personnel, money, orders, and information. Each of these six flows has its own symbol:

dashed arrows for information, solid arrows for materials, and so on. Flows have 'sources' (entry into the system) and 'sinks' (exit from the system), which are graphically denoted by 'clouds'. To facilitate the representation of complicated systems, auxiliary variables are used; they are represented by circles. Figure 4.18 gives an abstract example. This figure demonstrates that rates control physical inflows and outflows. Their settings are controlled by the information on the values of certain levels, namely the level to be controlled and the values of some other levels.

Figure 4.19 gives a specific model for the sales of air-conditioners. The symbol H stands for the number of households, y for the number of houses sold, x for the number

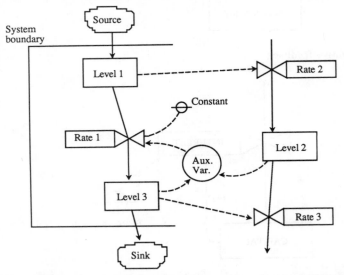

Figure 4.18 Structure of a system dynamics model (Source: Gordon, 1978, *System Simulation*, 2nd edn, Fig. 5.7, p. 93. Copyright © 1978 Prentice-Hall, Inc., Englewood Cliffs, NJ. Reproduced by permission)

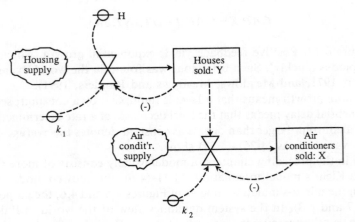

Figure 4.19 System dynamics model of air-conditioner sales (Source: Gordon, 1978, *System Simulation*, 2nd edn, Fig. 5.11, p. 97. Copyright © 1978 Prentice-Hall, Inc., Englewood Cliffs, NJ. Reproduced by permission)

Table 4.5 Air-conditioner sales example

T	H	Level$_y$	Level$_x$	Rate$_y$	Rate$_x$
	0	100	0.0		
1	100	40.0	0.0	40.0	0.0
2	100	64.0	20.0	24.0	20.0
3	100	78.4	42.0	14.4	22.0
4	100	87.0	60.2	8.6	18.2
5	100	92.2	73.6	5.2	13.4
6	100	95.3	82.9	3.1	9.3
7	100	97.2	89.1	1.9	6.2
8	100	98.3	93.2	1.1	4.0
9	100	99.0	95.7	0.7	2.6
10	100	99.4	97.4	0.4	1.6
11	100	99.6	98.4	0.2	1.0
12	100	99.8	99.0	0.1	0.6
13	100	99.9	99.4	0.1	0.4
14	100	99.9	99.6	0.1	0.2
15	100	100.0	99.8	0.0	0.1

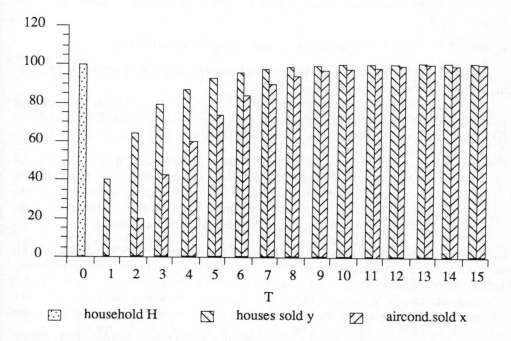

Figure 4.20 Number of houses sold (y) and number of air-conditioners sold (x)

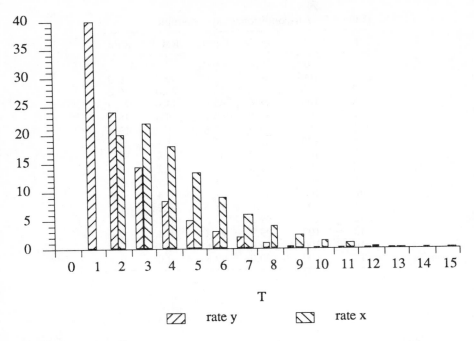

Figure 4.20 *(continued)*

of air-conditioners installed, *DEL1* and *DEL2* give the delays in the responses *y* and *x* respectively.

Exercise 4.8: Give the system dynamics equations for Figure 4.19.

Table 4.5 and Figure 4.20 give the time path for $H = 100$, $DEL1 = 2.5$, $DEL2 = 2.0$, and zero initial values for *x* and *y*.

The programming of system dynamics models was originally facilitated by a language called DYNAMO. Modern PC software is Professional DYNAMO, DYSMAP2 and STELLA. We shall further discuss simulation languages in a separate chapter.

Exercise 4.9: Consider a heating system with a thermostat. When *TEMP*, the temperature in the room, drops below a desired temperature (*DESTEMP*), the thermostat reacts by feeding oil to the heating system. When the temperature exceeds the desired temperature, the thermostat turns off the heating. Give the system dynamics figure and equations.

Well-known system dynamics applications are the studies by the Club of Rome. This committee relates the future development of the world's population, food production, pollution, and other variables with each other, and investigates measures for preventing a global catastrophe in the near future (see Meadows, Meadows and Randers, 1991). In general, system dynamics analysts study the effects of a change in policy. System dynamics analyses the qualitative behaviour of a system: does the system explode or does it settle down? The goal is not to compute exact results (other simulation models do aim to give exact results). System dynamics models are aggregated, since they concern very large systems. Forrester claims that many feedback systems respond counter-intuitively, so policy makers often fight symptoms instead of underlying causes.

Many realistic applications of system dynamics can be found in the literature. Kleijnen (1980, pp. 137–43) surveys several studies on the effects of different qualities of information; for example, a study at Philips in the Netherlands shows that delay and decentralization of information increase inventory fluctuations caused by an initial demand perturbation. More applications and details on the technical aspects of system dynamics are found in Forrester (1961, 1971), Goodman (1988), Hanneman (1988), Lyneis (1980), Pidd (1992), Richardson and Pugh (1981), Roberts et al. (1983), and Wolstenholme (1990). Dutch applications of system dynamics, including gaming, are given in Geurts and Vennix (1989).

REFERENCES

Adelman I. and F. L. Adelman (1959) The dynamic properties of the Klein–Goldberger model, *Econometrica*, **27**, 579–625.

Bonini C. P. (1963) *Simulations of Information and Decision Systems in the Firm*, Prentice-Hall, Englewood Cliffs, New Jersey. (Reprinted: Markham Publishing Company, Chicago, 1967.)

Cyert R. M. and J. G. March (1963) *A Behavioral Theory of the Firm*, Prentice-Hall, Englewood Cliffs.

De Kam C. A., C. J. Wiebrens and F. G. Van Herwaarden (1987) *Bouwstenen voor Inkomensbeleid en Sociale Zekerheid* (*Building Blocks for Income Policy and Social Security*), VUGA Uitgeverij B.V., The Hague.

Fishman G. S. (1978) *Principles of Discrete Event Simulation*, Wiley, New York.

Forrester J. W. (1961) *Industrial Dynamics*, The MIT Press, Cambridge, Massachusetts.

Forrester J. W. (1971) *World Dynamics*, Wright-Allen Press, Cambridge, Massachusetts.

Galler H. P. (ed.) (1980) *Handbuch zum Mikrosimulationsmodell des Sfb 3*. (*Handbook for the Micro-simulation Model of Sfb 3*), J. W. Goethe-Universität Frankfurt und Universität Mannheim.

Gandolfo G. (1980) *Economic Dynamics: Methods and Models* (2nd edn), North-Holland Publishing Company.

Geurts J. and J. Vennix (ed.) (1989) *Verkenningen in Beleidsanalyse: Theorie en Praktijk van Modelbouw en Simulatie.* (*Explorations of Policy Analysis: Theory and Practice of Model Building and Simulation.*) Kerckebosch, Zeist (Netherlands).

Goodman M. R. (1988) *Study Notes in System Dynamics* (fourth printing), MIT Press, Boston.

Gordon G. (1978) *System Simulation* (2nd edn), Prentice-Hall, Englewood Cliffs, New Jersey.

Hanneman R. A. (1988) *Computer-assisted Model Building; Modeling Dynamic Social Systems*, Sage, Beverly Hills, California.

Hertz D. (1964) Risk analysis in capital investment, *Harvard Business Review*, **42**, 95–106.

Hertz D. and H. Thomas (1983) *Risk Analysis and its Applications*, Wiley, Chichester.

Howrey E. P. (1966) *Stabilization Policy in Linear Stochastic Systems*, Econometric Research Program, Princeton University, Princeton, New Jersey.

Italianer A. (1986) *The HERMES Model: Complete Specification and First Estimation Results*, Commission of the European Communities, Report EUR 10669 EN.

Kleijnen J. P. C. (1980) *Computers and Profits: Quantifying Financial Benefits of Information*, Addison-Wesley, Reading, Massachusetts.

Klein L. R. (1950) *Economic Fluctuations in the United States 1921–1941*, Wiley, New York.

Lyneis J. M. (1980) *Corporate Planning and Policy Design: A System Dynamics Approach*, The MIT Press, Cambridge, Massachusetts.

Meadows D. H., D. Meadows and J. Randers (1991) *Beyond the Limits. Confronting Global Collapse; Envisioning a Sustainable Future*, Earthscan Publications Ltd., London.

Naylor T. H. (1971) *Computer Simulation Experiments with Models of Economic Systems*, Wiley, New York.

Naylor T. H. (1979) *Corporate Planning Models*, Addison-Wesley, Reading, Massachusetts.

Naylor T. H., J. L. Balintfy, D. S. Burdick and Kong Chu (1966) *Computer Simulation Techniques*, Wiley, New York.

Orcutt G. H., J. Merz and H. Quinke (1986) *Microanalytic Simulation Models to Support Social and Financial Policy*. North-Holland, Amsterdam.

Orcutt G. H., M. Greenberger, J. Korbel and A. M. Rivlin (1961) *Microanalysis of Socioeconomic Systems; A Simulation Study*, Harper and Row, New York.

Pidd M. (1992) *Computer Simulation in Management Science*, 3rd Edn, Wiley, Chichester.

Richardson G. P. and A. L. Pugh (1981) *System Dynamics Modeling with DYNAMO*, Productivity Press, Boston.

Richmond B., P. Vescuso and S. Peterson (1987) *STELLA for Business*, High Performance Systems, Inc., Lyme, New Hampshire.

Roberts N., D. Andersen, R. Deal, M. Garet and W. Shaffer (1983) *Introduction to Computer Simulation: a System Dynamics Modeling Approach*. Addison-Wesley, Reading, Massachusetts.

Simon H. A. (1982) *Models of Bounded Rationality* (Vols 1 and 2), The MIT Press, Cambridge, Massachusetts.

Theil H. (1971) *Principles of Econometrics*, Wiley, New York.

Turban E. (1990) *Decision Support and Expert Systems: Managerial Perspectives* (2nd edn), MacMillan Publishing Company, New York.

Turnovsky S. J. (1979) Futures markets, private storage, and price stabilization. *Journal of Public Economics*, **12**, 301–27.

Van der Giessen A. A. (1970) Solving non-linear systems by computer; a new method, *Statistica Neerlandica*, **24**, 41–50.

Van Fulpen H., F. Van Herwaarden, E. Hooijmans, F. De Kam, E. Pommer and C. Wiebrens (1985) *Berekend Beleid (Computed Policy)*, Sociale en Culturele Studies—5, Staatsuitgeverij, The Hague.

Wolstenholme E. F. (1990) *System Enquiry; a System Dynamics Approach*, Wiley, Chichester.

Chapter 5

Operations Research Models

Simulation is one of the most frequently applied techniques in operations research. In this chapter we concentrate on the simulation of inventory and queuing models. For didactic reasons we focus on simple models, but we do give an example of a more complicated queuing model, namely a model for a Rotterdam container harbour. We also briefly mention extensions of inventory and queuing models. The models in the preceding chapter were essentially deterministic, whereas the models in this chapter (for example, queuing models) are stochastic. The former type of models may be embellished with random disturbances, but without that noise they remain interesting. The latter type of models, however, make no sense without randomness; for example, a queuing model with deterministic arrival and service times turns into a 'sequencing' model (which determines when to serve which customer). The risk analysis models of the preceding chapter and the inventory models of the present chapter deserve some comment. In risk analysis, random sampling is used only to generate alternative time paths over time; each time path, however, may be ruled by deterministic 'laws'. The inventory models of this chapter concentrate on the buffer function of stocks, that is, stocks are cushions needed to compensate random variations in input (supply) and output (demand). The oldest inventory models, however, were deterministic; they were used to balance fixed set-up costs and variable inventory carrying costs.

This chapter is organized as follows.

—5.1 Fixed versus variable time increments
   Time may be sliced into segments of fixed, equal lengths (also see the preceding chapter). Alternatively, the simulation program jumps to the next event; it skips periods (of variable lengths) during which the system does not change its state.
—5.2 Inventory models
   We first summarize some analytical results on the economic order quantity and the reorder point. Next we simulate an inventory system with stochastic demand and stochastic lead time. We mention extensions of this basic inventory simulation.
—5.3 Queuing models
   First we discuss some elementary queuing concepts. Next we simulate the single-server queue in different ways: by hand, by fixed time increment programming, and by variable time increment programming. The third way leads to the 'next event' principle. That principle is demonstrated in simulations of systems with parallel servers, with repairmen, and with successive servers. Finally we discuss practical queuing simulations.

—5.4 Miscellaneous models, including combined continuous/discrete-event models
  We mention a few examples of models that represent some processes through
  differential equations and some other processes of the same system through discrete
  events. We finish this chapter with a case study, namely the Europe Container
  Terminus (ECT) in Rotterdam harbour.
—Appendix: Analytical solution of M/M/n models.
  We give some well-known formulae for analytical results of M/M/n models.

5.1 FIXED VERSUS VARIABLE TIME INCREMENTS

There are two ways to represent time in simulation models: fixed time increment approach
and variable time increment or next event approach.

(1) *Fixed time increment.* In the first approach we divide time into periods of fixed,
    equal length; see Figure 5.1(a). We mostly use this approach if the development
    of aggregates is of interest and the system's state changes continuously. For example,
    in an inventory model the development of the total inventory of a product is
    important, not the behaviour of the individual units of that product. All models
    in the preceding chapter were 'fixed time increment' models. (From that perspective,
    inventory models belong to the previous chapter.)
(2) *Variable time increment or next event.* In the second approach, we do not divide
    time into equal parts; the point in time at which the next event takes place is
    important; see Figure 5.1(b). In contrast to the first approach, the behaviour of
    individuals is now of interest. For example, in a queuing problem we simulate the
    individual customers.

Which approach is best? Usually the problem formulation determines the approach.
The models in the preceding chapter provide many examples. Sometimes, however, it
is not clear which method is best. For example, simulations of traffic across a street
intersection provide examples of both approaches. There are some rules of thumb; for

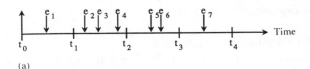

(a)

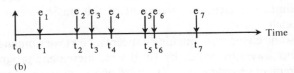

(b)

Figure 5.1 Time advancement: e_i is event i ($i = 1, 2, \ldots, 7$): (a) fixed time increment; (b) next
event

example, if events occur 'regularly' in time and there are many events, then a fixed time increment is more efficient. A disadvantage of a fixed time increment is that we must choose a time unit; we treat the events within a time unit as if they take place at the end of the time unit: aggregation principle. Figure 5.1(a) shows that in the 'fixed time increment' approach we process the events in batches; for example, in period 2 $(t_1 < t \leqslant t_2)$ there are three events, namely e_2, e_3, e_4. If we select a large time unit, we may get incorrect results and the simulation model may not be valid; the queuing models in Section 5.3.1 will provide examples. If we choose too small a time unit, we simulate many periods that show no activity of interest; that is, the system does not change its state within these periods, and we waste computer time. (The selection of a time unit was also discussed in the preceding chapter. Then, however, flows, not events, were simulated.)

5.2 INVENTORY MODELS

We first summarize some analytical results on the economic order quantity and the reorder point. Next we simulate an inventory system with stochastic demand and stochastic lead time. Finally we mention extensions of this basic inventory simulation.

Suppose we wish to model the behaviour of an inventory system over time, because we want to know on which day we should replenish the inventory, and—if we replenish the inventory—we wish to know how much we should order. In the model we ignore the effects of the exact timing of an event within a time unit (day). In Chapter 1 we have already discussed a simple example of such a system, but we did not account for the results of basic inventory theory. Now we first consider a classical inventory model, which assumes a single product and constant demand per time unit. Further total costs is composed of ordering costs, inventory carrying costs and out of stock costs. In inventory theory (for example, Tersine, 1982) it is proved that the optimal or economic order quantity (EOQ) is a square root function of fixed demand D per day, inventory carrying costs k_1 per product unit per day, out of stock costs k_2 per product unit (not per day; k_2 may be profit per product unit, which is forfeited if stock is depleted), and ordering costs k_3 fixed per order:

$$EOQ = \frac{\sqrt{(2 \times D \times k_3 \times (k_1 + k_2))}}{\sqrt{(k_1 \times k_2)}}. \tag{5.1}$$

The optimal reorder level or reorder point (ROP) equals demand during the lead time L (L is expressed in days and is a constant):

$$ROP = D \times L. \tag{5.2}$$

So much for the analytical results. In the simulation we may allow demand and lead time to be stochastic variables. We assume that demand $\underline{D}$ is independently and identically distributed or i.i.d. The independence assumption implies zero autocorrelation coefficients, and the assumption of identical distributions implies means and variances that remain constant over time. Lead time $\underline{L}$ is also assumed to be i.i.d. Moreover $\underline{L}$ and $\underline{D}$ are independent (no cross-correlation). We introduce the symbols

$$E(\underline{D}) = \mu_D \quad \text{and} \quad \text{var}(\underline{D}) = \sigma_D^2 \left.\vphantom{\begin{array}{c}a\\b\end{array}}\right\}$$
$$E(\underline{L}) = \mu_L \quad \text{and} \quad \text{var}(\underline{L}) = \sigma_L^2. \tag{5.3}$$

Inspired by (5.1) we use the following EOQ formula, where $\hat{\mu}_D$ is the simulation based estimator of μ_D (see eq. 5.6 later on):

$$\widehat{EOQ} = \frac{\sqrt{(2 \times \hat{\mu}_D \times k_3 \times (k_1 + k_2))}}{\sqrt{(k_1 \times k_2)}}. \tag{5.4}$$

Analogous to (5.2) we might use the stochastic reorder level $\underline{ROP} = \Sigma_{i=1}^{L} \underline{D}_i$. If, however, demand during the lead time $\underline{L}$ is distributed symmetrically, the out of stock probability with this $\underline{ROP}$ is 50%. We wish to fix this probability at a lower value, say α: $P(\text{out of stock} > 0) = \alpha$. Tersine (1982, pp. 148–61) shows that, if demand is normally distributed, then the reorder level should be estimated by

$$\widehat{ROP} = \hat{\mu}_L \hat{\mu}_D + z_{1-\alpha} \sqrt{(\hat{\mu}_L \hat{\sigma}_D^2 + \hat{\mu}_D^2 \hat{\sigma}_L^2)}, \tag{5.5}$$

where $z_{1-\alpha}$ is the $1 - \alpha$ quantile of $\underline{z} \sim N(0,1)$, which can be found in the table for the standard normal distribution; it makes the out of stock probability equal to α. The symbol $\hat{\sigma}_D^2$ denotes the estimated variance of demand in the periods $1, \ldots, T$, where T is the total number of periods to be simulated. The symbols $\hat{\mu}_L$ and $\hat{\sigma}_L^2$ denote the estimated expectation and variance of the lead time $\underline{L}_s$ with $s = 1, \ldots, \underline{S}$ and $\underline{S}$ the number of orders placed during the simulation: $0 \leqslant \underline{S} \leqslant T$ (if reordering does not occur in all periods, then $\underline{S} < T$). During the simulated history of the inventory system more information on $\underline{D}$ and $\underline{L}$ becomes available. So we should add the index t to all estimators in (5.4) and (5.5); for example, $\hat{\mu}_D$ should be replaced by $\hat{\mu}_D(t)$. However, for simplicity of notation we leave this index t implicit. These simple estimators may be defined as follows:

$$\hat{\mu}_D = \frac{1}{t} \sum_{i=1}^{t} \underline{D}_i \quad \text{and} \quad \hat{\sigma}_D^2 = \frac{\sum_{i=1}^{t} (\underline{D}_i - \hat{\mu}_D)^2}{t - 1} \quad (t = 2, \ldots, T). \tag{5.6}$$

Note that all observations $\underline{D}_i$ get the same weight, as $\underline{D}$ is i.i.d. When $\underline{s}$ denotes the number of replenishments that have already been simulated at the beginning of period t, we get

$$\hat{\mu}_L = \frac{1}{\underline{s}} \sum_{j=1}^{\underline{s}} \underline{L}_j \quad \text{and} \quad \hat{\sigma}_L^2 = \frac{\sum_{j=1}^{\underline{s}} (\underline{L}_j - \hat{\mu}_L)^2}{\underline{s} - 1} \quad (\underline{s} = 2, \ldots, \underline{S}). \tag{5.7}$$

We further assume that there is at most one order on its way; this implies an order size of at least $\hat{\mu}_L \times \hat{\mu}_D$.

Figure 5.2 gives a flowchart for this simulation. The flowchart, however, does not account for the variance in the lead time. To update the estimates for the mean and the variance of demand, which were given in (5.6), we use the recursive relationships (A.1) and (A.3) in the Appendix of Chapter 1 (pp. 12–13). In the flowchart these estimates are denoted by *ademand* and *ssdemand* respectively.

Exercise 5.1: Why is there a minus symbol in the following statement in Figure 5.2:
$out\_of\_stock = out\_of\_stock - k_2 \times stock$?

Exercise 5.2: Does this simulation represent a retailer without back ordering or a wholesaler with back ordering? Which instruction shows so?

Exercise 5.3: Is the economic or the technical inventory tested against ROP in Figure 5.2 (economic inventory = technical inventory + on order)?

Exercise 5.4: (a) Why would it be wrong to compute EOQ in the block where ROP is determined? (Naylor et al., 1966, p. 162, follow such an incorrect procedure!)
(b) And why would it be wrong to estimate the mean lead time in the block of Figure 5.2 where EOQ is calculated?

Exercise 5.5: (a) Simulate the same inventory system, now testing the economic inventory against ROP (delete the test: 'already ordered?'). Compute the total costs and the percentage of order cycles without stockouts, after one year of simulation. Repeat 100 times: is the stockout probability indeed α? Also compute the service percentage defined as total deliveries per year divided by total demand per year.
(b) Simulate a system with back-ordering, assuming late delivery costs are k_4 per product unit (not per day).

In inventory simulation we may drop assumptions that we introduced earlier in this section.

(1) We may allow more realistic cost functions. For example, several types of quantity discounts may be introduced: a discount is obtained if an individual order exceeds a minimum quantity; a bonus is earned if the total purchases of a calendar year exceed a minimum dollar amount, and so on.
(2) The probability functions of demand and lead time may be changed. Demand was assumed to be i.i.d. Actually demand may show autocorrelation (the concept of autocorrelation was discussed in Section 3.9). For example, a sales campaign may create positively correlated demands on successive days. Demand may also be non-normally distributed. For example, if only a small number of units is demanded per day (which may be demanded in order to repair larger systems), then a Poisson distribution may be realistic. The demand process may be nonstationary (so demand distributions on different days are not identical). Seasonality and trends may then be introduced. The forecasting of demand then becomes challenging: many procedures have been suggested, ranging from simple exponential smoothing to sophisticated Box–Jenkins (1976) methods. These procedures can be incorporated in the inventory simulation. We then postulate a certain seasonality and trend combined with a certain type of distribution function (say, Gaussian). Next we test the results of the forecast procedure. These results may be quantified through statistical measures like the mean squared error or through economic indicators such as total costs.

(3) The inventory model may be extended from a single item to multiple items. For example, a supermarket may have 100 000 stock-keeping units or SKUs (soft drink of brand A sold in a sixpack with small bottles forms one SKU; the same brand sold in one gallon bottles is a different SKU). There are many interdependencies among different SKUs. For example, they must compete for storage space. Certain ordering costs, such as transportation costs, can be shared by different SKUs.

define : inventory_costs, out_of_stock, order_costs,
                 total_costs, k1, k2, k3, stock, demand, $z_{1-\alpha}$, adel,
                 dev, ademand, ssdemand, orderno, EOQ, ROP   : REAL

                 maxday, day, deliver, del   : INTEGER

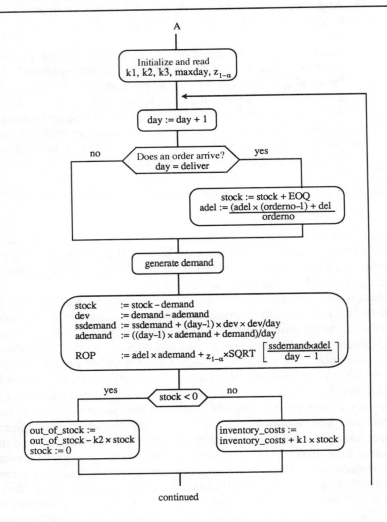

continued

Figure 5.2 Inventory model

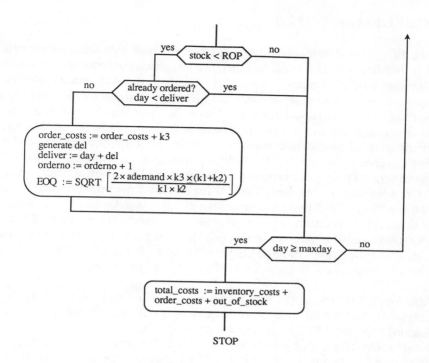

Figure 5.2 *(continued)*

Inventory theory suggests heuristics to reduce the total costs of these many SKUs. These heuristics can be tested in an inventory simulation.

(4) The inventories may be located in several places. For example, a supermarket company may have several stores, each with its own local inventories, besides a central warehouse. Again there are heuristics to decide where to store items, when to ship from the central warehouse or from the local warehouses (redistribution). Simulation is used to study such multi-echelon inventory systems.

(5) The orders that replenish the inventory may be placed with a factory that is part of the same company. For example, the supermarket company may have its own factory for certain SKUs. In general, factories can be modelled as a network of production subsystems, with inventories that buffer the input and output of each subsystem. At the boundaries of that network there are inventories for final products, which go to customers, and inventories for raw materials, which come from external suppliers. The resulting managerial problems are studied under names like logistics and materials management. Approaches for managing such complicated networks are manufacturing resource planning (MRP), just-in-time (JIT), and optimized production technology (OPT). The study of these approaches and their software uses simulation. An excellent textbook is Vollmann, Berry, and Whybark (1992). This book also discusses many aspects that we discussed under (1)–(4); so for additional literature we refer to that book. Actually manufacturing systems have not only inventory problems but also queuing problems.

5.3 QUEUING MODELS

First we discuss some elementary queuing concepts. Next we simulate the single-server queue in different ways: by hand, by fixed time increment programming, and by variable time increment programming. The third way leads to the 'next event' principle. That principle is demonstrated in simulations of systems with parallel servers, with repairmen, and with successive servers. Finally we discuss practical queuing simulations.

The common notation for queuing models is (a/b/c), where the symbol a refers to the distribution of interarrival times, b to the service time distribution, and c to the number of servers. For a and b the following symbols are common: M for a Poisson process of arrivals (that is, an exponential distribution of interarrival times, which results in a Markov process or Markov chain); D for deterministic times; and G for a general distribution. So M/M/1 denotes Markovian arrivals, Markovian service times, and a single server. This notation may be extended to (a/b/c):(d/e/f) where d denotes the priority rule (scheduler code, queue discipline), e is the maximum number of customers permitted into the system (limited buffer size), and f is the size of the total customer population. There are a large number of possible priority rules:

—'First come first served' (FCFS), also known as 'first in first out' (FIFO).
—'Last come first served' (LCFS) or 'last in first out' (LIFO, stack).
—'Shortest jobs first' (SJF): small jobs are served first.
—'Round robin' (RR): after each 'time slice' it is determined which job has not received any service for the longest time; that job will receive service first. RR is applied in 'time-sharing' computer systems, as we shall see.
—'Random service' (RS): an arbitrary customer is served next.
—'Pre-emption': the arrival of a customer of a particular type interrupts the service that a customer of the other type is receiving. In a medical system, for example, emergency patients require immediate attention; in a time-sharing system 'system jobs' pre-empt 'user jobs'. Pre-emption can be combined with all other priority rules such as FCFS and RR. If there is more than one pre-emptive customer in the system, 'first come first served' is usually applied to these customers.

Several behavioural patterns of the customers can be distinguished:

—'Balking': customers do not join the queue when it is too long.
—'Reneging': customers leave the queue when they have waited too long.
—'Jockeying': customers move from one queue to the other, when they think that they will be served sooner at the latter queue.

For analytical queuing models we refer to Gross and Harris (1985).

Exercise 5.6: Give examples of each queue discipline for systems that exist in practice.

In the remainder of this chapter we shall use the following symbols:

AT : interarrival time of a customer;
TAT : total arrival time;

ST : service time;
TST : total service time;
WT : waiting time excluding service time;
TWT : total waiting time;
IT : idle time of server;
TIT : total idle time;
QL : queue length, excluding the customer being served;
$TIME$: total time elapsed.

5.3.1 Single Server

In this subsection we consider systems of the type $(M/M/1):(FCFS/\infty/\infty)$ which denotes exponentially distributed interarrival and service times $(M/M/1)$, one server, FCFS priority rule, possibly an infinitely long queue (no limited capacity of the waiting room), and an infinite number of possible customers ($FCFS/\infty/\infty$ is often not explicitly stated). The behaviour of such a system is simulated manually in Figure 5.3, which shows the arrivals and the departures of a number of customers, using the example data of Table 5.1. The table gives the arrival times and the service times of the first five customers. This table shows that the first customer arrives at time 0, so the simulation begins when the first customer enters.

Exercise 5.7: In the simulation of shops and post offices, the simulation starts with the opening of the system, say at 8 a.m., and the first customer cannot arrive earlier. How would you simulate such a system, assuming Poisson arrivals?

The interarrival times AT can be derived by subtracting successive values for the time of arrival TAT in Table 5.1:

$$AT_2 = 3, \quad AT_3 = 2, \quad AT_4 = 6 \quad \text{and} \quad AT_5 = 3.$$

In general AT_i is the time between the arrivals of customers $i-1$ and i. The AT_i are sampled from the exponential distribution (in Chapter 3 we gave procedures for this sampling). Adding up the AT_i gives the total arrival time TAT; so TAT is merely an auxiliary variable (although Table 5.1 may suggest differently).

Table 5.1 Customer data

Customer number	1	2	3	4	5
Arrival time (TAT)	0	3	5	11	14
Service time (ST)	6	1	2	2	2

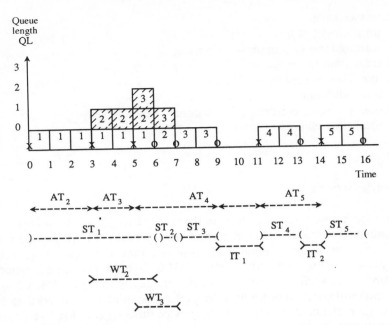

Figure 5.3 'Manual' simulation of (M/M/1):(FCFS/∞/∞). x customers arrival; if the system is empty, it also denotes the start of the service. o service end; if there is a queue, it also denotes the start of a new service. $\boxed{i}$ customer i is being served ($i = 1,2,3,4,5$). $\boxed{ii}$ customer i waits

After this 'manual' simulation, we show how to simulate the M/M/1 system on a computer. We discuss two methods (following Naylor et al., 1966, pp. 127–36).

Method 1: Fixed Time Increment

In the preceding chapter and in the inventory simulation we sliced the time into intervals of length Δt. For example, if we wish to simulate eight hours we may divide the hours into minutes; then Δt is one minute and the total time to be simulated (runlength), called (say) *SIMTIME*, is 480 minutes. For each interval we determine whether any events occur, and if so, what events take place. In Figure 5.4 we first initialize variables and read parameter values. The first customer enters the system (at time 0) and, for the time being, joins the queue: $QL := QL + 1$. Immediately we sample the time at which the next customer will arrive. We sample AT from the (negative) exponential distribution Ne and round the sampled value upwards to the next integer. We add AT to the total arrival time ($TAT := TAT + AT$). Then we check whether a preceding customer is being served ($ST > 0$). If this is not the case ($ST = 0$), we check whether there are any customers waiting ($QL > 0$). If there were no customers waiting ($QL = 0$), then the server would be idle during one time slice ($TIT := TIT + 1$). Actually, the first time we check the condition ($ST > 0$), the first customer is waiting ($QL = 1$). So we remove the customer from the queue ($QL := QL - 1$), and sample a service time ST; ST is rounded upwards again. The total time that customers have been waiting is recorded in the variable TWT: because we check per time unit whether there are any customers waiting, recording the total waiting time amounts to adding the queue length ($TWT := TWT + QL$). We also execute this instruction if $ST > 0$ holds (then the customers in the queue certainly have to wait). Next we decrease the remaining service time of the customer who is being served by one time unit ($ST := ST - 1$); so ST actually denotes the remaining service time; if ST is smaller than or equal to one, the server is idle (for didactic reasons we check whether $ST > 1$; the program is more efficient without this test). Because the latter step means that time has been increased with one unit, we update simulated elapsed time ($TIME := TIME + 1$). Next we check if the simulation finishes ($TIME \geqslant SIMTIME$). If this is the case, we check if there are still customers present in the system ($QL > 0$); if so, these customers are served. If, however, the desired simulation period has not elapsed ($TIME < SIMTIME$), we check whether a new customer arrives ($TAT = TIME$). If so, we add a new customer to the queue ($QL := QL + 1$, and so on); if not, we review the situation at the server ($ST > 0$).

Exercise 5.8: Write a computer program that corresponds with Figure 5.4

Method 2: Variable Time Increment

The example in the manual simulation of Figure 5.3 showed that customers 2 and 3 arrive while customer 1 is still being served. The resulting waiting time is $WT = 1 + 1 + 2 + 1 = 5$ time units. But we can also write the waiting time for customer 2 as

$$WT_2 = ST_1 - AT_2 = 6 - 3 = 3,$$

and for customer 3 as

$$WT_3 = (ST_1 + ST_2) - (AT_2 + AT_3)$$

$$= ST_2 - AT_3 + ST_1 - AT_2$$

$$= ST_2 - AT_3 + WT_2$$

$$= 1 - 2 + 3 = 2.$$

So the total waiting time of customers 2 and 3 is five, as we have already seen in Figure 5.3. Some reflection shows that in general the following recursive relationship holds:

$$WT_i = WT_{i-1} + ST_{i-1} - AT_i \qquad \text{if } WT_i \geqslant 0, \tag{5.8a}$$

or

$$WT_i = \max\{WT_{i-1} + ST_{i-1} - AT_i, \ 0\}. \tag{5.8b}$$

If we ignore the condition that waiting times must be non-negative, and apply this formula for $i = 4$ in the example of Figure 5.3, then the waiting time becomes

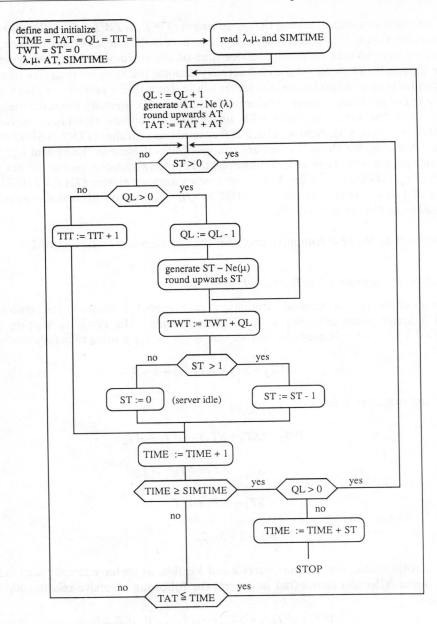

Figure 5.4 Fixed time increment simulation of $(M/M/1):(FCFS/\infty/\infty)$

$2 + 2 - 6 = -2$. Actually, its absolute value equals IT_1, the time the system is idle for the first time.

Figure 5.5 gives the flowchart for the variable time increment method. We now simulate a fixed number of arrivals, namely *NUMBER*. Customer # 1 has zero waiting time (we could have added zero to *TWT*); we initialize *CUSTNO*:= 2 (not 1). The

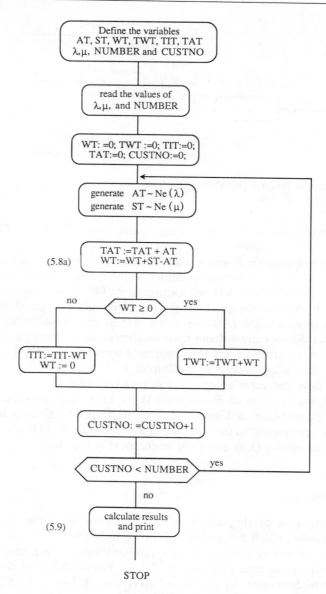

Figure 5.5 Variable time increment simulation $(M/M/1):(FCFS/\infty/\infty)$

flowchart gives as outputs: the total waiting time (TWT), the total idle time (TIT), and the total simulated time (TAT). (Observe that $TAT = TIME$ holds here.) From these outputs we compute

$$
\left.
\begin{aligned}
\text{average waiting time} &= TWT/NUMBER; \\
\text{average queue length} &= TWT/TIME; \\
\text{utilization rate} &= 1 - TIT/TIME.
\end{aligned}
\right\} \qquad (5.9)
$$

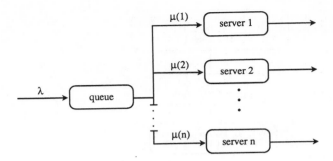

Figure 5.6 n Parallel servers: $(M/M/n){:}(FCFS/\infty/\infty)$

Exercise 5.9: Prove that indeed the average queue length is $TWT/TIME$.

Note that the average queue length equals the average waiting time multiplied by the arrival rate: Little's law. Obviously an upper limit for the total idle time (TIT) is the total simulated time ($TIME$). The total waiting time (TWT), however, exceeds the total simulated time if the average queue length per time unit is larger than one.

Actually the expected values of the responses in (5.9) are known for this simple system; see the Appendix. So we can confront these analytical results with the empirical results of the simulation, in order to test the program's correctness. (We shall return to the verification of simulation programs in Chapter 11.)

The variable time increment approach requires a more detailed analysis of the system to be simulated, as (5.8) showed. Because the M/M/1 system is so simple, the term 'next event' seems out of place in Figure 5.5. The next section gives a better example. Nevertheless we have presented the variable time method for the M/M/1 system, because we shall need the results (5.8) and (5.9) in the next subsection.

5.3.2 Parallel Servers

An obvious extension of the model in the preceding subsection is the $(M/M/n)$: $(FCFS, \infty, \infty)$ model, which is depicted in Figure 5.6. So there are $n \geqslant 2$ parallel servers; there is a single queue (the customer gets a number upon arrival); and each server has its own expected service time $\mu(i)$ ($i = 1, 2, \ldots, n$). The objective of simulating such a system may be to determine the number of servers needed to achieve a certain degree of service; for example, with 90% probability no customer waits longer than five minutes.

Using the variables that were defined earlier in this section, we give a flowchart in Figure 5.7. We start the simulation with n customers. Since the first customer is assumed to arrive at time zero, we initially sample only $n-1$ arrival times. The 'next event' principle implies that we determine which server will be idle first; that server is server # $IMIN$. That server will become idle at $TT(IMIN)$. This point in time is compared with the arrival time of the next customer: see the computation of the variable WT.

Exercise 5.10: Program and execute the flowchart of Figure 5.7.

In the next event approach we determine the next, imminent event, once we have processed the latest event. So *we jump from event to event*. During the intermediate periods the state of the system does not change, by definition. Hence these intervals are uninteresting for the simulation. The following model is also based on this principle.

5.3.3 Repairmen Model

We now discuss a classical model that may represent the maintenance of machines: the so-called repairmen problem. We assume there are n machines that are maintained by a crew of m mechanics ($1 \leqslant m \leqslant n$); each of the mechanics has the same expected speed (they can repair each of the machines in the same time, on the average). This problem may be formulated as a queuing problem, but now the machines are the customers and the mechanics are the servers. The number of customers is now finite (at most equal to n), whereas in the previous models the number of customers (and hence the queue length) could be infinite: (M/M/m)(FCFS/n/n). The repairmen model is presented in Figure 5.8 as a closed system.

The flowchart in Figure 5.9 uses the following symbols.

RT	: machine running time (mean time between failures or MTBF is $E(\underline{RT})$);
ST	: service or repair time;
$TIME$	: total simulated time;
$T(j)$	: point in time that has a change of state for machine j with $j = 1, \ldots, n$;
$WR(j)$	: identity number of the machine at place j in the 'waiting room' with $j = 1, \ldots, n-m$ and $WR \in \{j = 1, \ldots, n\}$. To implement the FCFS priority rule we always select $WR(1)$, the machine that waits at the first place in the waiting room (also see Exercise 5.12);
$IRP(j)$	: boolean variable that indicates whether machine j is under repair or not: $IRP(j) = TRUE$ and $IRP(j) = FALSE$ respectively;
$NUMBER$	: total number of repairs to be simulated;
L	: number of machines in repair with $L = 0, \ldots, m$;
I	: number of machines waiting with $I = 0, \ldots, n-m$;
K	: number of idle repairmen with $K = 0, \ldots, m$;
$REPNO$	: total number of repairs simulated so far;
D	: time during which the system does not change its state;
$JMIN$	: identity of machine that has next event.

We wish to know how much time we have zero machines in repair, how much time there is one machine under repair, and so on. Therefore we update the bookkeeping variables

$$TTR(L) = \text{total time with } L \text{ machines in repair;}$$

$$TTW(I) = \text{total time with } I \text{ machines waiting for repair;}$$

$$TTM(K) = \text{time with } K \text{ mechanics idle.}$$

The objective of the simulation may be to determine the number of repairmen needed to keep all or most machines running, with a certain probability.

Exercise 5.11: Write and run a computer program for the repairmen problem.

Exercise 5.12: How can you change the priority rule from *FCFS* into *LCFS*?

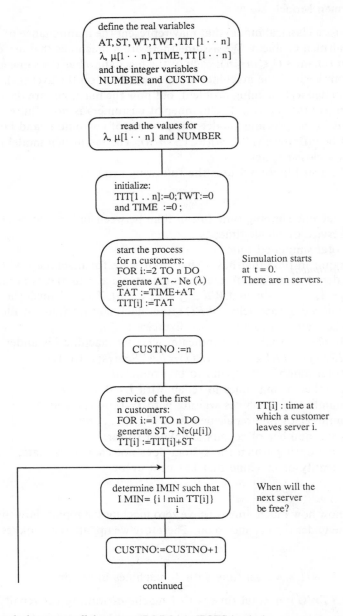

Figure 5.7 Simulating *n* parallel servers (M/M/*n*):(FCFS/∞/∞)

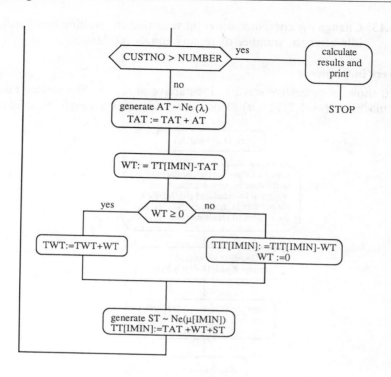

Figure 5.7 *(continued)*

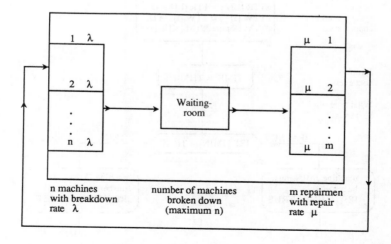

Figure 5.8 A closed system of servers (repairmen) and customers (machines)

Exercise 5.13: Change the computer program such that the waiting room will become idle after the number of repairs equals *NUMBER*.

5.3.4 Servers in Sequence

Figure 5.10 shows *n* successive servers. Jobs arrive at rate λ. The service rate μ_j may vary over machines ($j = 1, 2, \ldots, n$). This model describes a simple *flow shop*.

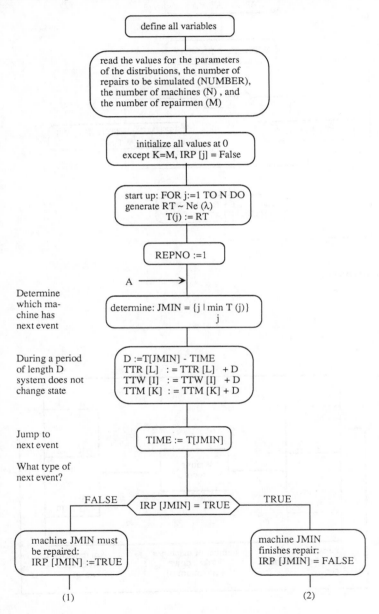

Figure 5.9 Repairmen simulation

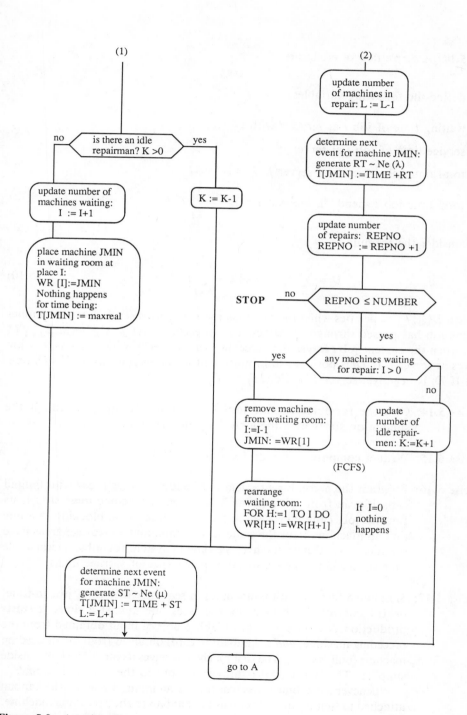

Figure 5.9 *(continued)*

Figure 5.10 A simple flow of production

We define the following variables.

WT_j^i: waiting time of job i at server j with $i = 1, 2, \ldots$;

ST_j^i: service time of job i at server j;

T_j^i: total time job i spends at server j: $T_j^i = W_j^i + ST_j^i$;

TS^i: total time job i spends in the system: $TS^i = \sum\limits_{j=1}^{n} T_j^i$.

Now consider the formula

$$D_j = \sum_{h=1}^{j} T_h^{i-1} - \left(AT_i + \sum_{h=1}^{j-1} T_h^i \right). \tag{5.10}$$

The term $\Sigma_{h=1}^{j} T_h^{i-1}$ specifies when the previous job $i-1$ leaves server j, which implies that this job has passed through all servers that precede server j. The term $\Sigma_{h=1}^{j-1} T_h^i$ shows when the current job i leaves the preceding server $(j-1)$, which means that job i arrives at server j. If D_j is positive, job i must wait at server j during $WT_j^i = D_j$ time units. If D_j is negative, server j is idle: $IT_j = -D_j$.

Exercise 5.14: Give the formulae for the initial conditions of this problem, if the simulation starts with the arrival of the first job.

Exercise 5.15: Write a computer program for this problem.

Exercise 5.16: Program the preceding problem but include storage areas with limited capacities in front of machine $2, 3, \ldots, n$. A machine must stop if its finished jobs cannot proceed to the next storage area: blocking. Assume that all machines have the same service rate, and all storage areas have the same size. Determine average time in system for jobs, average idle time of machines, and utilization percentage of storage areas.

Exercise 5.17: Simulate a factory with n machines in sequence that uses 'just-in-time' or JIT control. Each machine produces one unit at a time. It starts production as soon as it has available a unit of input obtained from the preceding machine, *and* a 'kanban' (a card) obtained from the succeeding machine (pull system). The first machine receives its input from an outside supplier. The last machine ships its output to the outside customer.

Whenever a machine starts working on an input, it releases the kanban attached to that input and returns the kanban to the preceding machine. Whenever a machine finishes the production of a unit, the machine sends that unit to the next machine, together with a kanban (which was originally received from the succeeding machine). The last machine in the production line receives kanbans from the outside customer; its number of kanbans equals the number of orders not yet delivered.

The initial conditions are: there are K kanbans at each machine, except for the last machine. No machine has inputs available. An order for K units has been placed with the outside supplier.

The following inputs are given: number of machines, exponential distribution of order arrivals, normally distributed service times. Compute the average delivery time per order, the utilization percentage of each machine, and the average inventory of input material per machine, for different values of K (number of kanbans).

5.3.5 Practical Queuing Simulations

In queuing simulations we may again drop assumptions, as we did for inventory simulations. (The programming of the resulting more complicated simulation models will be discussed in the next chapter.)

(1) The queuing discipline may be another rule than FCFS, which is usually assumed in analytical studies. In Manufacturing Resource Planning, for example, priority rules like 'shortest jobs first' and more complicated rules have been proposed for shop floor control (SFC); see Vollmann, Berry, and Whybark (1992) for a survey and Kleijnen (1992) for a case study. Furthermore, customer behaviour like balking, reneging, and jockeying is easily implemented in simulation.

(2) The probability functions of the interarrival and the service times were assumed to be exponential distributions. Traditionally these assumptions are used because otherwise the analytical solution is extremely difficult or impossible. In simulation, however, it is no problem at all to replace these distributions by (say) a lognormal distribution for service times and to include negative autocorrelation (this autocorrelation may account for faster service when the system fills up). Further, customers may arrive in 'busloads', at points of time that are normally distributed around scheduled points of time. Interarrival rates may be nonstationary and vary with the time of the day (peak hours), the day of the week (busy days), and so on.

(3) Queuing networks can be solved by numerical analysis, provided certain conditions hold. For example, buffer sizes are unlimited so that no blocking occurs; see Lavenberg (1983). In simulation, however, networks can have limited storage spaces. Moreover customers may follow paths through the network that depend on characteristics of the network (avoid busy nodes) and the customer (each job has its own specific resource requirements). Examples are simulations in Manufacturing Resource Planning, Flexible Manufacturing Systems (FMSs), communication systems (telephone lines, Local Area Networks, telematic systems), and so on.

We now return to the queuing situations listed in Chapter 1 (at the end of Section 1.1).

(1) Post offices and petrol stations are practical examples of the models discussed in the previous subsections.

(2) Street intersections may be modelled as queuing systems with traffic lights as servers. Typical priority rules in traffic systems may be priority for vehicles coming from the right or for pedestrians.
(3) Logistic problems have already been mentioned several times as classical topics of simulation studies. More examples are: identify resources that are bottlenecks (bottlenecks give excessive queue lengths), balance the work centres in the factory and determine the work-force required, quantify storage requirements (buffer sizes) for work in progress (WIP) on the factory floor, determine required transportation facilities, find effects of machine breakdowns and scrap (faulty products), and so on. Note that these problems occur at the strategic and the operational levels of the organization; that is, they range from investment analyses of different factory layouts and Computer Integrated Manufacturing (CIM) to daily problems on the work floor (determine the moment of the switch-over to a different batch of work and select a batch size). Also see Law and Kelton (1991, pp. 696–735).
(4) The processing of jobs within a computer will be discussed in detail in the next chapter.
(5) Project planning of a major dike in The Netherlands was simulated accounting for the manoeuvring space that ships need, the increasing water current as the dike nears completion so that the water must flow through a narrow gap, and so on.

Several more applications of simulation in the area of queuing analysis will be presented in later chapters, in order to illustrate the statistical techniques of those chapters.

5.4 MISCELLANEOUS MODELS, INCLUDING COMBINED CONTINUOUS/DISCRETE-EVENT MODELS

A system may have some processes that are modelled by physical laws that are specified by differential equations (also see the section on system dynamics in the preceding chapter), while some other processes are modelled as discrete events. Examples are systems with automatic guided vehicles (AGVs): the displacement of the AGV is determined by the laws of motion until the AGV reaches its point of destination, whereupon the loading and unloading events occur (the durations of these events are stochastic variables). The traffic applications mentioned in the preceding subsection are similar combined models. Another example is mine hunting at sea. The search for mines is done by ships equipped with sonar. The laws that govern the appearance of mines on the sonar screen are again ruled by physical laws. The detection of the signals by the human operator, however, is modelled as a random discrete event (see Chapter 11). Obviously the programming of combined continuous/discrete-event models is a challenge, which will be touched upon in the next chapter. For more details, including examples, we refer to Pegden, Shannon, and Sadowski (1990, pp. 495–528), and Pritsker (1986, pp. 342–79, 531–58).

Besides inventory and queuing models there are other kinds of simulation models,

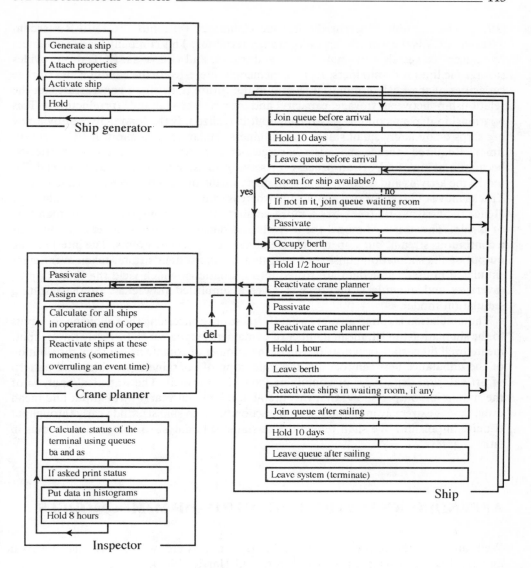

Figure 5.11 The simulation model in the Rotterdam case study

which might be called operations research models. Pritsker (1986, pp. 67–95) presents a number of simulation applications; the other references of this chapter also provide case studies.

5.4.1 Case Study: The Europe Container Terminus (ECT) in Rotterdam Harbour

The following example shows that simulation can indeed be applied to the study of complicated problems arising in the operation of real-life systems. We give only a survey of this case study; for details we refer to Kleijnen, van den Burg, and van der Ham

(1979). The example concerns the Europe Container Terminus (ECT) in Rotterdam harbour. ECT is the world's largest container terminus. This company loads containers from deep-sea vessels into smaller ships and trucks, and vice versa. ECT also provides storage facilities for containers. Its management is interested in the handling and storage capacities of the ECT terminal, now and in the future. Our study concentrates on the relationship between storage capacity and yearly 'throughput' (production). This relationship depends on the way throughput is realized: is the load delivered by a few big ships or by many small ships; do containers remain long or short at ECT ('dwell' time)? Required storage space is measured per day. An analytical model is rejected because it assumes a Poisson process for service times; simulation is used instead. To model the arrivals and departures of containers we distinguish between ships and trucks. Trucks move only one or two containers, whereas ships carry relatively many containers. Hence the arrival of a truck has a much smaller effect on the system's state than that of a ship. Therefore we model the arrivals and departures of containers by trucks as a continuous stream, but ship arrivals are modelled as discrete events. The intermediate output of the simulation consists of snapshots of the system's state, taken every eight simulated hours. These data are stored into histograms, which yield the final outputs (averages and quantiles). Figure 5.11 gives a simplified flow chart of the resulting simulation model.

The simulation is run to answer 'what if' questions concerning the following six inputs to the simulation model: mean number of containers moved per ship, yearly throughput, mean dwell time, statistical distribution of the number of containers per ship, distribution of the unbalance between loading and unloading of containers per ship, and pattern of arrivals and departures of containers from the terminal. The statistical analysis of the simulation output shows that the interaction between yearly throughput and mean dwell time is extremely important; the interaction between ship size and yearly throughput is quite important. We shall return to the statistical analysis of simulation models in later chapters.

APPENDIX: ANALYTICAL SOLUTION OF M/M/n MODELS

Well-known formulae for M/M/1 and M/M/n models are, with $1/\lambda$ the mean arrival and $1/\mu$ the mean service time (see Gross and Harris, 1985):

M/M/1

$$\frac{\lambda}{\mu(\mu-\lambda)} = \text{expected waiting time } E(\underline{WT})$$

$$\frac{\lambda^2}{\mu(\mu-\lambda)} = \text{expected queue length}$$

$$\frac{(\mu-\lambda)}{\mu} \times TIME = \text{expected idle time}$$

$$\frac{\lambda}{(\mu-\lambda)} \qquad = \text{expected number of customers in system}$$

$$\frac{1}{(\mu-\lambda)} \qquad = \text{expected total time in system}$$

$$\frac{\lambda}{\mu} \qquad = \text{expected traffic intensity}$$

$$\left(1-\frac{\lambda}{\mu}\right)\left(\frac{\lambda}{\mu}\right)^n = \text{probability of } n \text{ customers in system}$$

M/M/n

$$p_0 = \left\{\sum_{k=0}^{n-1}\frac{1}{k!}\left(\frac{\lambda}{\mu}\right)^k + \left(\frac{1}{n!}\right)\left(\frac{\lambda}{\mu}\right)^n\frac{n\mu}{(n\mu-\lambda)}\right\}^{-1} \quad \text{: probability of idle system at random point of time}$$

$$p_j = \frac{1}{j!}\left(\frac{\lambda}{\mu}\right)^j p_0 \qquad\qquad\qquad \text{: probability of } j<n \text{ customers in system}$$

$$p_j = \frac{1}{n!\mu^{(j-\mu)}}\left(\frac{\lambda}{\mu}\right)^j p_0 \qquad\qquad \text{: probability of } j\geqslant n \text{ customers in system}$$

$$P_{j\geqslant n} = \frac{\mu\left(\frac{\lambda}{\mu}\right)^n}{(\mu-1)!(n\mu-\lambda)}\, p_0 \qquad\qquad \text{: probability of all servers busy.}$$

REFERENCES

Box G. E. P. and G. M. Jenkins (1976) *Time Series Analysis: Forecasting and Control*, Holden Day, San Francisco.

Gross D. and C. M. Harris (1985) *Fundamentals of Queuing Theory*, Wiley, New York.

Kleijnen J. P. C. (1992) Simulation and Optimization in Production Planning: A Case Study, *Decision Support Systems* (in press).

Kleijnen J. P. C., A. J. van den Burg and R. T. van der Ham (1979) Generalization of simulation results: Practicality of statistical methods, *European Journal of Operational Research*, **3**, 50–64.

Lavenberg S. S. (ed.) (1983) *Computer Performance Modeling Handbook*, Academic Press, New York.

Law A. M. and W. D. Kelton (1991) *Simulation Modeling and Analysis* (2nd edn), McGraw-Hill, New York.

Naylor T. H., J. L. Balintfy, D. S. Burdick, and Kong Chu (1966) *Computer Simulation Techniques*, Wiley, New York.

Pegden C. P., R. E. Shannon and R. P. Sadowski (1990) *Introduction to Simulation Using SIMAN*, McGraw-Hill, New York.

Pritsker A. A. B. (1986) *Introduction to Simulation and SLAM II* (3rd edn), Halsted Press, New York.

Tersine R. J. (1982) *Principles of Inventory and Materials Management*, North-Holland, New York.

Vollmann T. E., W. L. Berry and D. C. Whybark (1992) *Manufacturing Planning and Control Systems* (3rd edn), Irwin, Homewood, Illinois.

Chapter 6

Simulation Software

The programming of a realistic simulation model may become so complicated as to make special software desirable. We give a detailed discussion of a particular software package that simplifies the simulation of queuing models with parallel servers. We also survey simulation software in general. This software simplifies the programming of simulation models.

This chapter is organized as follows.
—6.1 Simulation package for parallel servers
Based on Hellerman and Conroy (1975) we derive a general model for a queuing system with parallel servers. We include set-up and set-down times (besides service times) and various priority rules including round robin, which is used in time-sharing computer systems. For jobs we distinguish ten states, for servers four states. It is crucial to synchronize state changes of jobs and servers. Readers interested in the simulation of simple queuing systems only can skip Section 6.1.
—6.2 Simulation software: a survey
We survey simulation languages and packages for discrete-event systems and semi-continuous systems respectively, including software for economic and financial simulations.

6.1 SIMULATION PACKAGE FOR PARALLEL SERVERS

Our simulation package is based on Hellerman and Conroy (1975, pp. 112–18). They simulate a system of parallel servers, using the 'next event' principle. Their package was originally developed for the simulation of computer systems including terminals. These terminals are used interactively; each terminal transaction is an instruction (job) for the system of servers. The resulting simulation package can also be applied to many other problems.

6.1.1 System Components and Organization

We examine (1) servers, (2) transactions and (3) system organization.

(1) *Servers.* The model comprises a number of parallel servers: there are *NS* servers, where *NS* is a positive integer. These servers are not necessarily identical: each has

its own 'service factor' SF_j with $j = 1, \ldots, NS$ that determines how much faster server j is than the slowest server. Thus the slowest server has a service factor with value one.

(2) *Transactions.*   In the previous chapter we spoke of customers or jobs; now we talk about transactions. Each transaction is characterized by the following four attributes.

TAT_i: arrival time of transaction i at the system;
  ST_i: service time if processed by the slowest server;
  SU_i: set-up time, which is needed to fetch a transaction from the queue and to prepare it for processing;
  SD_i: set-down time, needed either to place a transaction back into the queue or to remove the transaction from the system.

For simplicity's sake we assume that SU_i equals SD_i: $SU_i = SD_i$. SU_i often has a constant value: $SU_i = SU$. If the system does not represent a computer but a bank, then SU may refer to the time needed to search for the file of a client or the time to store the file. From an economic viewpoint SU_i and SD_i are switchover costs.

(3) *System organization.*   The system has a finite *waiting room* with a known capacity, $MAXQ$. If the queue is full, the system turns away newly arriving transactions. If all servers are busy but $MAXQ$ has not yet been reached, then transactions do join the queue. There are two ways to organize queues:

(a) All transactions are placed in a *common queue*.
(b) Each server has its *own queue*. A newly arriving transaction joins the shortest 'effective' queue, which is calculated by dividing the queue length by the service rate. If two queues have the same effective length, then the transaction joins the server with the highest service rate. (If the actual service times in the actual queues are known, then we can use the effective waiting time instead of the effective queue length.)

Another system characteristic is the *priority rule* or scheduler code. Round robin (RR) is applied in time-sharing computer systems. RR uses the concept of a 'time slice': during one time slice the server processes one transaction; at the end of the time slice the operating system of the computer checks whether there is another transaction waiting; if a transaction is waiting, the operating system interrupts the current transaction and starts the next transaction. Round robin gives priority to the transaction that received service 'long ago'; transactions that have not been processed at all have top priority. To implement various priority rules in the simulation package, we use a service variable called SV: the transaction with the minimal SV is served first. Hence first come first served (FCFS) corresponds with $SV = TAT$; last come first served means $SV = -TAT$. Implementing round robin is more complicated (see Exercise 6.2 near the end of Subsection 6.1.2).

Exercise 6.1: How can the priority rule 'small jobs first' be implemented through SV?

There may also be *pre-emptive* transactions, that is, certain transactions interrupt an ongoing service. In a computer system the operating system itself generates transactions that are pre-emptive; these system jobs are necessary for the processing of the user jobs. Note that interrupting the *set-down* of a user job would be inefficient.

6.1.2 System States

Transactions and servers are the system's objects or entities. The object's state is determined by the values of the object's attributes. We distinguish ten different states for the transactions, and number these states from 0 to 9; we distinguish four states for the servers, numbered from 0 to 3. Table 6.1 shows the possible states of the transactions and Figure 6.1(a) shows the feasible state transitions for a transaction.

Table 6.1 Transaction states

0	transaction has not yet arrived ($TAT > CLOCK$); clock denotes current simulation time
1	transaction has arrived, but has not yet received any service
2	set-up of transaction
3	two possibilities:
	(a) transaction is ready for service (via state 2)
	(b) transaction has already been processed before, but has not been completed (via state 5)
4	transaction is being processed
5	transaction has been processed during a period of TS time units (TS = time slice length)
6	set-down of incomplete transaction (another transaction has higher priority and interrupts the processing of the current transaction)
7	transaction has been finished (the last time slice may not be used completely: transition from state 4 to state 7)
8	set-down of transaction that has been completed
9	transaction has left system

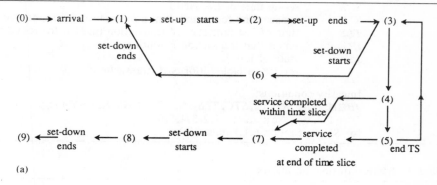

(a)

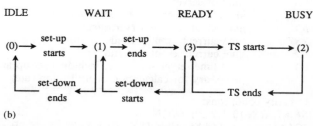

(b)

Figure 6.1 Feasible state transitions of system components: (a) transactions; (b) servers

In the previous chapter, servers had only two states: busy or idle. Now we also model set-up and set-down, which lead to the addition of the wait and ready states. The 'wait' state may be illustrated through a banking system: the server waits while the customer either unpacks or packs a briefcase. So the wait state occurs during set-up and set-down. When the server is in the 'ready' state, processing can start. Figure 6.1(b) shows the feasible state transitions for the servers.

The information on transactions is stored in state vectors, one vector per transaction. These vectors may be collected in a matrix with $MAXQ$ columns; see Table 6.2. The corresponding matrix for the servers is shown in Table 6.3; it has NS columns. The columns 'description' in these two tables clarify the symbols. The range conditions at the bottom of these tables enable us to guarantee the integrity or consistency of the information in the database.

The system state is completely characterized by the states of the servers and the transactions, at a certain point of time. Each transaction and each server is characterized by the set of attributes that were displayed in Tables 6.2 and 6.3. Some information in these tables is redundant; for example, either IP in Table 6.2 or JX in Table 6.4 suffices. Redundant variables may simplify programming, and serve didactic purposes.

Table 6.2 Transaction information matrix

$1, \ldots, MAXQ$	Symbol	Description
	JB	transaction or job identity number
	TAT	arrival time of transaction
	ST	service time of transaction
	SU	set-up time of transaction
	STC	service time completed until now (needed for round robin)
	TLS	time of last time slice of transaction (needed for round robin)
	IP	server that transaction is waiting at
	JS	state of job
	SV	service variable (priority of transaction)

Integrity conditions;
$JB \in \mathbf{N}$; $TAT, ST, SU, STC, TLS \in \mathbf{R}$, $STC < ST$, $TLS > TAT$;
$IP \in \{1, 2, \ldots, NS\}$; $JS \in \{0, 1, 2, 3, 4, 5, 6, 7, 8, 9\}$;
for SV see Section 6.1.1 (item (3))

Table 6.3 Server information matrix

$1, \ldots, NS$	Symbol	Description
	SF	speed factor of server
	RS	state of server
	JX	identity number of jobs being served
	IQL	number of jobs in server queue
	TST	time current event started
	EJ	time current event will end
	UT	total time server was busy, including set-up and set-down (necessary for calculation of utilization rate)

Integrity conditions:
$SF \geqslant 1$; $RS \in \{0, 1, 2, 3\}$; $JX \in \mathbf{N}$;
$IQL \in \{1, 2, \ldots, MAXQ\text{-}NS\}$; $TST \in R$; $EJ > TST$; $UT \in \mathbf{R}$.

Table 6.4 Synchronization of state transitions of servers and transactions

Current state		Next state		
Server	Trans-action	Server	Trans-action	Description
1	2	3	3	set-up completed
1	6	0	1	set-down completed; transaction not finished
1	8	0	9	set-down completed; transaction finished
2	4	3	5	time slice ends
2	4	3	7	service complete before time slice ends
3	5	3	3	transaction not finished after time slice
3	5	3	7	transaction ends and service is completed
0	0	0	1	arrival of transaction
0	1	1	2	set-up starts
3	3	2	4	service starts
3	3	1	6	set-down starts; service not completed
3	7	1	8	set-down starts; service completed

Note that, if the servers have a common queue, then IQL in Table 6.3 has the same value for all servers and IP in Table 6.2 is ignored.

Exercise 6.2: How can the priority rule round robin be implemented through SV?

Note that the waiting room is no object in this system. The system state would depend on the waiting room's state, if servers worked faster as the waiting room fills up.

6.1.3 Synchronization of Server and Transaction States

The states of transactions and servers must be compatible: a transaction and a server 'dance the tango together'. Table 6.4 shows which state changes go together. The upper part of the table refers to a service end; the lower part refers to a service start. To explain this table we suppose that the transaction is in state 2; see line 1 of Table 6.4. According to Figure 6.1(a) the transaction is then in the set-up state. Figure 6.1(b) shows that the server must then be in state 1 (wait). The next state of the transaction can be state 3 only: see the arrow in Figure 6.1(a). But if the transaction changes from state 2 to 3 (end of set-up), then according to Figure 6.1(b) the server changes from state 1 to 3.

Exercise 6.3: Explain the second line of Table 6.4: server from 1 to 0, and transaction
from 6 to 1.

The transaction got into state 2 (set-up completed; see first line of Table 6.4), because at an earlier point in time the simulation program executed line 4 from below in Table 6.4 (set-up starts).

Exercise 6.4: How did the transaction get into state 6?

6.1.4 Resulting Simulation Package

The computer implementation of this class of simulation models requires much programming. (Actually we had some students at our university implement this package successfully.) We do not present a detailed computer program or flowchart, but only the general flowchart of Figure 6.2. The blocks have the following functions.

Block 1: We read all parameter values, and initialize all variables.

Block 2: If the queue is not filled to capacity, we generate transactions to fill the queue up to its capacity *MAXQ*. (An alternative would be to look ahead one customer only, as we explained in the preceding chapter.)

Block 3: We determine the next event; that is, we find the minimum of the next arrival time (*TAT* in Table 6.2) and the next point in time at which a server becomes idle (*EJ* in Table 6.3).

Block 4: If the next arrival time does not exceed the service end, then the elapsed time or *CLOCK* becomes equal to the next arrival time. The transaction state becomes 1; see Figure 6.1(a). If the equality sign does not hold, we go to block 7.

Block 5: If in block 3 the next event is a service end, then *CLOCK* is set to this point in time. The transaction and the server states change, according to the upper part of Table 6.4.

Block 6: If the transaction is finished (state 9), we update the statistical summaries and check if this job was the last transaction. If so, we compute and print the statistical output variables; if not, we go to block 7.

Block 7: If no server is ready (state 3) or if no server is idle (state 0), we go back to block 2. If, however, a server has a completed transaction (ready; see Figure 6.1(b)), we start the set-down of that job (server state changes from 3 to 1; see the lower part of Table 6.4). If there are any other servers ready (state 3) or idle (state 0), we determine for these servers which transaction should be processed. If the transaction is already at the server, then service starts (server from state 3 to 2); otherwise set-up starts. If the server is ready but it does not contain the transaction that is next, then set-down of the current transaction begins (second half of Table 6.4).

Note that this general flowchart does not account for pre-emption (the arrival of a pre-emptive job cancels the future event time of the job that is being served).

Exercise 6.5: The 3.5 inch disk which is available for use with this book contains an implementation of the simulation package that follows Figure 6.2 and includes the following particulars.

(a) Servers may have different speeds.

(b) In round robin, new arrivals are placed in the regular queue; so they are not necessarily served before an old job gets its new time slice.

(c) If in round robin no other job is waiting, the current job gets a new time slice without first being set down and set up again.

(d) Pre-emption is allowed. Pre-emptive jobs must wait until the set-up

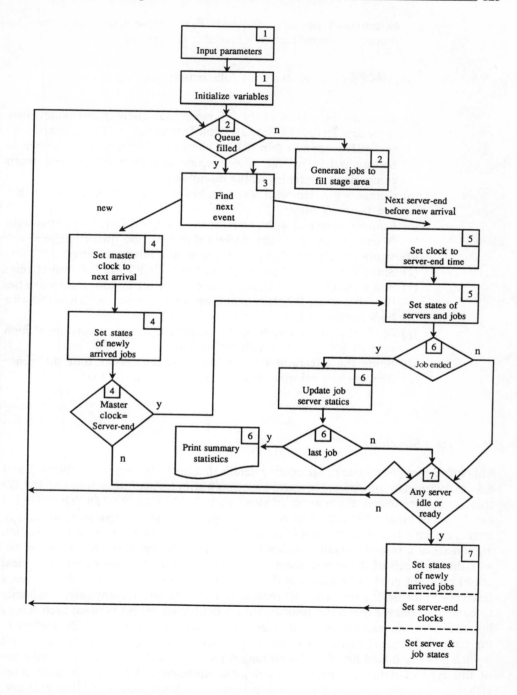

Figure 6.2 Basic logic of simulation package (Source: Hellerman and Conroy, 1975, *Computer System Performance*, Fig. 4.8.6, p. 117. Copyright ©1975 McGraw-Hill, Inc. Reproduced by permission)

or set-down has been finished. Pre-emptive jobs that cannot be processed immediately are placed in a separate queue.

Run this program to study the following issues.

(a) Compare the effects of the following four queuing disciplines: first come first served (FCFS), last come first served (LCFS), shortest jobs first (SJF), round robin (RR). (These queuing rules were defined in Section 5.3.) Use the same pseudorandom numbers seed when comparing different queuing disciplines.

(b) Compare a system with N servers to a system with a single server that is a factor N faster.

(c) Compare a system with N servers and a single queue, to a system with N servers and N queues. (Adapt the maximum queue length.)

(d) Study the effects of changing the maximum queue length.

(e) Study the effects of pre-emption, under FCFS and RR respectively.

(f) Study the effects of the magnitude of the set-up time relative to the time slice under RR. Distinguish between situations with low and with high traffic loads.

(g) Study the consequences of the magnitude of the percentage of high priority jobs, given a high traffic load.

(h) Study the effects of the magnitude of the service time difference between two priority classes, given a high traffic load.

*6.1.5 Data Structures

This subsection gives some programming details that might be skipped. Tables 6.2 and 6.3 use *matrices* to store data. Since there are nine attributes per transaction and $MAXQ$ transactions are stored, the number of elements in Table 6.2 is $9 \times MAXQ$; Table 6.3 has $7 \times NS$ elements. The computer reserves a fixed block of adjacent memory cells to store these data. It is more efficient to use a *linked list*. Then the attributes per transaction are placed in a record, together with a pointer. The pointer shows where the record with the attributes of the next transaction are stored. So the next record (in the logical sense) does not need to be stored in the adjacent memory place (physically). Given a reference to the first record, all other records can be retraced. In many cases it is handy to be able to retrace preceding records, then a doubly linked list is used; each record has two pointers, namely one that refers to the next record and one that refers to the preceding record. Adding new records is simpler with a doubly linked list than it is with a singly linked list. Simulation languages for discrete event models make use of this type of data structures. The computer implementation becomes even more efficient, if we select a different data structure for each scheduler code. For example, for first come first served we take a queue and for last come first served we use a stack. For details we refer to Law and Kelton (1991, pp. 133–233), and Stubbs and Webre (1985).

6.2 SIMULATION SOFTWARE: A SURVEY

In this section we give a survey of software for the simulation of different types of models, namely discrete-event, system dynamics, and economic and corporate models. We organize this survey as follows:

(1) software examples;
(2) functionality (*what* does the software do?);
(3) technical details (*how* does the software realize its functionality?); and
(4) literature references.

Technical details, mentioned under (3), are discussed only if deemed useful.

6.2.1 Discrete-event Simulation

A very general class of models is formed by *discrete-event models*, which change their state at discrete points of time that are not necessarily equidistant. To program such models efficiently we can use event scheduling (see Section 5.1 on fixed versus variable time increments, and Section 4.7 on system dynamics).

In the preceding section we gave a detailed example of a simulation package or *simulator*. Simulators are 'parameter driven', that is, all the user has to do is enter parameter values; no programming is needed. For example, in our simulator for parallel servers the user provides the values of the parameters of the distributions for the arrival and service times. Moreover the user must enter the number of servers and the time slice length. Note that we distinguish between parameters and exogenous variables (see the definitions in Section 1.2), whereas in computer science both types of inputs are called parameters. To get more flexibility, simulators may have an interface with a general-purpose language.

Our simulator for parallel servers could have been easily augmented to servers in sequence (not only in parallel). Then one more simulator for *queuing networks* would have been created. But there is already a number of packages for the analytical and the simulation modelling of computer and communication networks. Examples are IBM's RESQME, Bell's Q-PAS, and CACI's NETWORK and COMNET. A newsletter is devoted to these packages: *Q-passport* (see References at the end of this chapter). Also see Gordon et al. (1991).

Another interesting class of simulators has been developed for *manufacturing* applications. Examples are CACI's SIMFACTORY, Pritsker's XCELL+, ATT's WITNESS, and Production Modeling Corporation's ProModelPC. These simulators have features to represent material handling equipment such as automated guided vehicles (AGVs) and transport conveyors. Manufacturing simulators are discussed in Banks et al. (1991), and Law and Kelton (1991, pp. 699–703). These references are limited to American simulators. A European package, developed in the Netherlands, is 'Taylor'; see Kleijnen and Van Groenendaal (1988). A French simulator of Flexible Manufacturing Systems is FLEXSIM, developed by Gelenbe and Guennouni (1991).

Manufacturing Resource Planning (MRP) packages also have simulation capabilities, in order to evaluate weekly scheduling decisions. Alternatively, the MRP package may have an interface to a specially designed simulator; for example, Pritsker's FACTOR can be interfaced with IBM's COPICS.

Besides simulators there are *simulation languages*. A simulation language gives the user more modelling flexibility, that is, more general classes of systems can be modelled and simulated. Examples of these languages are Wolverine's GPSS/H and Minuteman's GPSS/PC, CACI's SIMSCRIPT, Pritsker's SLAM, and Systems Modeling Corporation's SIMAN; the latter three languages are based on FORTRAN. In Europe SIMULA is popular; it is based on ALGOL (for details on SIMULA we refer to Pritsker, 1986, p. 570). For Macintosh computers there is Extend, offered by Imagine That.

Simulation languages enable system analysts to develop simulation models and programs faster than general-purpose languages (such as FORTRAN) do; of course packages lead even faster to a running simulation program. Discrete-event simulation packages and languages provide the following *facilities*.

(1) Pseudorandom number generators (see Chapter 2).
(2) Sampling routines for random variables (Chapter 3).
(3) Automatic control of the event list and clock mechanism, which govern the progress of the simulated system over time (Chapter 5 and Section 6.1).
(4) Collection and processing of output statistics in the form of histograms and other statistical measures (Chapter 10).
(5) Error detection (for example, automatic 'tracing' of the history of an individual customer), which is important for program verification (Chapter 11).
(6) Animation (explained in the next paragraph), which helps verification and validation of the simulation model (Chapter 11).
(7) Interactive and graphical model specification (briefly discussed below).
(8) Combination of discrete-event and (semi)continuous models (Section 5.4).

With reference to (6) above, *animation* provides a 'cartoon movie' of the dynamic behaviour of the simulated system, as follows. Different types of resources (servers, nodes) and customers are represented by different icons that may change place and colour on the computer screen as the system state changes. The screen shows when customers arrive, which path they follow through the system (the system lay-out is shown as a static background), if and how long they must wait for service at the various system resources, and when they finally leave the system. For the resources the animation shows when they change state: (say) green means 'idle', amber means 'set-up', and red means 'busy' (also see the state transitions in Figure 6.1). The animation further shows how queue lengths change over time. Time may be compressed or expanded: the simulation may represent a system evolving over years or over microseconds. Obviously, *the* way to understand animation is to see an actual demonstration; Law and Kelton (1991, pp. 264–5) give colour plates (snapshots) of actual animations. Animation is a powerful tool to demonstrate and 'sell' a simulation model, but it does not solve all verification and validation problems, as we shall see in Chapter 11. Note that animations are available for both simulation languages (SIMAN/CINEMA, SLAM/TESS, SIMSCRIPT/SIMGRAPHICS) and simulators. Wolverine's Proof Animation can generate animations not only from GPSS/H but also from any other language that can produce ASCII data.

With reference to (7), simulators, but also simulation languages extended with additional software, enable the analyst to enter the model structure and the values for the parameters and exogenous variables in an interactive and graphical way. For example, SIMAN/CINEMA and SLAM/TESS offer these options. This user-friendly tool may be dangerous, since the amateur may easily build nonsense models that are syntactically correct.

Technically, three views can be distinguished within discrete-event simulation languages, namely event, activity, and process views. Many authors, however, distinguish only between event and process. The latter two views can be defined as follows.

(1) *Event view.* There are (say) k event types; for example, the arrival of a customer is a type 1 event, whereas the departure of a customer is a type 2 event. Each event type corresponds with a specific computer procedure. The flowchart in Figure 6.2 for our simulator gives an example. In general, the event list contains the times t_i that the next event of type i will occur, with $i = 1, 2, \ldots, k$. The minimal t_i is determined, and time is increased to that point of time. The procedure that corresponds with this type of event is executed. Events take no simulated time, that is, they are instantaneous.

(2) *Process view.* A process can be viewed as a series of related events that happen to an entity as it flows through the system; a process takes time. The process view is more macroscopic than the event view is. For example, a customer arrives, starts service, and finishes service; together these events form the customer process. Another example was given in the ECT example of the preceding chapter: Figure 5.11 displayed four types of process, namely ship generator, ship, crane planner, and inspector. That simulation was programmed in a process-oriented language called PROSIM, developed in the Netherlands. Modern languages for discrete-event simulation are based on the process view, even though they allow the event view. For details we refer to Law and Kelton (1991, pp. 237–40), Mitrani (1982, pp. 16–23), and Pritsker (1986, pp. 54–8).

Simulation languages run on many platforms: mainframes, microcomputers, workstations. These platforms are supplied by different hardware manufacturers and use different operating systems. On vector computers (such as the CRAY X-MP), however, there is not yet, to the best of our knowledge, special software for discrete-event simulation available; see Kleijnen and Annink (1992). On parallel computers (such as the Hypercube) discrete-event simulation software has started to become available; see Reiher (1990).

Learning a simulation language requires much effort, just as learning a general-purpose language does. So it takes a full course, a manual, and a textbook. We do not believe that a single chapter suffices to teach one or more simulation languages. For example, to discuss simulation in SLAM, Pritsker (1986) takes more than 800 pages; for SIMAN Pegden, Shannon, and Sadowski (1990) require more than 600 pages; and Schriber (1991) uses more than 400 pages to introduce GPSS/H. We refer to these textbooks for more details on simulation languages. The effort needed to learn a simulation language is worthwhile, if the analyst must program many simulation models of a type that fits into one specific language.

There are many more discrete-event simulation languages. For the United States we refer to the literature given in Section 6.2.4. In Europe, several simulation languages have been developed besides SIMULA. In The Netherlands, for example, we have PROSIM, TAYLOR, MUST, and COSMOS. (Addresses of Dutch software suppliers are given in Kleijnen and van Groenendaal, 1988, p. 226.) In England there is ESL, InterSIM, and Pascal-Sim (see Swain, 1991). And more discrete-event languages will become available, some of them based on new general-purpose languages such as object-oriented languages (for example, C + +). Moreover, in the field of artificial intelligence and expert systems, discrete-event simulation software is developed, for example, IntelliCorp's (1986) KEE; also see Swain (1991, p. 97).

6.2.2 System Dynamics Models

In Section 4.7 we saw that Forrester's system dynamics sees the world as a system of 'vessels' connected by 'pipes' with 'faucets' controlling the flows into and out of the vessels. Mathematically, these systems are modelled through difference equations; the system state is evaluated at equidistant points of time.

Examples of programming languages for system dynamics models are DYNAMO, DYSMAP2, and STELLA. We compare their *functionality* with that of the discrete-event languages of the preceding subsection, as follows.

(1)–(2) The generation of pseudorandom numbers and the sampling of stochastic variables is crucial in discrete-event systems but plays a minor role in system dynamics (also see the first paragraph of Chapter 5 on operations research models). Nevertheless randomness can be introduced into system dynamics, for example, to represent errors in the information that is used to control the system. System dynamics languages do provide pseudorandom numbers and sampling routines.

(3) The role of the event list and the clock mechanism in discrete-event systems is taken over by the integration routines in system dynamics. In our discussion of system dynamics in Section 4.7 we have already mentioned Euler and Runge–Kutta methods. Moreover, sort routines should place the recursive difference equations in the right order for computation.

(4) Collection and processing of output statistics remain important. In system dynamics the outputs are usually presented as time series and tables.

(5) Error detection is also provided, though the technical details differ: in discrete-event simulation individual transactions must be traced, whereas in system dynamics the difference equations should have the right format. For example, the level equation (4.25) implies that a level at time K cannot be determined by a rate during the (future) period from K to L: and levels must be connected through rates, not through other levels. In this way the consistency of the model is checked.

(6) Animation now means that the picture on the computer screen shows how levels and rates change over time.

(7) Interactive, graphical model specification is well developed in STELLA. (STELLA runs on the Apple–MacIntosh, which has an operating system especially developed to support such a user interface.)

(8) Discrete-event simulation languages have been extended to allow combined discrete-event/continuous models. For example, Pritsker (1986, pp. 519–25) gives an example

of a world dynamics simulation in SLAM. Of course, discrete-event languages do not provide the system dynamics terminology where, for example, KL denotes the time from 'now' ($K = t$) to the next point of time ($L = t + 1$).

System dynamics languages run on mainframes and microcomputers, with MS-DOS and Apple operating systems. For details on these languages we refer to Richmond, Vescuso, and Peterson (1987), and Wolstenholme (1990, pp. 57–8).

Note that in Section 4.7 on system dynamics we mentioned that in physics models, time is viewed as a truly continuous variable, which results in differential equations. In the past these models were simulated on analogue computers (which are composed of integrators and differentiators). Nowadays these models are simulated on digital computers, which means that continuous variables must be approximated through discretized variables. Hence differential equations are approximated through difference equations, so numerical integration routines become important. There are many languages for this application domain of simulation. Examples are CSMP, CSSL, ASCL, and DARE-P; see Pritsker (1986, pp. 578–9).

6.2.3 Economic and Corporate Models

In Chapter 5 we discussed economic models, ranging from macroeconomic to micro-economic, and corporate models. Mathematically, all these models consist of difference equations (and so do the system dynamics models of Section 4.7 and the inventory models of Chapter 5). Special simulation languages have been developed for this domain too. An example is MIT's TROLL for economic simulations. Statistical packages such as SAS and TSP have been extended so that economic models cannot only be estimated (through regression analysis, discussed in the next chapter) but can also be simulated. Big corporate models are easily simulated through languages like EPS's FCS, Execucom's IFPS, and Comshare's System-W (the company names may have changed in the meantime). Smaller corporate models and related business models can be simulated on microcomputers, using either the personal computer (PC) versions of the preceding mainframe languages or special PC languages like Lotus's 1-2-3 and Symphony, and Borland's Framework and Javelin.

We again discuss the *functionality* of these languages, now relative to that of system dynamics languages.

(1)–(2) Pseudorandom numbers and sampling of random variables is supported. This function also enables risk analysis (discussed in Section 4.6); @RISK is an add-on to 1-2-3, which simplifies risk analysis.
(3) Special integration routines are not needed, because of business conventions and periodic data collection, as we explained in Section 4.7 on system dynamics. Special routines enable the analyst to specify different types of growth rates, for example, an exponential growth of (say) ten per cent. This software also provides routines to compute financial functions like net present value (defined in equation (4.21)).
(4) Collection and processing of output is essential since high-quality presentations are required in business.

The other facilities mentioned in the preceding subsections are not so well supported (error detection, animation, interactive/graphical model specification, and combined discrete-event/continuous modelling).

Turban (1990, pp. 199–200) lists about 60 software packages for decision support systems (DSSs) that run on mainframes; he gives 20 packages for microcomputers.

6.2.4 Conclusions

There is a plethora of simulation software. There are different types of simulation models, which require different software functionality. But, given a certain class of simulation models, there is still much choice. Many years ago Shannon (1975) gave a decision tree to help select a discrete-event simulation language. Kreutzer (1986) discusses simulation languages at length in his monograph. In the preceding subsections we have referred to a number of recent textbooks on simulation software, especially discrete-event simulation software. Standard textbooks on simulation also contain a few chapters that introduce software; examples are Bratley, Fox, and Schrage (1983) and Fishman (1973, 1978). The 1990 Winter Simulation Conference Proceedings has as many as 24 tutorial papers on simulation software; see Balci, Sadowski, and Nance (1990). A recent survey of discrete event simulation software for personal computers and workstations is Swain (1991). In Chapter 12 we shall discuss how to keep up with the latest developments in the simulation field.

REFERENCES

Balci O., R. P. Sadowski, and R. E. Nance (eds) (1990) *Winter Simulation Conference Proceedings*, New York.

Banks E. A., E. Aviles, J. McLaughlin, and R. C. Yuan (1991) The simulator: new member of the simulation family, *Interfaces*, 2, 76–86.

Bratley P., B. L. Fox, and L. E. Schrage (1983) *A Guide to Simulation*, Springer-Verlag, New York.

Fishman G. S. (1973) *Concepts and Methods in Discrete Event Digital Simulation*, Wiley, New York.

Fishman G. S. (1978) *Principles of Discrete Event Simulation*, Wiley, New York.

Gelenbe E. and H. Guennouni (1991) FLEXIM: A Flexible Manufacturing System Simulator, *European Journal of Operational Research*, 53, 149–65.

Gordon K. J., R. F. Gordon, J. F. Kurose, and E. A. MacNair (1991) An extensible visual environment for construction and analysis of hierarchically-structured models of resource contention systems, *Management Science*, 37(6), 714–32.

Hellerman H. and T. F. Conroy (1975) *Computer System Performance*, McGraw-Hill, New York, 1975.

Intellicorp (1986) The SIMKIT System; Knowledge-Based Simulation Tools in Kee, *User Manual, Kee version 3.0*, Mountain View, California 94040-2216.

Kleijnen J. P. C. and B. Annink (1992) Vector Computers, Monte Carlo Simulation, and Regression Analysis: An Introduction, *Management Science*, 38(2), 170–81.

Kleijnen J. P. C. and W. J. H. van Groenendaal (1988) *Simulatie: Technieken en Toepassingen (Simulation: Techniques and Applications)*, Academic Service, Schoonhoven.

Kreutzer W. (1986) *System Simulation: Programming Styles and Languages*. Addison-Wesley, Sydney.

Law A. M. and W. S. Kelton (1991) *Simulation Modeling and Analysis* (2nd edn), McGraw-Hill, New York.

Mitrani I. (1982) *Simulation Techniques for Discrete Event Systems*, Cambridge University Press, Cambridge.

Pegden C. P., R. E. Shannon, and R. P. Sadowski (1990) *Introduction to Simulation using SIMAN*, McGraw-Hill, New York.

Pritsker A. A. B. (1986) *Introduction to Simulation and SLAM II* (3rd edn), Halsted Press, New York.

Q-passport (1987–90) Newsletter of the Dutch User Group Queueing/Performance Analysis Software (Q-PASS), Centre for Mathematics and Computer Science (CWI), Amsterdam.

Reiher P. J. (1990) Parallel simulation using the time warp operating system, *Proceedings of the 1990 Winter Simulation Conference*, New York.

Richmond B., P. Vescuso, and S. Peterson (1987) *STELLA for Business*, High Performance Systems, Inc., Lyme, New Hampshire.

Schriber T. L. (1991) *An Introduction to Simulation Using GPSS/H*, Wiley, New York.

Shannon R. E. (1975) *Systems Simulation: the Art and Science*, Prentice-Hall, Englewood Cliffs, New Jersey.

Stubbs D. F. and N. W. Webre (1985) *Data Structures*, Brooks/Cole, Monterey, California.

Swain J. (1991) Simulation software survey: world of choices, *OR/MS Today*, **18**(3), 81–102.

Turban E. (1990) *Decision Support and Expert Systems: Management Support Systems* (2nd edn), MacMillan, New York.

Wolstenholme E. F. (1990) *System Enquiry: A System Dynamics Approach*, Wiley, Chichester.

Chapter 7

Statistical Applications

In this chapter we review the use of Monte Carlo simulation in mathematical statistics. A simple example has already been discussed in Chapter 1, namely Student's t test. In mathematical statistics, simulation is applied to determine the consequences of violating the assumptions of a specific statistical model, for example, the effects of nonnormality. Further there are no analytical solutions yet for certain statistical problems; for example, what is the $1 - \alpha$ quantile of a newly proposed statistic? Often it is possible to give asymptotic answers, but then it is not clear how large a sample should be in order to use that solution. In practice, sample sizes are often small, and the Monte Carlo method is applied to compare the results of various statistical procedures in small samples. In this chapter we illustrate the use of the Monte Carlo method in mathematical statistics through a practical problem, namely the selection of a 'good' estimator in regression analysis. Moreover, we shall make extensive use of the results of this example in the next chapters.

Exercise 7.1: It is well-known (see Section 3.7.2) that the variance estimator $\underline{s}^2 = \Sigma_{i=1}^n$ $(\underline{x}_i - \bar{x})^2/(n-1)$ has a chi-square distribution, that is $(n-1)\underline{s}^2/\sigma^2 = \underline{\chi}_{n-1}^2$, assuming $\underline{x}_i$ is NID(μ, σ^2). Give a computer program (such as Figure 1.7) for investigating the effect of nonnormality, that is, assume $\underline{x}_i$ is independently *uniformly* distributed between zero and one (so var$(\underline{x}_i) = 1/12$).

This chapter is organized as follows.
— 7.1 Regression models
First we give an example of a regression model with a single explanatory variable, then a model with two explanatory variables. Next we discuss the linear regression model with q explanatory variables, including replications.
— 7.2 Ordinary least squares (OLS)
We present the OLS estimator $\underline{\hat{\beta}}$.
— 7.3 Estimated weighted least squares (EWLS)
If the response variances are not constant, then weighted least squares gives the best linear unbiased estimator (BLUE). In practice the (non-constant) response variance must be estimated, which gives EWLS.
— 7.4 Corrected least squares (CLS)
CLS uses the classic OLS point estimator $\underline{\hat{\beta}}$, but it corrects the traditional covariance matrix of $\underline{\hat{\beta}}$.

—7.5 Case study: simulation of EWLS and CLS
We present a Monte Carlo simulation program to compare the EWLS and CLS
estimators, but first we verify the correctness of the computer program statistically.

7.1 REGRESSION MODELS

We start with a simple example, illustrated in Figure 7.1. In this example x_i denotes
the midpoint of income class i, and y_{ij} denotes consumption of consumer j within
income class i; there are n income classes ($i = 1, \ldots, n$), and there are m_i consumers in
class i; the m_i are non-negative integers. (In econometrics, such a situation is called
cross-section analysis, not time series analysis.)

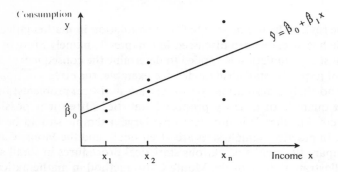

Figure 7.1 Simple regression analysis with replications

Exercise 7.2: How large are m_1 and m_2 in Figure 7.1?

We assume that consumption reacts linearly to income and that the noise is additive
and is normally independently distributed (NID) with zero mean and a variance that
varies with the income class:

$$\underline{y}_{ij} = \beta_0 + \beta_1 x_i + \underline{\epsilon}_{ij} \qquad i = 1, 2, \ldots, n \quad \text{and} \quad j = 1, 2, \ldots, m_i, \qquad (7.1)$$

$$\underline{\epsilon}_{ij} \sim \text{NID}(0, \sigma_i^2). \qquad (7.2)$$

A model with a single explanatory variable x is called a *simple* regression model. Before
we continue our discussion of regression analysis, we demonstrate how the Monte Carlo
method can be used to investigate regression models. We use the simple model of (7.1)
and (7.2). It is well known that the OLS estimator of the slope β_1 is

$$\underline{\hat{\beta}}_1 = \frac{\sum_{i=1}^{n} (x_i - \bar{x}) \sum_{j=1}^{m_i} (\underline{y}_{ij} - \underline{\bar{y}})}{\sum_{i=1}^{n} m_i (x_i - \bar{x})^2}, \qquad (7.3)$$

where $\bar{x} = \sum_{i=1}^{n} m_i x_i / N$ with $N = \sum_{i=1}^{n} m_i$, and $\underline{\bar{y}} = \sum_{i=1}^{n} \sum_{j=1}^{m_i} \underline{y}_{ij} / N$. The OLS estimator
of the intercept β_0 is

$$\underline{\hat{\beta}}_0 = \underline{\bar{y}} - \underline{\hat{\beta}}_1 \bar{x}. \qquad (7.4)$$

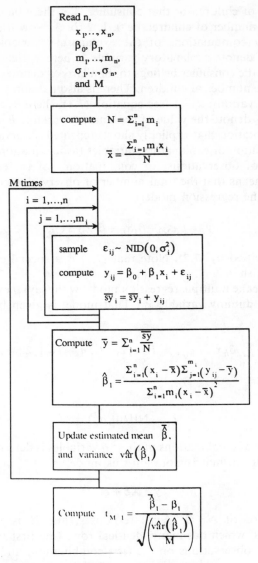

Figure 7.2 Monte Carlo simulation of simple regression models

Figure 7.2 gives a flowchart for a simulation that verifies whether indeed $\hat{\beta}_1$ is unbiased. Note that we can prove (analytically) that $\hat{\beta}_1$ is unbiased in this case, so we do not need Monte Carlo simulation for this simple example; it is only a demonstration. Note further that for the computation of $\hat{\beta}_1$ and the updating of $\widehat{var}(\hat{\beta}_1)$, we can use the formulae in the appendix of Chapter 1. If the computer program is correct, then the computed value of t_{M-1} has $1-\alpha$ probability of lying within the $1-\alpha$ confidence interval for that statistic $(-t_{M-1}^{\alpha/2}, t_{M-1}^{\alpha/2})$.

Now we discuss regression models with several explanatory variables: so-called *multiple regression analysis*. For example, suppose that we observe not only the consumer's income but also the number of children of that consumer. Let there be three income classes, and let the observed number of children be 0, 1, 2, or 3. Now n denotes the observed number of *different* combinations of the explanatory variables; in this example $n = 3 \times 4 = 12$. Let x_1 denote explanatory variable 1; here x_1 denotes the midrange of the income class that the consumer belongs to. Similarly x_2 denotes explanatory variable 2; here x_2 denotes the number of children. There is also a dummy variable that has the value one in all observations: $x_0 = 1$ (see equation (7.1) where β_0 may be multiplied by x_0). Let in general x_{ih} denote the value of explanatory variable h in observation i (here $h = 1, 2$). We use a notation that explicitly shows repeated observations or replications for the same combination of explanatory variables (as in equation (7.1)). Let m_i again denote the number of observations for combination i of the explanatory variables ($i = 1, \ldots, n$). This means that the total number of observations is $N = \Sigma_{i=1}^{n} m_i$. Then this example yields the regression model

$$\underline{y}_{ij} = \beta_0 x_{i0} + \beta_1 x_{i1} + \beta_2 x_{i2} + \underline{\epsilon}_{ij}, \tag{7.5}$$

where $\underline{\epsilon}_{ij}$ is still specified by (7.2). Note that (7.1) is a special case of (7.5); $x_{i0} = 1$, $x_{i1} = x_i$ and $\beta_2 x_{i2}$ vanishes.

Finally we consider the multiple regression model with (say) q explanatory variables, possibly including a dummy variable x_0. That model is given by the generalization of (7.5):

$$\underline{y}_{ij} = \sum_{h=0}^{q-1} \beta_h x_{ih} + \underline{\epsilon}_{ij} \qquad i = 1, 2, \ldots, n, \quad j = 1, 2, \ldots, m_i, \tag{7.6}$$

and

$$\underline{\epsilon}_{ij} \sim \text{NID}(0, \sigma_i^2). \tag{7.7}$$

Note that the number of combinations of these q variables is determined by the number of values per variable. In matrix notation this model is

$$\underline{y} = X\beta + \underline{\epsilon}, \tag{7.8}$$

where $\underline{y}$ is the vector of $N = (\Sigma_{i=1}^{n} m_i)$ responses, and X is the $N \times q$ matrix of explanatory variables, which has many identical rows (the first m_1 rows are identical because there are m_1 observations on the first combination, and so on):

$$
\underline{y} =
\begin{bmatrix}
\underline{y}_{11} \\
\vdots \\
\underline{y}_{1m_1} \\
\vdots \\
\underline{y}_{n1} \\
\vdots \\
\underline{y}_{nm_n}
\end{bmatrix}
\quad \text{and} \quad
X =
\begin{bmatrix}
1\ x_{11} x_{12} \ldots x_{1\,q-1} \\
\vdots \\
1\ x_{11} x_{12} \ldots x_{1\,q-1} \\
\vdots \\
1\ x_{n1} x_{n2} \ldots x_{n\,q-1} \\
\vdots \\
1\ x_{n1} x_{n2} \ldots x_{n\,q-1}
\end{bmatrix}
\begin{matrix}
\left.\begin{matrix} \\ \\ \end{matrix}\right\} m_1 \text{ rows} \\ \\ \\ \\ \left.\begin{matrix} \\ \\ \end{matrix}\right\} m_n \text{ rows}
\end{matrix}
\quad ; \tag{7.9}
$$

obviously $\boldsymbol{\beta} = (\beta_0, \beta_1, \ldots, \beta_{q-1})'$ is the vector of regression parameters and $\boldsymbol{\epsilon} = (\epsilon_{11}, \ldots, \underline{\epsilon}_{nm_n})'$ is the vector of N disturbances. We also speak of the dependent or endogenous variable $\mathbf{y}$ and of independent or exogenous variables $\mathbf{X}$. We assume that the noise or disturbance term $\underline{\epsilon}_i$ is normally independently distributed (NID) with expectation zero and variance σ_i^2. The traditional literature assumes constant variances: $\sigma_i^2 = \sigma^2$. In econometric time series there are no replications: $m_i = 1$. For example, a macroeconomic model may have one observation per period on total macroeconomic consumption. In simulation, however, $m_i > 1$ usually holds, as we shall see in later chapters.

7.2 ORDINARY LEAST SQUARES (OLS)

The OLS estimator of $\boldsymbol{\beta}$, the vector of regression parameters, is the estimator that minimizes the sum of the squared deviations between the observed responses $\mathbf{y}$ and the predicted or fitted values $\hat{\mathbf{y}}$ (see the straight line in Figure 7.1). In other words, the estimator (say) $\hat{\boldsymbol{\beta}}$ minimizes

$$\sum_{i=1}^{n} \sum_{j=1}^{m_i} (\underline{y}_{ij} - \underline{\hat{y}}_{ij})^2 = (\mathbf{y} - \mathbf{X}\hat{\boldsymbol{\beta}})'(\mathbf{y} - \mathbf{X}\hat{\boldsymbol{\beta}}), \tag{7.10}$$

where $\underline{\hat{y}}_{ij} = \underline{\hat{y}}_i = \sum_{h=0}^{q-1} \hat{\beta}_h x_{ih}$. We can prove that the OLS estimator is

$$\hat{\boldsymbol{\beta}} = (\mathbf{X}'\mathbf{X})^{-1} \mathbf{X}' \mathbf{y}, \tag{7.11}$$

provided $\mathbf{X}'\mathbf{X}$ is not singular (so the inverse of $\mathbf{X}'\mathbf{X}$ exists). The OLS criterion is a mathematical and not a statistical criterion. If, however, we further assume that the errors $\boldsymbol{\epsilon}$ in (7.8) are independently distributed with zero expectations and constant variances $(\sigma_i^2 = \sigma^2)$, then we can prove that the OLS estimator $\hat{\boldsymbol{\beta}}$ is the best linear unbiased estimator (BLUE). In other words, consider the class of linear estimators $\mathbf{Ly}$, where obviously $\mathbf{L}$ is a $q \times N$ matrix. Then choosing $\mathbf{L} = (\mathbf{X}'\mathbf{X})^{-1}\mathbf{X}'$ yields an unbiased estimator: $E(\hat{\boldsymbol{\beta}}) = \boldsymbol{\beta}$.

Exercise 7.3: Prove that $E(\hat{\boldsymbol{\beta}}) = \boldsymbol{\beta}$.

It can be proved that among all unbiased linear estimators, it is $\hat{\boldsymbol{\beta}}$ that has the minimum variance: $\hat{\boldsymbol{\beta}}$ is 'best'. The q individual variances follow from the main diagonal of the covariance matrix of $\hat{\boldsymbol{\beta}}$:

$$\mathbf{cov}(\hat{\boldsymbol{\beta}}) = \sigma^2 (\mathbf{X}'\mathbf{X})^{-1}. \tag{7.12}$$

Exercise 7.4: In Chapter 3 we gave the variance of a linear transformation; see (3.59). Apply this formula to (7.11) in order to derive (7.12).

Because σ^2 in (7.12) is unknown, we estimate this parameter through the mean squared residuals (MSR)

$$\hat{\underline{\sigma}}^2 = \frac{\sum_{i=1}^{n} \sum_{j=1}^{m_i} (\underline{y}_{ij} - \underline{\hat{y}}_{ij})^2}{N - q}, \tag{7.13}$$

where the numerator was given in (7.10). So the numerator is the sum of squared residuals (SSR). Combination of (7.12) and (7.13) gives the estimated covariance matrix $\widehat{\text{cov}}(\hat{\beta})$.

7.3 ESTIMATED WEIGHTED LEAST SQUARES (EWLS)

In many cases the assumption of equal variances is unrealistic. For example, in Figure 7.1 the noise usually increases with income; that is, larger deviations from the conditionally expected consumption $E(y|x_i)$ become more likely as x_i increases. The best linear unbiased estimator is then given by weighted least squares (WLS). The WLS estimator (say $\mathring{\beta}$) is

$$\mathring{\beta} = (\mathbf{X}' [\, \text{cov}(\underline{y})\,]^{-1}\mathbf{X})^{-1}\mathbf{X}' [\, \text{cov}(\underline{y})\,]^{-1}\underline{y}, \tag{7.14}$$

where $\text{cov}(\underline{y})$ is the $N \times N$ covariance matrix of the N responses $\underline{y}$, which is assumed to be non-singular. Because we assume that the observations are independent with heterogenous variances (see equation 7.2), we have

$$\text{cov}(\underline{y}) = \begin{bmatrix} \sigma_1^2 & & & & & \\ & \ddots & & & 0 & \\ & & \sigma_1^2 & & & \\ & & & \ddots & & \\ & & & & \sigma_n^2 & \\ 0 & & & & \ddots & \\ & & & & & \sigma_n^2 \end{bmatrix} \begin{array}{l} \left.\rule{0pt}{28pt}\right\} m_1 \text{ rows} \\ \\ \left.\rule{0pt}{28pt}\right\} m_n \text{ rows} \end{array} \tag{7.15}$$

Note that $\text{cov}(\underline{y}) = \text{cov}(\underline{e})$ because of (7.8). It can be proved that (7.14) and (7.15) imply that observations with a high variance get less weight; that is, the WLS estimator minimizes $\sum_{i=1}^{n} \sum_{j=1}^{m_i} (y_{ij} - \hat{y}_{ij})^2 / \sigma_i^2$ instead of (7.10). It is simple to prove that (7.14) results if standard OLS software is applied to the transformed data

$$\begin{aligned} y_{ij}^+ &= y_{ij}/\sigma_i && \text{with } i = 1, 2, \ldots, n \quad \text{and } j = 1, 2, \ldots, m_i; \\ x_{ih}^+ &= x_{ih}/\sigma_i && \text{with } h = 0, 1, \ldots, q-1. \end{aligned} \tag{7.16}$$

Note that the y_{ij}^+ have a constant variance, namely 1.

Exercise 7.5: Prove that (7.16) in combination with (7.11) yields (7.14).

Exercise 7.6: Derive the covariance matrix for the WLS estimator through (3.59).

Unfortunately WLS does not really solve our problems, since in practice the variances σ_i^2 are *unknown*. If there are replications ($m_i > 1$), we estimate the n different variances through the classical estimators.

$$\hat{\underline{\sigma}}_i^2 = \frac{\sum\limits_{j=1}^{m_i} (\underline{y}_{ij} - \underline{\bar{y}}_i)^2}{m_i - 1} \qquad \text{with } i = 1, \ldots, n, \tag{7.17}$$

where $\bar{y}_i = \sum_{j=1}^{m_i} y_{ij}/m_i$. Substitution of (7.17) into (7.14) gives

$$\tilde{\beta} = (\mathbf{X}' [\widehat{\mathrm{cov}}(\underline{y})]^{-1}\mathbf{X})^{-1}\mathbf{X}' [\widehat{\mathrm{cov}}(\underline{y})]^{-1}\underline{y}. \tag{7.18}$$

We call this the *estimated* WLS (EWLS) estimator; in econometrics this estimator is known as the Aitken estimator. This estimator is not linear: the transformation of $\underline{y}$ involves the random variables, $\widehat{\mathrm{cov}}(\underline{y})$. Under certain non-restrictive technical conditions and normality of the disturbances, its *asymptotic* covariance matrix can be derived:

$$\mathrm{cov}(\tilde{\beta}) = (\mathbf{X}' [\mathrm{cov}(\underline{y})]^{-1}\mathbf{X})^{-1} \quad \text{if } N \uparrow \infty; \tag{7.19}$$

see Arnold (1981) and Schmidt (1976, p. 71). An estimation method that holds for small examples is corrected least squares, which we examine now.

Note that if there are no replicates ($m_i = 1$), then other techniques are used to estimate $\mathrm{cov}(\underline{y})$. We refer to the textbooks on econometrics; for example, Schmidt (1976).

7.4 CORRECTED LEAST SQUARES (CLS)

Even if the variances are unequal, the OLS estimator $\hat{\beta}$ is still unbiased (see Exercise 7.3 again). So we may still use the classic OLS point estimator $\hat{\beta}$, but its estimated covariance matrix is no longer given by (7.12) and (7.13); it is now

$$\widehat{\mathrm{cov}}(\hat{\beta}) = (\mathbf{X}'\mathbf{X})^{-1}\mathbf{X}' [\widehat{\mathrm{cov}}(\underline{y})] \mathbf{X}(\mathbf{X}'\mathbf{X})^{-1}, \tag{7.20}$$

Exercise 7.7: Prove (7.20).

We call this approach corrected least squares (CLS).

Exercise 7.8: Consider again the simple regression model in (7.1) and (7.2). Assume $n > 2$ (otherwise perfect fit) and $m_i = m > 1$. Estimate σ_i^2 through the classic estimator (7.17). The OLS estimator is given by (7.3) and (7.4). The EWLS estimator can be computed through the combination of (7.3), (7.4), and the data transformation set of (7.16), where in (7.16) σ_i is replaced by $\hat{\sigma}_i$. Show by Monte Carlo simulation (see Kleijnen, 1992) that

    (a) the EWLS estimator is unbiased if the errors satisfy (7.2);
    (b) if the errors are lognormally distributed with zero mean, then OLS still gives unbiased estimators but EWLS gives a biased estimator of β_0.

7.5 CASE STUDY: SIMULATION OF EWLS AND CLS

If the additive disturbance term has zero expectation and is normally distributed (as in equations (7.6) and (7.7)), then we can easily prove that both OLS and EWLS give unbiased estimators of β (see Exercise 7.3 for OLS; for EWLS remember that under

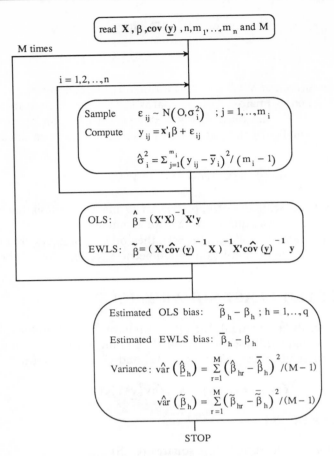

Figure 7.3 Monte Carlo simulation of EWLS and CLS

normality the estimators of the mean and variance are independent). So the question arises: which estimator has the smallest variance? Next question is: may we still use the t-test? Before we can answer these two questions, we must know if the asymptotic covariance matrix (7.19) holds for EWLS in small to moderate samples. To answer these questions, we perform the Monte Carlo experiment of Figure 7.3.

We wish to perform the Monte Carlo experiment for different combinations of $\mathbf{X}$, β, and $\mathbf{cov}(\mathbf{y})$. The layout of $\mathbf{X}$ in (7.9) shows that specifying $\mathbf{X}$ implies specifying n and m_1 to m_n. The matrix $\mathbf{X}$ should be non-singular, so a necessary but not sufficient condition is $n \geqslant q$. We may wish to study nearly singular (badly conditioned) matrices $\mathbf{X}$ versus orthogonal matrices $\mathbf{X}$. The magnitudes of the individual components β_h of the vector β are not important when we wish to answer the questions raised at the beginning of this section. So we might as well make all components zero: $\beta_h = 0$. The responses $\mathbf{y}$ are assumed to be independent so $\mathbf{cov}(\mathbf{y})$ is diagonal; see (7.15). Then it remains to specify the elements on the main diagonal, σ_1^2 to σ_n^2. We may wish to study different degrees of variance heterogeneity. We might specify this heterogeneity through the maximum standard deviation divided by the minimum standard deviation, (say)

$d = \max \sigma_i / \min \sigma_i$. Whether the (absolute) magnitudes of the standard deviations σ_i are considered to be big depends on the magnitudes of the regression parameters β_h: consider $\beta_h / \bar{\sigma}$ with $\bar{\sigma} = \Sigma_{i=1}^{n} \sigma_i / n$. Moreover, it can be proved that the least squares algorithm fits the regression model to the *average* responses $\bar{y}_i (= \Sigma_{j=1}^{m_i} y_{ij} / m_i)$. Since $\mathrm{var}(\bar{y}_i) = \sigma_i^2 / m_i$, the noise in this fitting process depends on both σ_i and m_i. Kleijnen (1992) discusses in detail how to select $\mathbf{X}$ (and hence n and m_i), β, and $\mathrm{cov}(\mathbf{y})$.

Besides specifying how representative the Monte Carlo experiment is for the various situations met in practice, we must specify how accurate the results are, that is, how often the simulation is to be replicated for every combination of $\mathbf{X}$, β, and $\mathrm{cov}(\mathbf{y})$. In Figure 7.3 we read the number of macro replications (say) M. In Chapter 10 we shall further discuss how to determine an appropriate value for M. Kleijnen (1992) takes $M = 100$.

The second block in Figure 7.3 specifies that for the noise we take m_i independent samples from the normal distribution with mean zero and variance σ_i^2. To get the m_i independent responses y_{ij} we add the m_i noise terms to the expected response (for combination i of the explanatory variables) $\Sigma_{h=0}^{q} \beta_h x_{ih}$; see (7.6). From these replicated responses we also compute the estimated response variance, using (7.17). We repeat these computations for all n combinations of explanatory variables.

Exercise 7.9: Prove that (7.17) is equivalent to the more efficient formula

$$\hat{\sigma}_i^2 = \sum_{j=1}^{m_i} (\epsilon_{ij} - \bar{\epsilon}_i)^2 / (m_i - 1).$$

The third block of Figure 7.3 shows that now we are ready to compute the OLS estimate $\hat{\beta}$: we have read $\mathbf{X}$ in block 1 and sampled $\mathbf{y}$ in block 2. To compute the EWLS estimate $\hat{\beta}$ we use (7.18), where $\widehat{\mathrm{cov}}(\mathbf{y})$ is a diagonal matrix with elements $\hat{\sigma}_i^2$ computed in block 2.

After M replications of the Monte Carlo experiment, we have M OLS estimates for (say) β_1, namely $\hat{\beta}_{11}, \hat{\beta}_{12}, \ldots, \hat{\beta}_{1M}$. We compare their average $\bar{\hat{\beta}}_1 = \Sigma_{r=1}^{M} \hat{\beta}_{1r} / M$ with the true value β_1, which was read in block 1. This gives the Monte Carlo estimator of the bias, namely $\bar{\hat{\beta}}_1 - \beta_1$. The Monte Carlo estimator of $\mathrm{var}(\hat{\beta}_1)$ is $\Sigma_{r=1}^{M} (\hat{\beta}_{1r} - \bar{\hat{\beta}}_1)^2 / (M-1)$ (not equation (7.20)). So block 4 gives the Monte Carlo estimates of the bias and the covariance matrices of the OLS and EWLS estimators.

Before we further analyse the Monte Carlo results of block 4, we summarize Figure 7.3. (1) We 'plug in' a value for the parameter vector of interest, namely β, plus some 'nuisance' parameters, namely $\mathbf{X}$ and $\mathrm{cov}(\mathbf{y})$, which imply n and m_i. (2) Using all these parameters we generate observations $\mathbf{y}$ including noise. (3) Next the two estimators (CLS and EWLS) try to 'guess' the correct value of β. (4) Since we ourselves plugged in the correct value β, we can estimate how well CLS and EWLS behave; that is, we estimate the bias and (co)variances of these two estimators. To reduce the noise in our conclusions, we repeat steps (2) and (3) M times before we go to step (4).

7.5.1 Verification of the Computer Program

Before we decide which estimator (CLS or EWLS) is best, we verify the correctness of the computer program implied by Figure 7.3. So we calculate for each individual parameter β_h:

$$z_h = (\bar{\hat{\beta}}_h - \beta_h)/\sqrt{(\text{var}(\hat{\underline{\beta}}_h)/M)}, \tag{7.21}$$

where $\bar{\hat{\beta}}_h$ is the average of the M observations $\hat{\beta}_{hr}$; in a Monte Carlo experiment we know β_h and $\text{var}(\hat{\underline{\beta}}_h)$; in (7.20) we replace $\widehat{\text{cov}}(\mathbf{y})$ by $\text{cov}(\mathbf{y})$. Because the disturbance term $\underline{\epsilon}$ is distributed normally, $\underline{z}_h$ has a standard normal distribution. So there is a 90% probability that $\underline{z}_h$ lies between -1.645 and 1.645. If the realization of $\underline{z}_h$ falls outside that interval, we conclude that our computer program has a 'bug'; the probability that we reject our computer program erroneously is only 10% (so-called α error or type I error).

Unfortunately, there is a complication. We are dealing with q parameters $(\beta_1, \ldots, \beta_q)$. For example, if in block 1 of Figure 7.3 we read $\boldsymbol{\beta}' = (0,0,0)$ then q is 3. Moreover we also study a second case, say $\boldsymbol{\beta}' = (0,0,0,0)$, where q is 4. Furthermore we use several values for the inputs $\text{cov}(\mathbf{y})$ and $\mathbf{X}$. (We also read M, but that is not relevant now.) Suppose we have 20 observations on $\underline{z}_h$ of (7.21). Even if our computer program operates correctly, we expect that, if α is 0.10, then $0.10 \times 20 = 2$ realizations of (7.21) fall outside the interval $[-1.645, 1.645]$. These 'significant' values cause a *false alarm*. To avoid such a false alarm, we do not test the 20 individual values z_h with the classic α value of 10% but with a value of only $(10/20)\%$ or 0.5%. This is the so-called *Bonferroni* approach, which we shall further discuss in the next chapter.

Exercise 7.10: If we follow the Bonferroni approach, do we reject an individual value of z_h sooner than with 'classic' testing, that is, testing with $\alpha = 10\%$?

To further verify the correctness of the computer program we perform additional tests. So we compare the known variances $\text{var}(\hat{\underline{\beta}}_h)$ (see equation (7.21)) with the estimated variances $\widehat{\text{var}}(\hat{\underline{\beta}}_h)$ of the last block in Figure 7.3. For this comparison we use the χ^2 test with M degrees of freedom:

$$\chi^2_{M-1} = \frac{\widehat{\text{var}}(\hat{\underline{\beta}}_h)}{\text{var}(\hat{\underline{\beta}}_h)}. \tag{7.22}$$

Moreover we know that the *EWLS estimator* $\tilde{\boldsymbol{\beta}}$ is also unbiased in this study. The variance of $\tilde{\boldsymbol{\beta}}$, however, is known only asymptotically; so an expression analogous to (7.21)—with $\hat{\boldsymbol{\beta}}$ replaced by $\tilde{\boldsymbol{\beta}}$—holds for large m_i only. Fortunately, the Monte Carlo experiment gives an unbiased estimator of $\text{var}(\tilde{\boldsymbol{\beta}})$ (which also holds for small samples):

$$\widehat{\text{var}}(\tilde{\underline{\beta}}_h) = \frac{\sum_{r=1}^{M} (\tilde{\underline{\beta}}_{hr} - \bar{\tilde{\underline{\beta}}}_h)^2}{M-1}, \tag{7.23}$$

which is computed in the last block of Figure 7.3 (the main diagonal of $\widehat{\text{cov}}(\tilde{\underline{\beta}})$. Through the t test we check whether the program for EWLS indeed yields an unbiased estimator of β (analogous to equation (7.21)):

$$t_{M-1} = \frac{\bar{\tilde{\beta}}_h - \beta_h}{\sqrt{(\widehat{\text{var}}(\tilde{\underline{\beta}}_h)/M)}}. \tag{7.24}$$

Strictly speaking, the t test assumes that $\tilde{\beta}_h$ is normally distributed. But $\tilde{\beta}_h$ is a nonlinear estimator, as we saw. So even if y is distributed normally, $\tilde{\beta}_h$ is not distributed normally. Fortunately, it is common knowledge that for large degrees of freedom the t test is not sensitive to nonnormality. Since M is large, we may test the correctness of our program for EWLS by means of (7.24).

Fortunately all these statistics are not significant in our case study. Only after we are convinced of the correctness of our computer program, can we discuss the following interesting question.

7.5.2 Asymptotic Covariances in EWLS

Our null hypothesis is that we may apply the asymptotic formula (7.19). Let d_{hh} be its hth diagonal element. Our test statistic is then

$$\chi^2_{M-1} = \widehat{\text{var}}(\tilde{\underline{\beta}}_h)/d_{hh}, \tag{7.25}$$

where the numerator was specified in (7.23). If χ^2_{M-1} is very large, the true variance is larger than the asymptotic formula suggests; in other words, this formula then underestimates the variance of $\tilde{\beta}$. The results in Kleijnen (1992) indicate that the asymptotic formula holds for really large samples only.

7.5.3 Relative Efficiency of EWLS and CLS

We compare the estimated variance of the EWLS estimator (see equation (7.23); we do not rely on the asymptotic variance) with the known variance of the OLS/CLS estimator:

$$\chi^2_{M-1} = \frac{\widehat{\text{var}}(\tilde{\underline{\beta}}_h)}{\text{var}(\hat{\underline{\beta}}_h)}. \tag{7.26}$$

Kleijnen (1992) concludes that the EWLS estimator has a smaller variance than the OLS estimator has.

It is not enough, however, to know that the EWLS estimator is more efficient. After all, besides the point estimator of β_h, we need a confidence interval.

7.5.4 Confidence Intervals in EWLS and CLS

Because we wish to base our confidence intervals on the Student t statistic, we expand Figure 7.3 with the statistics

$$t_v = \frac{\hat{\beta}_h - \beta_h}{\sqrt{\widehat{\text{var}}(\hat{\underline{\beta}}_h)}} \quad \text{and} \quad \tilde{t}_v = \frac{\tilde{\beta}_h - \beta_h}{\sqrt{\widehat{\text{var}}(\tilde{\underline{\beta}}_h)}}, \tag{7.27}$$

which deserve the following comments. We have M observations on $\underline{t}_v$ and $\underline{\tilde{t}}_v$ per parameter β_h $(h = 1, \ldots, q)$, but we have suppressed the indices h and r $(r = 1, \ldots, M)$ of $\underline{t}_v$ and $\underline{\tilde{t}}_v$. In the expression for $\underline{t}_v$ we compute $\hat{\beta}_h$ from (7.11), and $\widehat{\text{var}}(\hat{\beta}_h)$ from (7.17) and (7.20). These formulae use variables that are indeed observed in practice, namely $\mathbf{y}$ and $\mathbf{X}$; they do not use $\text{cov}(\mathbf{y})$, which is only known in the Monte Carlo experiment. For $\underline{\tilde{t}}_v$ we compute $\tilde{\beta}_h$ from (7.18), and $\widehat{\text{var}}(\tilde{\beta}_h)$ from the asymptotic formula (7.19) with $\text{cov}(\mathbf{y})$ replaced by $\widehat{\text{cov}}(\mathbf{y})$; so ultimately $\underline{\tilde{t}}$ follows from $\mathbf{y}$ and $\mathbf{X}$.

The question is: do $\underline{t}_v$ and $\underline{\tilde{t}}_v$ have a t distribution, and if so, what is the value of v (the number of degrees of freedom)? Kleijnen (1992) concludes that $\underline{t}_v$ of (7.27) has indeed a t distribution; it has $m - 1$ degrees of freedom (assuming a common $m_i = m$). EWLS does not give a t distribution, if m is small. Rao (1959) gives an alternative confidence interval, which is further investigated in Kleijnen (1992).

Note that we can improve EWLS through the jackknife, which is a simple but computer-intensive technique to be discussed in Chapter 10; see Kleijnen et al. (1987).

Exercise 7.11: (a) Write a Monte Carlo program to test if $E(\hat{\sigma}^2) = \sigma^2$, where σ^2 is estimated through the mean squared residuals (MSR; see equation (7.13)). Restrict the regression model to the simple model of (7.1) and (7.2) *without* replications $(m_i = 1)$ and with *constant* variance $(\sigma_i^2 = \sigma^2)$.

(b) Repeat the experiment with $\underline{\epsilon} \sim U(-5, +5)$, where $U(-5, +5)$ denotes the uniform distribution over the interval $[-5, +5]$.

REFERENCES

Arnold S. F. (1981) *The Theory of Linear Models and Multivariate Analysis*, Wiley, New York.

Kleijnen J. P. C. (1987) *Statistical Tools for Simulation Practitioners*, Marcel Dekker, New York.

Kleijnen J. P. C. (1992) Regression metamodels for simulation with common random numbers: comparison of validation tests and confidence intervals, *Management Science*, **38**(8).

Kleijnen J. P. C., P. C. A. Karremans, W. K. Oortwijn, and W. J. H. Van Groenendaal (1987) Jackknifing estimated weighted least squares: JEWLS, *Communications in Statistics, Theory and Methods*, **16**(3), 747–64.

Rao C. R. (1959) Some problems involving linear hypotheses in multivariate analysis, *Biometrika*, **46**, 49–58.

Schmidt P. (1976) *Econometrics*, Marcel Dekker, New York.

Chapter 8

Regression Metamodels

In this chapter we show how to analyse the results of both *deterministic* and *stochastic* simulations. Figure 8.1 illustrates that in the analysis of simulation results we often make a graph of the input and output data. The visual analysis of the resulting 'cloud' of observed points should provide insight into the global effect an input change has on the output. Moreover, we can interpolate and extrapolate so we get a quick estimate of the expected simulation response at an input value not yet observed. Note that in Figure 8.1 the observations at low utilization rates show so little variation that they coincide, given the scale of that figure.

The visual analysis becomes impractical when there are several input variables. We then replace the graphical analysis by an algebraic analysis: we use regression analysis. Why is such an analysis useful? Most important is the resulting insight into the general behaviour of the simulated system. As we have already remarked in Chapter 1, a major disadvantage of simulation is its *ad hoc* character: we observe the simulation responses only for the selected input combinations. In this chapter we simultaneously examine all input/output combinations used in the simulation experiment, and hope to gain more insight, while we use a 'minimum' of computer time. Computer time plays an important role in the search for optimal input combinations and in sensitivity analysis. (The search for the optimal input combination will be discussed in the next chapter.) We will show that the *linear* regression model, presented in the previous chapter, is an adequate model to gain insight into simulation models. Because we make a (regression) model of the simulation model, we speak of (regression) *metamodels*.

This chapter is organized as follows.

—8.1 Metamodel concept

We introduce a hierarchy of models: simulation models approximate reality, and regressive models approximate simulation models.

—8.2 Simulation data for regression analysis

We show how the simulation input and output data correspond with the regression model's independent and dependent variables.

—8.3 Least squares estimation

We derive the statistical distribution of the 'error' term for stochastic simulation models. The regression parameters can be estimated through different least squares algorithms, which have already been presented in the preceding chapter. For deterministic simulation, ordinary least squares (OLS) may suffice.

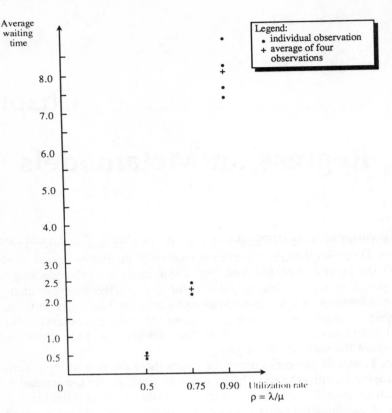

Figure 8.1 Average waiting time versus utilization rate in simulated M/M/1 with $1/\lambda = 1.0$, $1/\mu = 0.50$, 0.75, 0.90, 4 times 100 000 customers simulated per (λ, μ) combination

—8.4 Validation of metamodels
To validate the metamodel we use that model to forecast the response of the simulation model for 'new' combinations of inputs for the simulation model, that is, combinations not used to specify and estimate the metamodel. We derive different validation techniques for stochastic and deterministic simulations respectively. Further refinements are cross validation, which saves simulation computer time, and Rao's test.

—8.5 Use of metamodels
Once the regression metamodel has been validated, the individual regression parameters can be used for sensitivity and 'what if' analysis . An M/M/s example with SAS results is analysed using SAS, a statistical package.

—8.6 Higher-order metamodels: interactions and quadratic effects
The metamodel does not need to be additive. Through a case study we illustrate the role of interactions among simulation inputs.

—8.7 Epilogue
We briefly discuss metamodelling for simulation models with several output variables.

8.1 THE METAMODEL CONCEPT

The relationship between the output (say) w and the inputs v_1, v_2, ..., of the *real* system can be represented through the function f_0:

$$w = f_0(v_1, v_2, \ldots). \tag{8.1}$$

There may be an infinite number of input variables in (8.1) or there may be stochastic variables; we will not dwell on this fundamental question, which is discussed in the philosophy of science.

As Figure 8.2 suggests we can make a simulation model of the real system. The simulation model attempts to describe the relationship f_0 through a few input variables and parameters, say $z_1, \ldots, z_K$. After all, in reality most variables v in (8.1) have only marginal effects. Hopefully, these unimportant variables do not occur in the simulation model; the simulation tries to represent only the most important variables and parameters. We distinguish between variables and parameters, following Zeigler (1976). So we define a parameter as a quantity that cannot be observed in the real system, whereas a variable can be observed directly. Examples of variables are customer arrival times and number of servers; examples of parameters are the arrival rate λ of the Poisson arrival process, and the service rate μ (also see Section 1.2). When we run the simulation program, the parameters are known inputs. The output variable (say) y of the simulation model represents the output w of the real system. In stochastic simulation we introduce

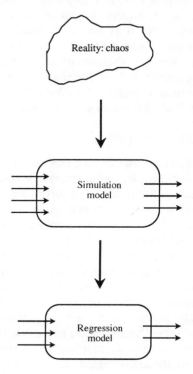

Figure 8.2 Hierarchy of models

randomness by means of pseudorandom numbers $\underline{r}$. We may interpret $\underline{r}$ either as a vector of random numbers or as the randomly selected starting value or seed of the pseudorandom number generator (see Chapter 2). So the simulation program can be represented by the mathematical function f_1:

$$\underline{y} = f_1(z_1, \ldots, z_K, \underline{r}). \tag{8.2}$$

A special case of (8.2) is deterministic simulation; then $\underline{y}$ has the degenerated density function $P(\underline{y} = y) = 1$.

Consider the regression metamodel, which we have already seen in (7.6),

$$\underline{y}_{ij} = \beta_0 + \sum_{h=1}^{q-1} \beta_h x_{ih} + \underline{\epsilon}_{ij} \qquad \text{with } \underline{\epsilon}_{ij} \sim \text{NID}(0, \sigma^2). \tag{8.3}$$

In some cases a regression variable x_h in (8.3) is identical to a simulation parameter or variable z_k in (8.2). For example, x_1 equals the arrival rate λ (assuming the service rate μ and the number of servers remain constant in the simulation). In other cases x_h is a transformation of one or more z_k; for example $x_1 = \log(z_1)$ or $x_1 = z_1/z_2$ (assuming a logarithmic scale is better when studying the effect of a change in $z_1 = \lambda$, or assuming the ratio $\rho = \lambda/\mu$ gives a better explanation). So parameters and input variables z of the simulation model (8.2) determine the independent variables x of the metamodel. The coefficients β of the regression model are the parameters of the metamodel, and must be estimated. We might interpret (8.3) as a first-order Taylor series approximation to (8.2), with $x_h = z_h$ and $q = K + 1$; to this Taylor approximation we add the noise $\underline{\epsilon}$. However, to use a Taylor series it is necessary that the variables z_k in (8.2) be continuous, that f_1 be a function that can be differentiated twice, and that the random component $\underline{r}$ be ignored. Because these mathematical conditions are not met in practice, we first postulate a specific form for the regression model (8.3), and next we test the validity of the postulated metamodel. We will examine this procedure in the remainder of this chapter, but first we discuss an example.

EXAMPLE 8.1: THE M/M/s MODEL

In Chapter 5 we discussed Markov systems with exponential interarrival and service times with means $1/\lambda$ and $1/\mu$ respectively, and s servers: M/M/s. Note that a mean value $1/\lambda$ implies a rate λ (sometimes the symbols λ and $1/\lambda$ are interchanged so $1/\lambda$ denotes the rate). Now we model a delicatessen store as a system with one queue and s employees. Variables that are ignored are, for example, the employees' marital status and the number of slicing machines. Possible criteria, which summarize the results of the simulation, could be the utilization rate of the servers, the mean queue length, and the mean waiting time of customers, in the steady state. Suppose we concentrate on the average waiting time $\overline{w}$. Then we summarize the time series formed by the individual waiting times $\underline{w}_1, \underline{w}_2, \ldots$ through a single number, namely the average $\overline{w}$. We formulate the regression metamodel (8.3); for example $y = \beta x^2 + \underline{\epsilon}$, where y represents the average waiting time $\overline{w}$, and x represents the utilization rate $\rho = \lambda/(s\mu)$. This yields a figure that resembles Figure 8.1. Note that the average queue length (say $\overline{v}$) equals the average waiting time $\overline{w}$ multiplied by the arrival rate λ, as we saw in Chapter 5. We shall return to this example later in this chapter.

8.2 SIMULATION DATA FOR REGRESSION ANALYSIS

Table 8.1 shows some simulation input and output data for the M/M/s example. We study six combinations of simulation inputs, selected intuitively as follows. We simulate three values for the arrival rate λ, six values for the service rate μ, and either two or four servers ($s = 2$ and 4). We select λ and μ such that the utilization factor ρ lies between 0.5 and 0.7, where ρ is defined as $\lambda/(s\mu)$. Hence if we increase the number of servers, we also decrease the service rate. We decide to simulate each input combination for 2000 customers, and to replicate this 20 times; each of these 20 macroreplications starts in the empty state (no customers waiting); in Chapter 10 we shall return to decisions of this type. The output is the average queue length $\bar{y}$ (which is closely related to the average waiting time $\bar{w}$, as we saw at the end of the preceding section).

To estimate the parameters β of the regression metamodel we apply linear regression analysis. Table 8.2 shows the general layout of the simulation data for this regression analysis. As we said before, the independent variables x of the regression model can be identical to the simulation parameters and input variables z, but they can also be transformations of z. Several replications are obtained per combination of $(z_1, \ldots, z_K)$. The standard deviation of the output $\underline{y}_{ij}$ is estimated from m_i replications, with $m_i > 1$, through

$$\hat{\sigma}_i = \left[\frac{\sum_{j=1}^{m_i} (\underline{y}_{ij} - \bar{\underline{y}}_i)^2}{m_i - 1} \right]^{1/2}. \tag{8.4}$$

Note that σ_i^2 denotes the variance of $\underline{y}_{ij}$, not the variance of $\bar{\underline{y}}_i$, the average of the m_i replications; obviously $\text{var}(\bar{\underline{y}}_i) = \text{var}(\underline{y}_{ij})/m_i$ if the replications are independent. By definition, different replications use identical values for the independent variables (x_{ih}) but different pseudorandom number seeds. In deterministic simulation, replication makes no sense since the same output results. Observe further that the rows $\mathbf{x}_i'$ in Table 8.2 correspond to the inputs of the simulation model. These rows cannot be identical; in other words, two rows have at least one element that is different. In the preceding chapter

Table 8.1 Average queue length $\bar{v}$ of M/M/s simulation

Comb.	λ	μ	s	Replication									
				1 11	2 12	3 13	4 14	5 15	6 16	7 17	8 18	9 19	10 20
1	1	0.9	2	0.56 0.38	0.55 0.56	0.47 0.66	0.52 0.64	0.42 0.56	0.55 0.45	0.44 0.51	0.46 0.49	0.31 0.38	0.52 0.47
2	1	0.38	4	1.14 0.82	0.72 0.71	0.78 0.63	0.74 0.81	1.14 0.60	0.67 0.67	0.51 0.49	1.04 0.47	0.86 0.66	0.97 0.62
3	2	1.6	2	1.18 0.69	0.78 1.15	0.80 0.98	1.60 1.00	0.87 0.72	0.81 0.84	0.93 0.67	0.71 0.99	0.62 0.90	0.87 0.69
4	2	1	4	0.11 0.17	0.19 0.18	0.16 0.18	0.14 0.23	0.20 0.12	0.14 0.14	0.13 0.16	0.11 0.13	0.20 0.18	0.16 0.23
5	4	2.9	2	1.74 1.07	1.10 1.27	1.24 0.90	1.23 1.12	1.31 1.29	1.27 1.13	1.07 1.08	1.64 1.41	1.70 1.19	1.57 1.17
6	4	1.69	4	0.41 0.43	0.39 0.57	0.60 0.27	0.31 0.36	0.37 0.38	0.36 0.35	0.42 0.29	0.26 0.29	0.42 0.32	0.40 0.41

Table 8.2 Simulation data for regression models

Combina-tion i	Independent variables x_{ih}					Dependent variable y_{ij}					Estimated standard deviation $\hat{\sigma}_i$
	0	1	... h	... $q-1$		1	2	... j	... m_i	
1	1	x_{11}	... x_{1h}	... $x_{1\,q-1}$		y_{11}	y_{12}	... y_{1j}	...y_{1m_1}	$\hat{\sigma}_1$
.		.	.	.			.	.	.	.
i	1	x_{i1}	... x_{ih}	... $x_{i\,q-1}$		y_{i1}	y_{i2}	... y_{ij}	... y_{im_i}	$\hat{\sigma}_i$
.		.	.	.		.	.	.	.	.
.		.	.	.		.	.	.		.
n	1	x_{n1}	... x_{nh}	... $x_{n\,q-1}$		y_{n1}	y_{n2}	... y_{nj}	... y_{nm_n}	$\hat{\sigma}_n$

the dependent variable **y** was a vector. We can easily transform Table 8.2 into that notation. We then rearrange its elements y_{ij} into the vector **y** with $N = \Sigma_{i=1}^{n} m_i$ elements, as specified by (7.9). Consequently in the matrix of independent variables **X** we must repeat row $\mathbf{x}_i$ of Table 8.2 m_i times, so that **X** is an $N \times q$ matrix.

If and only if each input combination is replicated an equal number of times ($m_i = m$), we may replace the individual observations y_{ij} by their averages $\bar{y}_i$ and apply least squares to the vector with the n averages $\bar{y}_i$. Obviously **X** shrinks then to the $n \times q$ matrix that corresponds with Table 8.2. See Kleijnen (1987, p. 195).

EXAMPLE 8.1: THE M/M/s MODEL CONTINUED

In the previous section we presented a simulation experiment with a delicatessen store. We might introduce a complication, in that we do not simulate a fixed number of customers (namely 2000), but T_j customers arriving between 9 a.m. and 6 p.m. Then the average waiting time in replication j of combination i is

$$\bar{w}_{ij} = \sum_{t=1}^{T_j} \frac{w_{ijt}}{T_j} \quad \text{with } i = 1, \ldots, n \quad \text{and} \quad j = 1, \ldots, m_i. \tag{8.5}$$

For combination i of the simulation parameters and input variables we simulate $m_i = 20$ days. So the total number of observations on $\bar{w}$ equals $\Sigma_{i=1}^{n} m_i = N = 120$. Obviously the y_{ij} of Table 8.2 equal the $\bar{w}_{ij}$ of Table 8.1. The standard deviation of the average waiting time $\bar{w}_i$ can still be estimated through (8.4) (but if $\bar{w}_i$ is computed from a stochastic number of observations T, then its variance increases). As independent variables we could take the number of employees $x_1 = s$, the expected interarrival time $x_2 = 1/\lambda$, and the expected service time $x_3 = 1/\mu$ (in the simulation experiment we indeed know not only the input variable s but also the parameters λ and μ used to sample from the exponential distributions). However, queuing theory suggests that it is better to use the utilization rate $x_1 = \rho = \lambda/(\mu s)$. This is an example of a function that combines several simulation parameters and input variables into a single explanatory variable in the regression metamodel. Suppose further that we introduce two priority rules, namely first come first served (FCFS) and random service (RS), which means that customers are served in random order. We represent priority rules in the regression metamodel by means of a *binary* variable (say) x_2:

$$x_{i2} = \begin{cases} 0 \text{ if the priority rule is FCFS in combination } i \\ 1 \text{ if the priority rule is RS in combination } i. \end{cases} \qquad (8.6)$$

If there are more than two priority rules, we must use several binary variables to represent 'the' queuing discipline (so if there are three priority rules, then we do not represent them by $x_{i2} = -1, 0, +1$). For an extensive treatment of qualitative variables we refer to Kleijnen (1987). If there are only two priority rules, we may replace the binary variable with the values 0 and 1 (see equation (8.6)) by a binary variable with the values -1 and $+1$, as we shall see in Chapter 9.

8.3 LEAST SQUARES ESTIMATION

We can apply the least squares technique to estimate the parameters β in the regression model. In the previous chapter we saw that the ordinary least squares (OLS) criterion results in the following estimator for β, the vector of parameters:

$$\hat{\underline{\beta}} = (\mathbf{X}'\mathbf{X})^{-1}\mathbf{X}'\underline{y}. \qquad (8.7)$$

The simulation model (f_1 in equation (8.2)) defines a statistical population of observations ($\underline{y}$) that has characteristics that vary with the input ($x_{i0}, x_{i1}, \ldots, x_{i\,q-1}$). The members of that population correspond with all possible pseudorandom number seeds; that is, in theory there is an infinitely large population. The classical assumption is that this population is Gaussian (we shall return to this assumption). If the linear regression model of (8.3) holds, then that population's conditional expectation and variance are

$$\left. \begin{array}{l} E(\underline{y}_i | x_{i0}, x_{i1}, \ldots, x_{i\,q-1}) = \displaystyle\sum_{h=0}^{q-1} x_{ih}\beta_h = \mathbf{x}_i'\,\beta = \mu_i \\[2mm] \mathrm{var}(\underline{y}_i | \underline{x}_{i0}, x_{i1}, \ldots, x_{i\,q-1}) = \sigma_i^2 \quad \text{with } i = 1, 2, \ldots, n \end{array} \right\} . \qquad (8.8)$$

So Table 8.2 implies that the simulation outputs $\underline{y}_{ij}$ are interpreted as m_i independent observations from the normal distribution $N(\mu_i, \sigma_i^2)$. If each combination i uses different random numbers, then the variables $\underline{y}_{11}, \ldots, \underline{y}_{i1}, \ldots, \underline{y}_{n1}$ are mutually independent. In general, the observations within column j of Table 8.2 ($\underline{y}_{1j}, \ldots, \underline{y}_{ij}, \ldots, \underline{y}_{nj}$) are independent with $j = 1, 2, \ldots$. This yields (8.3), or in matrix notation,

$$\underline{y} = \mathbf{X}\beta + \underline{\epsilon} \qquad \text{and} \qquad \underline{\epsilon} \sim N(0, \mathrm{cov}(\underline{y})), \qquad (8.9)$$

where $\underline{y}$ is the response vector with $N = \Sigma_{i=1}^{n} m_i$ elements, $\mathbf{X}$ is the $N \times q$ matrix of independent variables, β is the vector with q parameters, $\mathrm{cov}(\underline{y})$ is a diagonal matrix with the main-diagonal elements σ_i^2 (also see equation (7.15)). For this model we can now apply the estimation techniques of Chapter 7: not only ordinary least squares (OLS), but also estimated weighted least squares (EWLS), and corrected least squares (CLS) (and jack-knifed EWLS). If, however, different combinations use the same seed, then $\mathrm{cov}(\underline{y})$ is no longer diagonal. We can estimate the elements of this symmetric matrix by

$$\widehat{\text{cov}}(\underline{y}_i, \underline{y}_{i'}) = \frac{\sum\limits_{j=1}^{m} (y_{ij} - \bar{y}_i)(y_{i'j} - \bar{y}_{i'})}{(m-1)} \qquad \text{with } i, i' = 1, \ldots, n, \qquad (8.10)$$

where we assume a constant number of replications m (replication j of combination i uses seed r_{0j}). For $i = i'$ this equation reduces to $\hat{\sigma}_i^2$; see (8.4). It can be proved that $\widehat{\text{cov}}(\underline{y})$ is singular if $m \leqslant n$. Common seeds in regression metamodelling are further discussed in Kleijnen (1992b).

As we saw in the preceding chapter, the OLS point estimator $\hat{\underline{\beta}}$ is unbiased, even if the distribution of the simulation responses is not Gaussian. Normality usually holds if the simulation responses are averages, such as average queuing times.

In *deterministic* simulation we can also apply linear regression metamodels. Then we assume that the deviations between the simulation outputs and the metamodel predictions are normally distributed, again with zero means but now with constant variance σ^2. The simplest model assumes that these deviations are independent; see Kleijnen (1990). Then OLS suffices. A more sophisticated metamodel assumes that these deviations form a stationary covariance process; see Sacks et al. (1989).

8.4 VALIDATION OF METAMODELS

Suppose we have specified and 'calibrated' a metamodel, that is, we have estimated the regression parameters β. For the time being we assume that OLS is used, which yields the estimator $\hat{\underline{\beta}}$. We can then use this metamodel to predict the output for a *new* combination of independent variables $\mathbf{x}'_{(n+1)} = (1, x_{(n+1)1}, \ldots, x_{(n+1)q-1})$:

$$\hat{\underline{y}}_{n+1} = \hat{\underline{\beta}}_0 + \sum_{h=1}^{q-1} \hat{\underline{\beta}}_h x_{(n+1)h} = \mathbf{x}'_{n+1} \hat{\underline{\beta}}. \qquad (8.11)$$

We can easily quantify the inaccuracy of this prediction: since the predictor $\hat{\underline{y}}_{n+1}$ is a linear transformation of $\hat{\underline{\beta}}$, its estimated variance is

$$\widehat{\text{var}}(\hat{\underline{y}}_{n+1}) = \mathbf{x}'_{n+1} \widehat{\text{cov}}(\hat{\underline{\beta}}) \mathbf{x}_{n+1}, \qquad (8.12)$$

where $\widehat{\text{cov}}(\hat{\underline{\beta}})$ was given in (7.20) if we assume stochastic simulation with replications (we shall discuss deterministic simulation later).

Exercise 8.1: Prove (8.12).

To test whether the predictor (8.11) is accurate (so the metamodel is valid), we actually run the simulation program with the new input combination $\mathbf{x}_{n+1}$, using m_{n+1} independent seeds with $m_{n+1} > 1$. Then $\bar{\underline{y}}_{n+1}$ is the average of the m_{n+1} replications of the new combination:

$$\bar{\underline{y}}_{n+1} = \frac{1}{m_{n+1}} \sum_{j=1}^{m_{n+1}} \underline{y}_{n+1, j}. \qquad (8.13)$$

The estimated variance of $\bar{\underline{y}}_{n+1}$ is

$$\widehat{\text{var}}(\bar{\underline{y}}_{n+1}) = \sum_{j=1}^{m_{n+1}} \frac{(\underline{y}_{n+1,j} - \bar{\underline{y}}_{n+1})^2}{(m_{n+1}-1)m_{n+1}}; \tag{8.14}$$

see (8.4). Finally we calculate the standardized or *Studentized prediction error*:

$$\underline{z} = \frac{\hat{\underline{y}}_{n+1} - \bar{\underline{y}}_{n+1}}{\{\widehat{\text{var}}(\hat{\underline{y}}_{n+1}) + \widehat{\text{var}}(\bar{\underline{y}}_{n+1})\}^{1/2}}. \tag{8.15}$$

We compare the absolute value of $\underline{z}$ with $z_{1-\alpha/2}$, the $1-\alpha/2$ quantile of the standard normal variable. If this value is significance, we can *not* use the metamodel for prediction. Obviously if we apply EWLS, then $\hat{\beta}$ becomes $\tilde{\beta}$ in (8.11) and (8.12); the equations for $\tilde{\beta}$ and its asymptotic covariance matrix were given in (7.18) and (7.19).

We can compute the statistic $\underline{z}$ of (8.15) for *several* new combinations of independent variables. Suppose we select G new combinations, where G is a positive integer. We then have available z_1 to z_G. Given a significance level of $\alpha = 0.05$ we expect 0.05 times G significant values of $\underline{z}$, even if the metamodel is perfect. So the more new combinations, the higher the probability that we *erroneously* reject the correct metamodel. Therefore we use *Bonferroni's inequality* as follows. Let A_g be a random event, which has probability $P(A_g)$; for example, A_g denotes the statement 'this metamodel is not valid for input combination g'; this statement may happen to be true or false. Events may be statistically dependent. Bonferroni's inequality states that the probability of the 'joint' event (A_1 or $A_2 \ldots$ or A_G) does not exceed the sum of the probabilities of the individual events:

$$P(A_1 \vee A_2 \vee \cdots \vee A_i \vee \cdots \vee A_G) \leqslant \sum_{i=1}^{G} P(A_i), \tag{8.16}$$

where $\vee$ represents the Boolean operator 'or'. We apply this inequality as follows. Let α_g be the probability that the absolute value of $\underline{z}_g$ is significant while the metamodel is correct: false alarm or type I error. The probability of one or more false alarms is

$$P\{(|\underline{z}_1| \geqslant z_{1-\alpha_1/2}|H_0) \vee \cdots \vee (|\underline{z}_G| \geqslant z_{1-\alpha_n/2}|H_0)\} \leqslant \sum_{g=1}^{G} P\{|\underline{z}_g| \geqslant z_{1-\alpha_g/2}|H_0\}, \tag{8.17}$$

where H_0 is the null-hypothesis that states the metamodel is correct. We test each individual input combination g at the level α_g. Then (8.17) implies that 'the' probability of rejecting the metamodel, denoted by (say) α_E, satisfies the following upperbound:

$$\alpha_E \leqslant \sum_{g=1}^{G} \alpha_g. \tag{8.18}$$

In the literature α_E is called the 'experimentwise error rate', and α_g the 'error rate per comparison g'. The inequality (8.18) implies that if we test each combination with $\alpha_g = \alpha/G$, then the experimentwise error rate α_E is at most α. For example, if $G = 10$ and $\alpha_E = 20\%$, then we test each individual combination at the level $\alpha_g = 2\%$. In other words, the more combinations, the smaller α_g is and the higher the critical value $z_{1-\alpha_g/2}$ is. Kleijnen (1987) discusses error rates in more detail.

In *deterministic* simulation the responses show no noise; so (8.14) is replaced by $\widehat{\text{var}}(\bar{y}_{n+1})=0$. Because we assume that the fitting errors have constant variances, we could compute $\widehat{\text{var}}(\hat{y}_{n+1})$ from (8.12) with $\widehat{\text{cov}}(\hat{\underline{\beta}})=\hat{\sigma}^2(\mathbf{X}'\mathbf{X})^{-1}$, where $\hat{\sigma}^2=\Sigma_{i=1}^n$ $\Sigma_{j=1}^{m_i}(y_{ij}-\hat{y}_{ij})^2/(N-q)$; see (7.12) and (7.13). But that would mean that, the worse the model is, the larger the mean squared residual $\hat{\sigma}^2$ becomes; thus the smaller the test statistic z in (8.15) becomes, and the smaller is the probability that we reject the bad model (low power or high type II error). Therefore we propose to replace (8.15) by $\hat{y}/y$, the relative prediction error, and to 'eyeball' this error: is this error 'acceptable'? Examples are given in Kleijnen and Standridge (1988) and Kleijnen, van Ham, and Rotmans (1992).

8.4.1 Cross-validation

A disadvantage of the method described above is that we have to run the simulation program for G extra input combinations ($G \geqslant 1$). An alternative is the next procedure, which is called *cross-validation*. We first discuss stochastic simulation.

(1) We eliminate one combination, say i, from the old data in Table 8.2. So we eliminate its m_i replications.
(2) We estimate the regression parameters β from the remaining data. If we use OLS, this gives

$$\hat{\underline{\beta}}_{-i}=(\mathbf{X}'_{-i}\mathbf{X}_{-i})^{-1}\mathbf{X}'_{-i}\underline{y}_{-i}, \tag{8.19}$$

where the index $-i$ means that combination i has been eliminated. We assume that there are more input combinations than regression parameters: $n>q$ (otherwise $\mathbf{X}_{-i}$ would certainly be singular).
(3) We predict the response for the eliminated combination through

$$\hat{\underline{y}}_{-i}=\hat{\beta}_{0(-i)}+\sum_{h=1}^{q-1}\hat{\beta}_{h(-i)}x_{ih}=\mathbf{x}'_i\hat{\underline{\beta}}_{-i}, \tag{8.20}$$

which is the analogue of (8.11). We compute its variance through the analogue of (8.12):

$$\widehat{\text{var}}(\hat{\underline{y}}_{-i})=\mathbf{x}'_i\,\widehat{\text{cov}}(\hat{\underline{\beta}}_{-i})\,\mathbf{x}_i, \tag{8.21}$$

where $\widehat{\text{cov}}(\hat{\underline{\beta}}_{-i})$ follows from (7.20) if we replace $\mathbf{X}$ by $\mathbf{X}_{-i}$ and in the $N \times N$ matrix $\widehat{\text{cov}}(\mathbf{y})$ we remove the m_i rows and the m_i columns that correspond with input combination i.
(4) We calculate the test variable $\underline{z}_{-i}$, that is, we replace (8.15) by

$$\underline{z}_{-i}=\frac{\hat{\underline{y}}_{-i}-\bar{y}_i}{\{\widehat{\text{var}}(\hat{\underline{y}}_{-i})+\widehat{\text{var}}(\bar{y}_i)\}^{1/2}}. \tag{8.22}$$

(5) We repeat steps (1)–(4) for all values of $i=1,\ldots,n$.

So without any extra simulation effort, we have n values of the test statistic $\underline{z}$ at our disposal. To these n values we apply Bonferroni's inequality; see (8.18) with G replaced by n.

It is not necessary to recompute the whole regression model n times, in cross-validation. It can be proved that the residual upon deletion of observation i is determined by the original residual, divided by $1 - h_{ii}$, where h_{ii} is the ith element on the main diagonal of the hat matrix $\mathbf{H} = \mathbf{X}(\mathbf{X}'\mathbf{X})^{-1}\mathbf{X}'$:

$$\hat{\underline{y}}_{-i} - \underline{y}_i = \frac{\hat{y}_i - y_i}{1 - h_{ii}}. \tag{8.23}$$

It can be further proved that

$$\underline{z}_i = \frac{\hat{y}_i - y_i}{\hat{\sigma}_i (1 - h_{ii})^{1/2}}. \tag{8.24}$$

In EWLS, $\hat{y}$ is replaced by its EWLS estimator, and h_{ii} is replaced by the ith diagonal elements of $_i$

$$\mathbf{H}^* = \hat{\mathbf{W}}\mathbf{X}(\mathbf{X}'\,\hat{\mathbf{V}}^{-1}\mathbf{X})^{-1}\mathbf{X}'\,\hat{\mathbf{W}}, \tag{8.25}$$

where $\hat{\mathbf{W}}$ and $\hat{\mathbf{V}}$ are diagonal matrices with the elements $1/\hat{\sigma}_i$ and $\hat{\sigma}_i^2$ respectively. Alternatively, the EWLS estimates may be computed using (7.16). Modern statistical software provides the diagnostic statistics mentioned earlier. For details we refer to Panis et al. (1991); see also Grier (1992).

The idea of cross-validation has become well accepted in regression analysis. One of the first publications in the statistics literature was Stone (1974). Since then a number of test statistics have been proposed that are related to the statistic in (8.22). These statistics include *PRESS, DEFITS, DFBETAS*, and Cook's *D*. In this literature, cross-validation and its associated statistics are called *diagnostics*. This literature also discusses the influence of outlying combinations in the matrix $\mathbf{X}$. In simulation, however, we should use experimental design principles to select these combinations, so the problem of such outliers is much smaller. A complication in simulation is that often common pseudorandom number streams are used; the simulation responses then become correlated whereas the standard regression literature assumes independent responses. Moreover, this literature assumes a common variance, whereas we wish to account for heterogenous variances. For more details in a simulation context, including EWLS and CLS, we refer to Kleijnen (1987, pp. 179, 185–96). For regression analysis including diagnostics we refer to textbooks such as Atkinson (1985), Belsley, Kuh, and Welsch (1980), Chatterjee and Hadi (1988), Cook and Weisberg (1982), and Myers (1990). Articles on diagnostics appear virtually every day.

In *deterministic* simulation to proceed analogously:

(1) We eliminate combination i ($i = 1, \ldots, n$).
(2) We estimate β through the OLS estimator $\hat{\beta}$ of (8.19).
(3) We predict y_i through $\hat{\underline{y}}_{-i}$ of (8.20). This predictor has a variance given by (8.21) with $\widehat{\text{cov}}(\hat{\beta}_{-i})$ specified not by (7.20) but by the classical formula (7.12) where $\mathbf{X}$ is replaced by $\mathbf{X}_{-i}$.
(4) Instead of $\underline{z}_{-i}$ we compute the relative prediction error $\hat{\underline{y}}_{-i}/y_i$.
(5) We repeat steps (1) through (4) for all values of i.

8.4.2 Rao's Lack-of-Fit Test

For random simulation models with Gaussian responses there is a more powerful validation test, namely the lack-of-fit F test. This test compares two variance estimators. One estimator uses the mean squared residuals, which we defined in (7.13). This estimator is unbiased only if the model is correct; otherwise it overestimates the variance. The other estimator is based on replication; see (7.17) or (8.4). The latter estimator does not depend on the regression model. The model is rejected if the ratio of these two estimators exceeds F_{ν_1, ν_2} with $\nu_1 = N - q$ and $\nu_2 = \Sigma_1^n (m_i - 1)$. This test is based on the classical assumptions: $\epsilon_{ij} \sim \text{NID}(0, \sigma^2)$. If the responses have different variances, then we apply Rao's (1959) lack-of-fit test, assuming $m_i = m$,

$$\underline{F}_{n-q,\, m-n+q} = \frac{m-n+q}{n-q} \frac{1}{(m-1)} (\bar{\mathbf{y}} - \mathbf{X}\tilde{\boldsymbol{\beta}})' [\, \widehat{\mathbf{cov}}(\bar{\mathbf{y}}) \,]^{-1} (\bar{\mathbf{y}} - \mathbf{X}\tilde{\boldsymbol{\beta}}), \qquad (8.26)$$

where $\mathbf{X}$ is $n \times q$ (see Table 8.2) and $\tilde{\boldsymbol{\beta}}$ denotes the estimated *generalized* least squares estimator (EGLS). This estimator follows from (7.14), provided the covariance matrix $\mathbf{cov}(\mathbf{y})$ in (7.15) is replaced by a nondiagonal matrix with elements estimated through (8.10).

If the responses are skewly distributed, then Rao's procedure performs less well than cross-validation does; see Kleijnen (1992b).

8.5 USE OF METAMODELS

Only after we have validated the metamodel can we use it to explain the behaviour of the simulation model. We can test if an estimated regression parameter differs significantly from zero. An exact $1 - \alpha$ confidence interval for the OLS estimator is

$$\underline{\hat{\beta}}_h \pm t_m^{\alpha/2} \sqrt{\widehat{\text{var}}(\underline{\hat{\beta}}_h)}, \qquad (8.27)$$

where $\widehat{\text{var}}(\underline{\hat{\beta}}_h)$ is the hth diagonal element of $\widehat{\mathbf{cov}}(\hat{\boldsymbol{\beta}})$ given in (7.20), which uses $\mathbf{cov}(\mathbf{y})$ estimated through (8.10) (m still denotes the number of replicates). Rao (1959) gives an exact $1 - \alpha$ confidence interval for EGLS:

$$\tilde{\underline{\beta}}_j \pm t_\nu^{\alpha/2} \,\hat{\sigma}(\tilde{\underline{\beta}}_j) \left[\frac{1 + \underline{F}(n-q)/(m-n+q)}{1 - (n-q)/(m-1)} \right]^{1/2}, \qquad (8.28)$$

where $\nu = (m-1) - (n-q)$, $\hat{\sigma}(\tilde{\underline{\beta}}_j) = \{\widehat{\text{var}}(\tilde{\underline{\beta}}_j)\}^{1/2}$ with $\widehat{\text{var}}(\tilde{\underline{\beta}}_j)$ estimated from (7.19) (for any N) and (8.10), and $\underline{F} = \underline{F}_{n-q,\, m-n+q}$ as given by (8.26). Kleijnen (1992b) found that if the response $\underline{y}$ is asymmetrically distributed, then $\tilde{\beta}_0$ (the estimator of the intercept) is biased.

We test if the estimator of β_h is significantly different from zero (H_0: $\beta_{h=0}$). Of course, in general β_h is not exactly zero, so the null-hypothesis is false, strictly speaking. Nevertheless, if $|\hat{\beta}_h|$ is so small that this hypothesis is not rejected, then the corresponding variable x_h is 'unimportant'. If the estimator of β_h differs from zero significantly, then x_h is important. This is the information we seek in *what-if* analysis. If x_h represents a parameter or a variable that can be influenced by the user, then to improve the system the user increases or decreases that parameter or variable, dependent on the sign of the estimated regression coefficient. The user may even try to optimize the system, as we shall see in the next chapter.

We can also give predictions for new input combinations; that is, we can interpolate and extrapolate from old simulation data. This is important if a simulation run costs much computer time.

8.5.1 Detailed Example of Metamodelling: M/M/s

We return to the M/M/s example of Table 8.1. The input variables z_k in this model are the Poisson interarrival rate λ, the Poisson service rate μ, and the number of servers s. The output is the average queue length $\bar{y}$ after 2000 customers have been simulated, starting with an empty system. For each of the $n = 6$ combinations (λ_i, μ_i, s_i) we have $m_i = 20$ macroreplications $(i = 1, 2, \ldots, n)$. In this way we get $N = \sum_{i=1}^{n} m_i = 120$ observations on the average number of waiting customers.

To specify the metamodel we start from the well-known formula for the utilization rate:

$$\rho_i = \frac{\lambda_i}{(\mu_i \times s_i)} \qquad \text{with } i = 1, \ldots, n. \tag{8.29}$$

Friedman and Friedman (1985) propose the following metamodel for the mean queue length:

$$\bar{y}_{ij} = \beta_0^* \left[\frac{\lambda_i^{\beta_1}}{\mu_i^{\beta_2} \times s_i^{\beta_3}} \right] \underline{v}_{ij} \qquad \text{with } j = 1, \ldots, m_i \quad \text{and} \quad \underline{v}_{ij} \sim LN(\mu, \sigma_i^2), \tag{8.30}$$

where LN stands for 'lognormal' (see also Chapter 3). Taking logarithms, we get a *linear* regression model with $\beta_0 = \ln(\beta_0^*)$ and $\underline{\epsilon}_{ij} \sim N(\mu, \sigma_i^2)$:

$$\ln(\bar{y}_{ij}) = \beta_0 + \beta_1 \ln(\lambda_i) - \beta_2 \ln(\mu_i) - \beta_3 \ln(s_i) + \underline{\epsilon}_{ij}. \tag{8.31}$$

We wish to check whether the number of servers s and the service rate μ can be combined into a single variable, namely service $(\mu \times s)$; see the denominator of (8.29). Therefore we test the null-hypothesis H_0: $\beta_2 = \beta_3$. If this simplification is permitted, we further test if $\beta_1 = -\beta_2 = -\beta_3 = \beta$ holds. Finally if $\beta_0 = 0$ or $\beta_0^* = 1$, then the utilization rate ρ become the single explanatory variable: (8.30) reduces to

$$E(\bar{y}_i) = \rho_i^{\beta}. \tag{8.32}$$

To analyse the simulation results of Table 8.1 we use SAS, which yields Table 8.3. We apply OLS, CLS, and EWLS respectively. The total number of observations is $N = 6 \times 20 = 120$. There are three explanatory variables besides the dummy variable: the 'model' has three degrees of freedom (DF). This leaves $120 - 4 = 116$ DF for 'error'. OLS yields $\hat{\beta}_0 = 2.8$, $\hat{\beta}_1 = 5.1$, $\hat{\beta}_2 = -5.2$, and $\hat{\beta}_3 = -5.9$. By definition, CLS gives point estimates identical to the OLS values. The correct standard errors turn out to be slightly bigger than the traditional OLS formula gives. EWLS yields point estimates not much different from the OLS estimates; the standard errors are somewhat smaller: the logarithmic transformation reduces the variance heterogeneity so EWLS does not differ so much from OLS. The model is not validated in the way we proposed in the preceding section. Instead SAS uses the traditional R^2 criterion:

$$R^2 = \frac{\sum_i \sum_j (\hat{y}_{ij} - \bar{y})^2}{\sum_i \sum_j (y_{ij} - \bar{y})^2} = 1 - \frac{\sum\sum (y_{ij} - \hat{y}_{ij})^2}{\sum\sum (y_{ij} - \bar{y})^2}, \tag{8.33}$$

where $\bar{y} = \sum\sum y_{ij}/N$. This criterion suggests that the model is adequate whenever R^2 approaches one. Since R^2 always improves if more explanatory variables are added, R^2 may be adjusted for the number of parameters q:

$$R^2_{adj} = 1 - (N-1)(1-R^2)/(N-q). \tag{8.34}$$

In Table 8.3 all R^2 values are very high. The hypothesis $H_0: \beta_2 = \beta_3$ is rejected ($F = 130$) because the standard errors of $\hat{\beta}_2$ and $\hat{\beta}_3$ are very small. In a related experiment not reported here, we simulated the system with higher traffic loads. Then the noise increases (lower power) and H_0 is not rejected. We then ended with the model presented in (8.32).

Exercise 8.2: Derive that in the logarithmic model (8.31) the elasticity coefficient $(\partial \bar{w}/\bar{w})/(\partial \lambda/\lambda)$ is β_1.

8.6 HIGHER-ORDER METAMODELS: INTERACTIONS AND QUADRATIC EFFECTS

In a first-order or *additive* metamodel the effect of a particular input variable does not depend on the other input variables (we also refer back to Exercise 8.2). If the additive model does not pass the validation test, we may switch to a model with interactions between the simulation input variables z_j and z_g, denoted by β_{jg}, and with purely quadratic effects β_{jj}:

$$y = \beta_0 + \sum_{j=1}^{K} \beta_j z_j + \sum_{j=1}^{K-1} \sum_{g=j+1}^{K} \beta_{jg} z_j z_g + \sum_{j=1}^{K} \beta_{jj} z_j^2 + \varepsilon. \tag{8.35}$$

We may interpret this equation as a second-order Taylor series approximation to the simulation model. The *linear* regression model still applies. For example, for $K = 2$ (8.35) gives

$$y = \beta_0 + \beta_1 z_1 + \beta_2 z_2 + \beta_{11} z_1^2 + \beta_{12} z_1 z_2 + \beta_{22} z_2^2 + \varepsilon. \tag{8.36}$$

This model is identical to the following model if we define $z_1 = x_1$, $z_2 = x_2$, $z_1^2 = x_3$, $z_1 z_2 = x_4$, $z_2^2 = x_5$, and $\beta_{11} = \beta_3$, $\beta_{12} = \beta_4$, $\beta_{22} = \beta_5$:

$$y = \beta_0 + \beta_1 x_1 + \beta_2 x_2 + \beta_3 x_3 + \beta_4 x_4 + \beta_5 x_5 + \varepsilon. \tag{8.37}$$

The latter model is linear in the parameters β (also see equation (8.3)).

Table 8.3 SAS analysis of M/M/s example

Linear regression: OLS
var(log($\bar{v}$))

0.182921
0.2584141
0.2270683
0.2280807
0.1741199
0.2170907

Dependent variable: log($\bar{v}$)

Analysis of variance

Source	D.F.	Sum of squares	Mean square	F value	Prob > F
Model	3	53.32683455	17.77561152	380.812	0.0001
Error	116	5.41467432	0.04667823		
C total	119	58.74150887			

Root MSE	0.2160514	R-square	0.9078	
Dep mean	− 0.629453	ADJ R-SQ	0.9054	
C.V.	− 34.3237			

Parameter estimates

Variable	D.F.	Parameter estimate	Standard error	T for HO: parameter = 0	Prob > |T|
INTERCEPT	1	2.82523873	0.10951557	25.798	0.0001
LOGLABDA	1	5.10760536	0.19460843	26.246	0.0001
LOGMU	1	− 5.21545	0.19938765	− 26.157	0.0001
LOGSERVERS	1	− 5.90304	0.18832235	− 31.345	0.0001

Covariance of estimates

COVB	INTERCEPT	LOGLABDA	LOGMU	LOGSERVERS
INTERCEPT	0.01199366	0.01576176	− 0.0172908	− 0.0189349
LOGLABDA	0.01576176	0.03787244	− 0.0381753	− 0.034371
LOGMU	− 0.0172908	− 0.0381753	0.03975544	0.0357937
LOGSERVERS	− 0.0189349	− 0.034371	0.0357937	0.03546531

Test: LOGMU = LOGSERVERS

Numerator:	6.0738	DF:	1	F value:	130.1212
Denominator:	0.046678	DF: 116		Prob > F:	0.0001

Linear regression: CLS

Parameter	Standard errors	T statistic
2.82524	0.11376	24.83509
5.10761	0.20000	25.53805
− 5.21545	0.21361	− 24.41576
− 5.90304	0.19607	− 30.10680

(continued)

Table 8.3 *(continued)*

R-square

0.9491

COVB

0.012942	0.0180258	−0.020285	−0.02091
0.018026	0.0399989	−0.042134	−0.03712
−0.020285	−0.042134	0.045630	0.040085
−0.020909	−0.03712	0.040085	0.038444

Linear regression: EWLS

Parameter	Standard errors	T statistic
2.80905	0.11300	24.85885
5.08647	0.19873	25.59488
−5.19890	0.21285	−24.42518
−5.87790	0.19492	−30.15545

R-square

0.9477

ADJ R-SQ

0.9463

COVB

0.0127697	0.0178555	−0.020153	−0.020676
0.0178555	0.0394948	−0.04173	−0.036675
−0.020153	−0.04173	0.0453059	0.0397319
−0.020676	−0.036675	0.0397319	0.0379927

8.6.1 Case Study: FMS Example

Kleijnen and Standridge (1988) apply regression analysis to a deterministic simulation model of a flexible manufacturing system (FMS). They wish to select x_i, the number of machines of type i with $i = 1, \ldots, 4$, such that a given production volume is realized. Preliminary analysis shows that the inputs to the simulation may vary over the following 'experimental domain': $x_1 \in (5,6)$, $x_2 \in (1,2)$, $x_3 \in (2,3)$, and $x_4 \in (0,1,2)$; that is, 24 combinations are of interest. Actually they simulate only eight combinations and estimate the first-order metamodel. If one combination is deleted from the data (see the subsection on cross-validation), then the OLS estimates $\hat{\beta}_{-i}$ change. Especially the values of the non-significant effects change since they represent noise. Upon deletion of a combination, the degrees of freedom are $v = N - q = 7 - 5$. Table 8.4 displays only the effects that are significant at $\alpha = 0.30$. Such a high α value is used in order to reduce the probability of eliminating important factors. The price paid for reducing this probability is the increased risk of including unimportant factors, but these factors will be identified later on, probably.

Table 8.4 Estimates of β upon deleting a combination; only significant effects are displayed

Combination deleted	$\hat{\beta}_1$	$\hat{\beta}_2$	$\hat{\beta}_3$	$\hat{\beta}_4$	$\hat{\beta}_0$
1		557		557	
2		712		500	2032
3		640		700	
4		629		694	1962
5				658	
6				736	
7				536	
8				541	3288
none				541	3288

Table 8.5 Cross-validation: relative prediction errors $(y_i - \hat{y}_i)/y_i$

Combination deleted:	1	2	3	4	5	6	7	8
Error (in %):	10	27	−19	−18	13	33	−38	−35

Table 8.6 Estimates of γ upon deleting a combination

Combination deleted	$\hat{\gamma}_2$	$\hat{\gamma}_4$	$\hat{\gamma}_{24}$	$\hat{\gamma}_0$
1	952	1364	−492	776
2	952	1300	−460	776
3	952	1324	−468	776
4	952	1340	−484	776
5	1152	1432	−576	576
6	752	1232	−376	976
7	952	1332	−476	776
8	952	1332	−476	776
none	952	1332	−476	776

Table 8.7 Cross-validation: relative prediction errors in new model

Combination deleted:	1	2	3	4	5	6	7	8
Error (in %):	2	2	−1	1	−16	14	0	0

The effects of deleting a combination can be shown more compactly by concentrating on the responses; that is, the criterion becomes prediction instead of explanation. Table 8.5 displays the relative prediction errors $(y_i - \hat{y}_{-i})/y_i$ in cross-validation.

Upon 'eyeballing' the prediction errors of Table 8.5 and the instabilities of Table 8.4, the additive metamodel is rejected, and a new model is specified. The calibration of this model still uses the old data of the simulation experiment ($\mathbf{X}$ and $\mathbf{y}$). Table 8.4 suggested that the factors 1 and 3 are unimportant. Therefore a regression model in the remaining factors is formulated, but now interaction is included:

$$\hat{y} = \hat{\gamma}_0 + \hat{\gamma}_2 x_2 + \hat{\gamma}_4 x_4 + \hat{\gamma}_{24} x_2 x_4. \tag{8.38}$$

In this model all estimated effects remain significant upon run deletion: see Table 8.6. The relative prediction errors become much smaller, as Table 8.7 shows.

The new metamodel suggests that type 2 and type 4 machines are the bottle-necks in the FMS. The negative sign of the interaction $\hat{\gamma}_{24}$ means that there is a trade-off between these two machine types. In the next chapter we shall discuss interactions in detail.

Exercise 8.3: Determine the marginal output $\partial\hat{y}/\partial x_2$ in (8.38). When is there complementarity, independence, and substitution between x_2 and x_4?

8.7 EPILOGUE

We have restricted ourselves to univariate models, that is, we analyse a single output per simulation run. If there are several output variables, we can still apply regression analysis per output variable, possibly combined with Bonferroni's inequality. We could also use multivariate regression analysis. Some outputs may not be criteria but may occur in sideconditions; see Kleijnen (1992a).

Exercise 8.4: Simulate a single-server system with fixed service times $1/\mu$ and a Poisson arrival process with rate $\lambda = 1$. Estimate the expected queue length as a function of $1/\mu$ with $0.90 \leqslant 1/\mu \leqslant 0.98$.

Many applications of metamodelling are referenced in Kleijnen (1987), who also gives two more case studies. One case concerns the Europe Container Terminus (ECT) in Rotterdam harbour; the other case is keypunching at the computer centre of Tilburg University.

REFERENCES

Atkinson A. C. (1985) *Plots, Transformations and Regression*, Clarendon Press, Oxford.

Belsley D. A., E. Kuh, and R. E. Welsch (1980) *Regression Diagnostics, Identifying Influential Data and Sources of Collinearity*, Wiley, New York.

Chatterjee S. and A. S. Hadi (1988) *Sensitivity Analysis in Linear Regression*, Wiley, New York.

Cook R. D. and S. Weisberg (1982) *Residuals and Influence in Regression*, Chapman and Hall, New York.

Friedman L. W. and H. H. Friedman (1985) Validating the simulation metamodel; some practical approaches, *Simulation*, **45**(3), 144–6.

Grier D. A. (1992) An extended sweep operator for the cross validation of variable selection in linear regression, Dep. of Statistics/Computer and Information Systems, George Washington University, Washington D.C. 20052.

Kleijnen J. P. C. (1987) *Statistical Tools for Simulation Practitioners*, Marcel Dekker, New York.

Kleijnen J. P. C. (1990) Statistics and deterministic simulation models: why not? *Proceedings Winter Simulation Conference*, edited by O. Balci, 344–6.

Kleijnen J. P. C. (1992a) Simulation and optimization in production planning: a case study, *Decision Support Systems*, **8**.

Kleijnen J. P. C. (1992b) Regression metamodels for simulation with common seeds: comparison of validation tests and confidence intervals, *Management Science,* **38**(8).

Kleijnen J. P. C. and C. R. Standridge (1988) Experimental design and regression analysis in simulation: an FMS case study, *European Journal of Operational Research*, 33, 257–61.

Kleijnen J. P. C., G. van Ham, and J. Rotmans (1992) Techniques for sensitivity analysis of simulation models: a case study of the CO_2 greenhouse effect, *Simulation*.

Myers R. H. (1990) *Classical and Modern Regression with Applications* (2nd edn), PWS-Kent Publishing Company, Boston.

Panis R. P., R. H. Meyers, and E. C. Houck (1992) Combining regression diagnostics with simulation metamodels, *European Journal of Operational Research*, (accepted 1992).

Rao C. R. (1959) Some problems involving linear hypotheses in multivariate analysis, *Biometrika*, **46**, 49–58.

Sacks J., W. J. Welch, T. J. Mitchell, and H. P. Wynn (1989) Design and analysis of computer experiments (includes comments and rejoinder), *Statistical Science*, 4(4), 409–35.

Stone M. (1974) Cross-validatory choice and assessment of statistical predication, *Journal of Royal Statistical Society*, Series B, **36**(2), 111–47.

Zeigler B. (1976) *Theory of Modelling and Simulation*, Wiley Interscience, New York.

Chapter 9

Design of Experiments

In simulation experiments we change the values of parameters and input variables, and the model structure, in order to analyse the effects of such changes. For example, in a multi-server system we may vary the following factors: number of servers s, arrival and service parameters λ and μ_j ($j = 1, 2, \ldots, s$), and priority rule. We wish to estimate the effects of these $s + 3$ factors on the average waiting time $\overline{w}$. Per combination i of factor 'levels' we simulate m_i days; that is, the number of runs for combination i is m_i with positive integer m_i. Thus the total number of observations is $N = \sum_{i=1}^{n} m_i$, where n denotes the number of combinations of factor levels actually simulated. In most experiments the examination of all factor combinations would take too much computer time. An experimental design is a set of combinations of factor levels. The goal of experimental design theory is to gain insight into the system's behaviour while observing relatively few factor combinations.

This chapter is organized as follows.

—9.1 Classical experimental designs

Factors, factor levels, and interactions can be expressed through a linear regression model. We introduce three classical designs: (1) one factor at a time design; (2) full factorial designs, which are proved to be more efficient; (3) incomplete factorial designs, such as 2^{k-p} designs, which require fewer combinations than full factorial designs do and yet are efficient. The role of interactions is highlighted. We illustrate some issues through a flexible manufacturing system (FMS) case study. We also discuss the classic assumption of constant variances, and coding or scaling of factors.

—9.2 Screening

In the early phase of a simulation study, the number of potentially important factors may be so high as to prohibit the use of classical designs. One solution is to aggregate the individual factors. Alternative techniques are referenced only. (For didactic reasons, screening is discussed *after* the classical designs have been presented.)

—9.3 Response surface methodology

If factors are quantitative, we can optimize the simulated system through the application of experimental designs, regression analysis, and steepest ascent (a heuristic search procedure). A production planning case study illustrates these techniques.

There is a vast literature on experimental designs. In the 1930s Sir Ronald Fisher started developing experimental designs and their analysis, in agriculture experimentation. In the 1950s George Box further developed these techniques, inspired by their applications in chemistry. Currently there is a growing interest for these techniques in order to improve the quality of the western industrial complex. The application of experimental design in simulation means the elimination of certain complications that arise in real-life applications because of lack of experimental control. On the other hand, simulation models may have hundreds of controllable factors, which in real-life experimentation would be impossible. Standard references on experimental designs are Box, Hunter, and Hunter (1978) and Box and Draper (1987). Experimental design in simulation is discussed in detail in Kleijnen (1987, pp. 257–363). This chapter gives a summary and update of the latter reference. Many articles on experimental design appear in *Technometrics*.

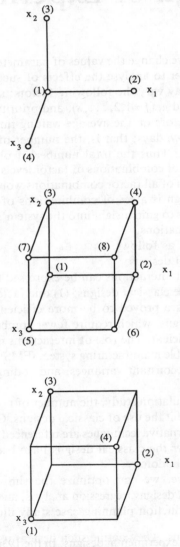

Figure 9.1 Experimental design for three factors. The numbers (1), . . ., (8) correspond with the combinations of Table 9.1.

Table 9.1 Experimental design for three factors

(1) One factor at a time

Combination	x_1	x_2	x_3
1	-1	-1	-1
2	1	-1	-1
3	-1	1	-1
4	-1	-1	1

(2) Full factorial design

Combination	x_1	x_2	x_3
1	-1	-1	-1
2	1	-1	-1
3	-1	1	-1
4	1	1	-1
5	-1	-1	1
6	1	-1	1
7	-1	1	1
8	1	1	1

(3) Fractional design: 2^{3-1} factors

Combination	x_1	x_2	x_3
1	-1	-1	1
2	1	-1	-1
3	-1	1	-1
4	1	1	1

9.1 CLASSICAL EXPERIMENTAL DESIGNS

Figure 9.1 and Table 9.1 illustrate the following experimental designs that are often used in practice.

(1) Change a single factor at a time: 'one factor at a time designs'.
(2) Examine all possible combinations of factor levels: 'full factorial designs'.
(3) Examine only part of all possible combinations: 'incomplete factorial designs', in particular, 'fractional designs'.

We shall show that designs of type (3) can give the same information as types (1) and (2); yet type (3) requires fewer observations. In contrast to type (1), type (3) gives information on interactions in certain situations (see Section 9.3).

Note that some statisticians—for example, Morris (1991)—use a different definition of one factor at a time designs. They define such designs as plans that switch on one factor after another, without resetting the previous factor back to its base value. For instance, $k = 3$ gives

$$
\begin{array}{rrr}
-1 & -1 & -1 \\
1 & -1 & -1 \\
1 & 1 & -1 \\
1 & 1 & 1
\end{array}
$$

These designs give less precise estimators than designs of type (2) and (3), and they do not give unbiased estimators of interactions.

Except for Section 9.3 we assume that each factor is observed at only two 'levels' or values. Therefore the independent variables x (introduced in the preceding chapter on regression models) satisfy

$$
x_{ij} = \begin{cases} -1 & \text{if factor } j \text{ is } \textit{off} \text{ in combination } i \text{ with } j=1,2,\ldots,k \text{ and } i=1,2,\ldots,n; \\ +1 & \text{if factor } j \text{ is } \textit{on} \text{ in combination } i. \end{cases}
$$

$$(9.1)$$

For quantitative factors, 'off' may mean that the factor has a low value (we may also randomly associate 'off' with either 'low' or 'high'; see Section 9.1.1). The coding in (9.1) also holds for qualitative factors, which have only nominal values. For example, if factor 1 denotes the priority rule and if in combination 3 the priority rule is first come first served (FCFS), we may say $x_{31} = 1$; if in combination 4 the priority rule is last come first served (LCFS), then $x_{41} = -1$. (We could also have associated FCFS with -1, and LCFS with $+1$.) For qualitative factors with more than two levels we refer to Kleijnen (1987, pp. 275–8).

Exercise 9.1: How many combinations can at least be observed when there are seven factors?

Exercise 9.2: Suppose that in an M/M/s model the utilization rate or traffic load ρ ranges between 0.5 and 0.8, and the number of servers s ranges between 1 and 3. Construct an experimental design for these two factors with only four combinations; give the design in the coded variables of (9.1) and in the original variables ρ and s respectively.

In the example of Figure 9.1 and Table 9.1 there are three factors, each with two levels. The underlying simulation model may be a queuing system with the following factors and levels: priority rule is either FCFS or LCFS, number of servers is 1 or 3, and utilization degree is 0.5 or 0.8. Table 9.1 gives the matrices $\mathbf{X} = (x_{ij})$ for the three designs; we do not show the dummy variable x_0 because it is always $+1$. (In all designs we may consider -1 to represent the 'base' value, but this is not essential; the 'base' value may be the value currently in use.)

In this section we assume the regression *metamodel* or *response surface*

$$
\underline{y}_i = \beta_0 + \sum_{j=1}^{k} \beta_j x_{ij} + \sum_{j=1}^{k-1} \sum_{h=j+1}^{k} \beta_{jh} x_{ij} x_{ih} + \underline{\epsilon}_i \qquad \text{with } \underline{\epsilon}_i \sim \text{NID}(0,\sigma^2), \qquad (9.2)
$$

which has k first-order or main effects β_j and $k(k-1)/2$ two-factor interactions β_{jh}, and normally independently distributed (NID) errors $\underline{\epsilon}$ with zero means and constant variances. The example of Table 9.1 has $k=3$. (In Chapter 8 we used a slightly different

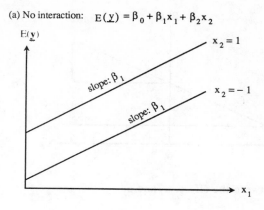

(a) No interaction: $E(\underline{y}) = \beta_0 + \beta_1 x_1 + \beta_2 x_2$

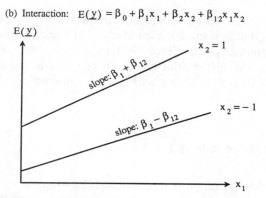

(b) Interaction: $E(\underline{y}) = \beta_0 + \beta_1 x_1 + \beta_2 x_2 + \beta_{12} x_1 x_2$

Figure 9.2 The effect of interaction

notation; regression analysis and experimental design have their own conventions.) *Interaction* between (say) factors 1 and 2 means that the effect of a change in factor 1 depends on the level of factor 2. In other words, the response curves do not run parallel; see Figure 9.2, which ignores the noise ϵ in (9.2). If the factors x_1 and x_2 are complementary, then β_{12} is positive. If these factors can be substituted for each other, then β_{12} is negative.

Exercise 9.3: Give relationship (9.2) for $k = 3$.

Exercise 9.4: Prove that the slope in Figure 9.2(b) equals $\beta_1 + \beta_{12}$ if $x_2 = 1$.

9.1.1 One Factor at a Time Designs

In the example with three factors ($k = 3$), changing one factor at a time yields four combinations ($n = k + 1 = 4$), namely the base variant ($i = 1$) and three more variants; see Table 9.1 (1). For this design we must assume that there are no interactions: $\beta_{jh} = 0$. Intuitively we estimate the main effects of the factors as follows:

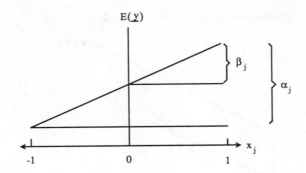

Figure 9.3 Relation between the effects α_j and β_j

$$\hat{\underline{\alpha}}_j = \underline{y}_i - \underline{y}_1 \quad \text{with } i = j+1 \quad (j = 1, \ldots, k). \tag{9.3}$$

Figure 9.3 illustrates the relation between the main effect β_j in (9.2) and $E(\hat{\underline{\alpha}}_j) = \alpha_j$. Equation (9.2) implies that β_j is the differential effect of factor j, when the other factors h are fixed at the origin ($x_{ih} = 0$). Since (9.2) means that the response surface has no curvature ($\beta_{jj} = 0$), the differential effect ($\partial/\partial x_j$) equals the difference quotient $\Delta E(\underline{y})/\Delta x_j$. If $\Delta x_j = 1$ then $\beta_j = \Delta E(\underline{y})$, as Figure 9.3 illustrates. The estimator

$$\hat{\underline{\beta}}_j = \hat{\underline{\alpha}}_j/2 \tag{9.4}$$

is an unbiased estimator of β_j in (9.2).

Exercise 9.5: Prove that $\hat{\underline{\beta}}_j$ of (9.4) is an unbiased estimator of β_j in (9.2), if one factor is changed at a time and interactions are zero. (Consider only $j = 1$ and $k = 3$.)

Equations (9.2) and (9.3) imply that the variance of the estimator $\hat{\underline{\alpha}}$ is $2\sigma^2$; so $\text{var}(\hat{\underline{\beta}}_j) = \sigma^2/2$. The intuitive estimator of β_0 is the overall average

$$\hat{\underline{\beta}}_0 = \sum_{i=1}^{n} \underline{y}_i/n. \tag{9.5}$$

Note that we may randomly associate the values $+1$ and -1 with the actual factor levels, so the sign of the estimator is arbitrary.

9.1.2 Full Factorial Designs

A full factorial design consists of all possible combinations of factor levels. In case of two levels per factor, this design results in 2^k combinations (the one factor at a time design requires only $k+1$ combinations). To estimate the main effect intuitively we adapt (9.3) as follows. We take the difference between the average result for $x_j = -1$ and $x_j = 1$ respectively. So the example of Table 9.1(2) yields

$$\left.\begin{array}{l} \hat{\alpha}_1 = (y_2 + y_4 + y_6 + y_8)/4 - (y_1 + y_3 + y_5 + y_7)/4; \\ \hat{\alpha}_2 = (y_3 + y_4 + y_7 + y_8)/4 - (y_1 + y_2 + y_5 + y_6)/4; \\ \hat{\alpha}_3 = (y_5 + y_6 + y_7 + y_8)/4 - (y_1 + y_2 + y_3 + y_4)/4. \end{array}\right\} \quad (9.6)$$

In the general case there are k factors, each observed at two levels (so x_{ij} is $+1$ or -1 according to equation (9.1)), and the intuitive estimators become

$$\hat{\alpha}_j = \frac{\sum\limits_{i=1}^{n} x_{ij} y_i}{(n/2)} \qquad \text{with } n = 2^k. \qquad (9.7)$$

We now prove that the *intuitive* estimator is identical to the OLS estimator. The matrix X for the 'additive' model (no interactions) consists of the dummy column with $n = 2^k$ elements equal to $+1$, and the k columns of the experimental design. In the example of Table 9.1(2) X is an 8×4 matrix. In a full factorial design this X is *orthogonal*: $X'X = n I$. In the preceding chapter we presented $\hat{\beta}$, the OLS estimator of the vector of regression parameters $\beta = (\beta_0, \beta_1, \ldots, \beta_k)'$, which simplifies, for orthogonal X:

$$\hat{\beta} = (X'X)^{-1} X' y = \frac{1}{n} X' y \qquad \text{or in scalar notation} \qquad (9.8a)$$

$$\hat{\beta}_j = \frac{1}{n} \sum_{i=1}^{n} x_{ij} y_i \qquad \text{with } j = 0, \ldots, k \text{ and } n = 2^k. \qquad (9.8b)$$

Its covariance matrix becomes

$$\text{cov}(\hat{\beta}) = \sigma^2 (X'X)^{-1} = \frac{\sigma^2}{n} I, \qquad (9.9)$$

which implies $\text{var}(\hat{\beta}_j) = \sigma^2/n$. So (9.7) specifies the intuitive estimator $\hat{\alpha}_j$ for a 2^k design; (9.8) proves that the intuitive estimator equals the OLS estimator $\hat{\beta}_j$ multiplied by two; (9.4) relates $\hat{\alpha}_j$ and $\hat{\beta}_j$. Hence the OLS estimator and the intuitive estimator are indeed identical. Equation (9.9) proves that the estimators have a constant variance and they are independent.

Exercise 9.6: (a) Prove that the OLS estimators for the one factor at a time design with two factors are
$$\hat{\beta}_0 = (y_2 + y_3)/2;$$
$$\hat{\beta}_1 = (y_2 - y_1)/2;$$
$$\hat{\beta}_2 = (y_3 - y_1)/2.$$
(b) Prove that these estimators are positively correlated, and their variances are $\sigma^2/2$.

To see which experimental design is more *efficient*, we compare the variances of $\hat{\beta}_j^{(1)}$ and $\hat{\beta}_j^{(2)}$, which denote the estimators for designs (1) and (2) respectively, but we account for the different numbers of observations, $k+1$ and 2^k respectively:

$$\frac{(k+1)\text{var}(\hat{\beta}_j^{(1)})}{2^k \text{var}(\hat{\beta}_j^{(2)})} = \frac{(k+1)(\sigma^2/2)}{n(\sigma^2/n)} = \frac{k+1}{2}. \qquad (9.10)$$

In other words, type (2) designs are more efficient, provided $k > 1$ (more than one factor). This can be explained intuitively. In type (1) designs the variance remains the same (namely $\sigma^2/2$) for all k values, whereas in type (2) designs the variance decreases as $n = 2^k$ increases, because in the latter designs we use each observation i when we estimate an effect β_j. It can be proved that an orthogonal matrix $\mathbf{X}$ minimizes the variances of the OLS estimator, provided $\mathbf{cov}(\underline{\epsilon}) = \sigma^2 \mathbf{I}$ (as in equation (9.2)).

Type (2) designs are not only more efficient; they are also more *effective* since they enable the estimation of *interactions*. To estimate the interaction between x_j and x_h we derive the new matrix of independent variables, that is, we multiply the vectors of these two independent variables elementwise. For example, Table 9.2 follows from the design in Table 9.1 (2) and the model in (9.2). We emphasize that the columns for the interactions are completely determined by the columns for the main effects, which are identical to the columns in the design matrix (Table 9.1). Each column in Table 9.2, except for the x_0 column, has an equal number of plus signs and minus signs. All vectors of the new matrix of independent variables $\mathbf{X}$ remain orthogonal. So analogous to (9.8), the OLS estimator of the two-factor interaction β_{jh} becomes

$$\hat{\underline{\beta}}_{jh} = \frac{1}{n} \sum_{i=1}^{n} (x_{ij} x_{ih}) \underline{y}_i \qquad \text{with } n = 2^k. \tag{9.11}$$

Equation (9.9) still holds. So the estimators of main effects and interactions remain independent with constant variance σ^2/n.

Upon including two-factor interactions, the number of effects q becomes

$$q = 1 + k + k(k-1)/2. \tag{9.12}$$

So $q < n = 2^k$ holds for $k > 2$. For example, Table 9.2 shows $q = 7 < n = 8$; and for $k = 7$ we have $q = 29 \ll n = 128$. But, if $q < n$ holds, then we could estimate regression models with more parameters, in particular models with interactions among three or more factors. These higher-order interactions, however, are difficult to interpret. Therefore we suggest not to add higher-order interactions to the metamodel (9.2) (although books on analysis of variance often do include high-order interactions). Ignoring high-order interactions allows us to use the experimental designs of the next subsection.

Table 9.2 Independent variables for the 2^3 experimental design including interactions between two factors

Combination	x_0	x_1	x_2	x_3	$x_1 x_2$	$x_1 x_3$	$x_2 x_3$
1	1	-1	-1	-1	1	1	1
2	1	1	-1	-1	-1	-1	1
3	1	-1	1	-1	-1	1	-1
4	1	1	1	-1	1	-1	-1
5	1	-1	-1	1	1	-1	-1
6	1	1	-1	1	-1	1	-1
7	1	-1	1	1	-1	-1	1
8	1	1	1	1	1	1	1

9.1.3 Incomplete Factorial Designs

A disadvantage of 2^k designs is that if there are no interactions at all, then we have 2^k observations to estimate only $k+1$ effects; these $k+1$ effects could also have been estimated with only a fraction, namely 2^{-p}, of these 2^k observations. For $k+1$ effects it suffices to take $k+1$ observations, as is illustrated by the example of Table 9.1 (3). In that example the intuitive estimators are analogous to (9.6):

$$\left.\begin{array}{l} \hat{\underline{\alpha}}_1 = (\underline{y}_2 + \underline{y}_4)/2 - (\underline{y}_1 + \underline{y}_3)/2; \\ \hat{\underline{\alpha}}_2 = (\underline{y}_3 + \underline{y}_4)/2 - (\underline{y}_1 + \underline{y}_2)/2; \\ \hat{\underline{\alpha}}_3 = (\underline{y}_1 + \underline{y}_4)/2 - (\underline{y}_2 + \underline{y}_3)/2. \end{array}\right\} \qquad (9.13)$$

The new matrix $\mathbf{X}$ remains orthogonal. So the OLS formulae of (9.8) and (9.9) still apply, but now with $n = 2^k/2^p = 2^{k-p}$.

Designs of types (2) and (3) are equally efficient, if we account for the number of observations:

$$\frac{2^{k-p}\text{var}(\hat{\underline{\beta}}_j^{(3)})}{2^k\text{var}(\hat{\underline{\beta}}_j^{(2)})} = \frac{2^{k-p}(\sigma^2/2^{k-p})}{2^k(\sigma^2/2^k)} = 1. \qquad (9.14)$$

In practice, however, fractional designs are often preferred, because their number of combinations is considerably smaller, so less computer time is needed for the simulation experiment. Table 9.1 showed $n = 8$ and 4 for the 2^3 and the 2^{3-1} experiment respectively; for $k = 7$ the full factorial design needs 128 combinations whereas a fractional design may need only 8 combinations (see Table 9.7, which we shall discuss later). On the other hand, the full factorial design has a smaller variance because of the larger number of observations. In comparison with the one at a time design, the fractional design becomes more efficient, the more factors there are; see (9.10). Both types may require an equal number of observations (namely $k+1$). In the example of Table 9.1 we have $n = 4$ and $\text{var}(\hat{\underline{\alpha}}_j) = 2\sigma^2$ and σ^2 in the type (1) and type (3) designs respectively.

Exercise 9.7: Prove that (9.3) and (9.13) imply $\text{var}(\hat{\underline{\alpha}}_j) = 2\sigma^2$ and σ^2 respectively.

Kleijnen and Standridge (1988) study a flexible manufacturing system (FMS) simulation model, as we saw in the preceding chapter. Table 9.3 specifies an intuitively selected fraction of 24 possible input combinations. If a first-order regression metamodel is assumed, then the four main effects β_1 to β_4 and the overall effect β_0 can also be estimated from the fractional design in Table 9.4. The difference between the two designs is the x_4 values in combinations 2, 3, 6, and 7. The two designs specify two sets of simulation inputs; this results in two output vectors $\mathbf{y}$. OLS yields the estimated covariance matrices $\widehat{\text{cov}}(\hat{\underline{\beta}})$; their main-diagonal elements are shown in Table 9.5, which demonstrates that the fractional design gives more accurate estimators.

The fractional factorial designs of the 2^{k-p} type imply that the number of combinations is a power of two: $n = 2, 4, 8, 16, 32$, and so on. For first-order metamodels, there are also so-called *Plackett–Burman designs*, where n is only a multiple of four. An example is shown in Table 9.6, where $k = 11$ and $n = 12$. The Plackett–Burman designs have been tabulated; these tables are reproduced in Kleijnen (1975, pp. 332–3).

Table 9.3 Intuitive fractional design for four factors

Combination	x_1	x_2	x_3	x_4
1	−	−	−	−
2	+	−	+	M
3	−	+	+	M
4	+	+	−	−
5	−	−	+	+
6	+	−	−	M
7	−	+	−	M
8	+	+	+	+

Legend: − denotes minimum value of x_j with $j = 1, \ldots, 4$
  + denotes maximum value of x_j
  M denotes medium value of x_4

Table 9.4 2^{4-1} fractional factorial design

Combination	x_1	x_2	$x_3{}^*$	x_4
1	−	−	−	−
2	+	−	+	−
3	−	+	+	−
4	+	+	−	−
5	−	−	+	+
6	+	−	−	+
7	−	+	−	+
8	+	+	+	+

$*x_{i3} = x_{i1} x_{i2} x_{i4}$ with $i = 1, \ldots, 8$.

Table 9.5 Estimated variances $\widehat{\mathrm{var}}(\hat{\beta}_j)$

Effect	Intuitive design	Fractional design
$\hat{\beta}_1$	0.5	0.5
$\hat{\beta}_2$	0.5	0.5
$\hat{\beta}_3$	1.0	0.5
$\hat{\beta}_4$	0.5	0.13
$\hat{\beta}_0$	20.6	19.6

If the number of effects $k + 1$ is not a multiple of four, then n is rounded upwards to the next multiple of four. For example, if k is 4, 5, 6 or 7 then n becomes 8; see Table 9.7. So for $k = 4$ we eliminate the columns x_5, x_6 and x_7; for $k = 5$ we do not use the columns x_6 and x_7; for $k = 6$ we eliminate the column x_7.

If there are *interactions*, then fractional factorials may give false conclusions. For example, in Table 9.1(3) we have $x_3 = x_1 x_2$ (hence we have $x_{i2} = x_{i1} x_{i3}$, $x_{i1} = x_{i2} x_{i3}$, and $x_{i0} = x_{i1} x_{i2} x_{i3}$). It can be proved that, for example, $\hat{\underline{\alpha}}_3$ in (9.13) does not estimate α_3; it estimates $\alpha_3 + \alpha_{12}$. Hence if the interaction α_{12} is important, then $\hat{\underline{\alpha}}_3$ is a biased estimator of α_3. (Likewise $E(\hat{\underline{\alpha}}_2) = \alpha_2 + \alpha_{13}$, $E(\hat{\underline{\alpha}}_1) = \alpha_1 + \alpha_{23}$, and $E(\hat{\alpha}_0) = \alpha_0 + \alpha_{123}$, where α_{123} is the three-factor interaction.) Therefore we should validate the metamodel

Table 9.6 Plackett–Burman design for eleven factors

Combination	1	2	3	4	5	6	7	8	9	10	11
1	+	−	+	−	−	−	+	+	+	−	+
2	+	+	−	+	−	−	−	+	+	+	−
3	−	+	+	−	+	−	−	−	+	+	+
4	+	−	+	+	−	+	−	−	−	+	+
5	+	+	−	+	+	−	+	−	−	−	+
6	+	+	+	−	+	+	−	+	−	−	−
7	−	+	+	+	−	+	+	−	+	−	−
8	−	−	+	+	+	−	+	+	−	+	−
9	−	−	−	+	+	+	−	+	+	−	+
10	+	−	−	−	+	+	+	−	+	+	+
11	−	+	−	−	−	+	+	+	−	+	+
12	−	−	−	−	−	−	−	−	−	−	−

Table 9.7 2^{7-4} experimental design

Combination	x_1	x_2	x_3	$x_4 = x_1x_2$*	$x_5 = x_1x_3$	$x_6 = x_2x_3$	$x_7 = x_1x_2x_3$
1	−1	−1	−1	1	1	1	−1
2	1	−1	−1	−1	−1	1	1
3	−1	1	−1	−1	1	−1	1
4	1	1	−1	1	−1	−1	−1
5	−1	−1	1	1	−1	−1	1
6	1	−1	1	−1	1	−1	−1
7	−1	1	1	−1	−1	1	−1
8	1	1	1	1	1	1	1

*$x_4 = x_1x_2$ stands for $x_{i4} = x_{i1}x_{i2}$, and so on.

that guides the choice of the experimental design. That validation was discussed in the previous chapter. For a further discussion of experimental designs we refer to Kleijnen (1987, pp. 259–357).

Exercise 9.8: Consider a situation with five factors ($k = 5$).
(a) If there are no interactions, which experimental design would you recommend?
(b) Assume that all two-factor interactions are important. How many effects should we estimate in that case?
(c) Check that for (b) the following 2^{5-1} experimental design is adequate: write down a full factorial design for the first four factors, and define the column $x_5 = x_1x_2x_3x_4$.

9.1.4 Comments: Replications and Scaling Effects

The classic theory on experimental designs assumes that the *noise* ϵ is normally and independently distributed with constant variance; see (9.2). We can estimate this constant variance from the mean squared residuals, as we saw in the preceding chapter. In practice, the variances may differ very much. We can estimate the heterogenous variances σ_i^2, provided we have $m_i \geqslant 2$ replicates of combination i (m_i simulation runs for system variant i). We can then apply corrected least squares and estimated weighted least squares, as we saw in the preceding chapter. In that chapter we also discuss non-normal and correlated responses.

The literature presents the metamodel and the experimental design in the form of *standardized* variables, x, that is, x is either $+1$ or -1; see (9.1) and (9.2). We may also formulate the model in terms of the original variables (say) z_j, centred around their averages $\bar{z}_j = (1/n) \sum_{i=1}^{n} z_{ij}$:

$$\underline{y} = \delta_0 + \sum_{j=1}^{k} \delta_j (z_j - \bar{z}_j) + \sum_{j=1}^{k-1} \sum_{h=j+1}^{k} \delta_{jh} (z_j - \bar{z}_j)(z_h - \bar{z}_h) + \underline{\epsilon}. \tag{9.15}$$

To interpret this model, we assume a balanced experimental design; that is, in the experiment there are as many 'low' values L_j as there are 'high' values H_j for factor j. Such a design implies

$$\bar{z}_j = \frac{1}{n} \sum_{i=1}^{n} z_{ij} = \frac{1}{n} \left(\frac{n}{2} L_j + \frac{n}{2} H_j \right) = \frac{L_j + H_j}{2}. \tag{9.16}$$

Then the marginal or main effect of factor j is δ_j. The total effect over the range $L_j \leqslant z_j \leqslant H_j$ is

$$\delta_j (H_j - L_j) = 2\beta_j = \alpha_j; \tag{9.17}$$

see also Bettonvil and Kleijnen (1990). In the example of Figure 9.4 factor 1 has a larger marginal effect than factor 2; yet factor 2 is more important, given the experimental domain. In sensitivity analysis we are interested in α_j (or β_j); then we should apply the standardized variables x and the regression metamodel (9.2), which is expressed in x and β.

Exercise 9.9: Formulate three different designs, namely (a) a one factor at a time design, (b) the 2^k design, and (c) a 2^{k-p} design. Use these designs to investigate

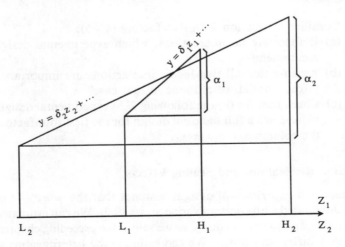

Figure 9.4 Scaling effects

a simulation model. For didactic reasons that model might be a simulation model you are familiar with, for example, an M/M/s queuing model or some other simulation model that is available to you. However, from the viewpoint of statistical design theory the simulation model is a black box: the design determines the standardized variables x_{ij}, which must be transformed into the original simulation inputs z_{ij}, which are used by the simulation model (f_1) to generate the output $\underline{y}_i$ (using a new seed $\underline{r}_{0i}$ or a common seed $\underline{r}_0$). Generating $\underline{y}_i$ usually takes relatively much computer time. For the purpose of this exercise we replace the complicated simulation model (f_1) by the simpler function

$$\underline{y}_i = \gamma_0 + \gamma_1 z_{i1} + \gamma_2 z_{i2} + \gamma_3 z_{i3} + \gamma_{12} z_{i1} z_{i2} + \gamma_{13} z_{i1} z_{i3} + \gamma_{23} z_{i2} z_{i3} + \underline{\epsilon},$$

where $10 \leqslant z_{i1} \leqslant 25$, $100 \leqslant z_{i2} \leqslant 200$, $-10 \leqslant z_{i3} \leqslant +10$, $\underline{\epsilon}_i \sim \text{NID}(0, \sigma^2)$ and $i = 1, \ldots, n$; n is determined by the design, that is (1) $n = 1 + 3 = 4$, (2) $n = 2^3$, and (3) $n = 2^{3-1} = 4$ (see Table 9.1). We further take $\sigma = 1$ (whether the effects γ_1 through γ_{23} are 'big' is determined by their magnitudes relative to σ); $\gamma_0 = 100$, $\gamma_1 = 3$, $\gamma_2 = 2$, $\gamma_{12} = 1.5$, and all other effects are zero (of course, in the design and analysis of the simulation experiment, you cannot use your knowledge about the values of γ and σ: you perform a Monte Carlo experiment). So you must first formulate a design, translate the design into the original variables (z_1, z_2, z_3), 'run' the simulation program n times (that is, generate ϵ_i, which together with z_{i1}, z_{i2}, and z_{i3} yields y_i using the equation given above). Note that designs (1) and (3) assume a regression model without interactions; that is, the effects γ_0 through γ_3 are estimated using observations that are also determined by the interactions, especially γ_{12}. Repeat the exercise with a 'simulation' model that has *all* interactions (including γ_{12}) zero. In both experiments, you should estimate the standardized effects β (or $\alpha = 2\beta$), not the effects γ or δ (see equation (9.15)).

9.2 SCREENING

In the beginning of a simulation study there may be very many factors. Obviously we assume that not all these (say) k factors are important; unfortunately, we do not know which factors are really important. If there is such a large number of factors, then the designs discussed so far require too many combinations n and hence too much computer time: they all require $n > k$. The following method may provide a solution.

We partition the k factors into G groups. A 'group factor' w_g ($g = 1, 2, \ldots, G$) has the value 1 (and -1 respectively) if all its component factors x have the value 1 (and -1 respectively); Table 9.8 gives an example with $k = 100$ and $G = 2$ (we shall discuss the last column of this table in a moment). For each group we test the significance of the estimated group effect $\hat{\gamma}_g$. If the estimated group effect is not significant, we eliminate all factors of that group in the next phase. It can be proved, under not too stringent assumptions, that if the group effect is not important, then none of the individual factors is important. Group screening allows us to quickly reduce the number of factors in the pilot phase of our research.

Table 9.8 Group screening

Combination	Group factor		Individual factors	Result
i	w_1	w_2	$x_1, \ldots, x_{50}, x_{51}, \ldots, x_{100}$	$E(y)$
1	-1	-1	$-1 \ldots -1 \quad -1 \ldots -1$	$-\beta_1 - \beta_2$
2	-1	1	$-1 \ldots -1 \quad 1 \ldots 1$	$-\beta_1 - \beta_2$
3	1	-1	$1 \ldots 1 \quad -1 \ldots -1$	$\beta_1 + \beta_2$
4	1	1	$1 \ldots 1 \quad 1 \ldots 1$	$\beta_1 + \beta_2$

EXAMPLE 9.1: GROUP SCREENING

Suppose that there are 100 factors and no dummy factor x_0 (so $\beta_0 = 0$). We decide to partition these factors into two groups ($G = 2$), each of 50 factors. We analyse these two groups through a 2^2 design. Also see Table 9.8. Suppose that only x_1 and x_2 are important; that is, only β_1 and β_2 are not zero, there are no interactions, and all other factors are unimportant (of course, in practice we do not have this prior knowledge). This yields the last column of Table 9.8. The OLS estimator for the main effects of the groups follow from the general formulae for OLS in (9.8):

$$\hat{\gamma}_1 = \frac{\sum_{i=1}^{4} w_{i1} \underline{y}_i}{4} = \frac{-\underline{y}_1 - \underline{y}_2 + \underline{y}_3 + \underline{y}_4}{4}, \tag{9.18}$$

and

$$\hat{\gamma}_2 = \frac{\sum_{i=1}^{4} w_{i2} \underline{y}_i}{4} = \frac{-\underline{y}_1 + \underline{y}_2 - \underline{y}_3 + \underline{y}_4}{4}. \tag{9.19}$$

It is simple to prove that $E(\hat{\gamma}_1) = \beta_1 + \beta_2$ and $E(\hat{\gamma}_2) = 0$.

Exercise 9.10: Prove that $E(\hat{\gamma}_1) = \beta_1 + \beta_2$ and $E(\hat{\gamma}_2) = 0$.

Next we test if the estimates $\hat{\gamma}_1$ and $\hat{\gamma}_2$ differ significantly from zero, as we saw in the preceding chapter. Suppose we test each group effect at level α. Because $E(\hat{\gamma}_2) = 0$, the probability of finding a significant $\hat{\gamma}_2$ is α. The larger $\beta_1 + \beta_2$ is, the higher the probability of a significant $\hat{\gamma}_1$. Obviously this approach fails if β_1 and β_2 happen to have opposite signs, and they are of the same absolute magnitude: $\beta_1 + \beta_2 = 0$. Therefore we try to code the variables x such that they have non-negative effects, if they have any effects at all. For example, in a study of waiting times we take $x_1 = +1$ if arrival rate is high, $x_2 = +1$ if service rate is low, $x_3 = +1$ if number of servers is low, and so on. Table 9.8 means that after only four runs we probably eliminate the 50 individual factors that form group 2 (so we eliminate the factors $51, 52, \ldots, 100$). In the next stage of the investigation (not shown in the table) we further examine group 1; for example, we apply group screening to the factors $1, 2, \ldots, 50$. We continue, until so few individual factors remain, that we can apply the classical designs of the previous section. For further details we refer to Kleijnen (1987, pp. 320–8).

Exercise 9.11: Consider a simulation model with 90 potentially important factors. Suppose you have more time and money than in the example of Table 9.8: you can investigate five to ten simulation runs. Give a group screening design for this situation.

Recently the following alternative techniques for screening have been developed.

(1) Sequential bifurcation by Bettonvil (1990) is a more efficient variation on group screening. He applied his technique to a deterministic simulation model of the greenhouse effect, with 281 factors. His dissertation is summarized in Bettonvil and Kleijnen (1992).
(2) Search linear models by Ghosh (1987) are based on Srivastava's (1975) designs.
(3) The frequency domain technique by Schruben and Cogliano (1987) uses spectral analysis. It is criticized by Sargent and Som (1991).
(4) Instead of treating the simulation model as a black box to which experimental design theory is applied, mathematical analysis can be applied to derive marginal effects. This results in Ho's perturbation analysis (see Ho and Cao, 1991, and Suri, 1989) and Rubinstein's score function (see Rubinstein, 1989).

9.3 OPTIMIZATION: RESPONSE SURFACE METHODOLOGY

The goal of response surface methodology (RSM) is to estimate optimum values for quantitative inputs of a system. The method is heuristic; so it is not certain that the answer is optimal; for example, a *local* optimum may result. RSM uses the *steepest ascent* algorithm, which determines in which direction factors should be changed in order to reach the optimum; it does not give the step size along this path.

We now sketch how RSM works; for illustrative purposes we take a problem with only two controllable variables, x_1 and x_2.

(1) We vary the inputs x_1 and x_2 over a small range only. In Figure 9.5 this corresponds with the rectangle with $a \leqslant x_1 \leqslant b$ and $c \leqslant x_2 \leqslant d$.

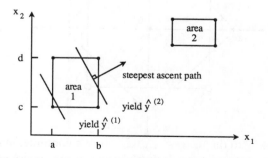

Figure 9.5 Steepest ascent

(2) Because this area is small relative to the total area that x_1 and x_2 can vary over, we apply the local first-order approximation

$$\hat{y} = \hat{\beta}_0 + \hat{\beta}_1 x_1 + \hat{\beta}_2 x_2 \quad \text{with } a \leqslant x_1 \leqslant b \quad \text{and} \quad c \leqslant x_2 \leqslant d, \quad (9.20)$$

where the three regression parameters $(\beta_0, \beta_1, \beta_2)$ are estimated from the four observations corresponding with the four corners of 'area 1'.

(3) Next we change x_1 and x_2 according to the ratio $\hat{\beta}_1 / \hat{\beta}_2$. It can be proved that the steepest ascent path is perpendicular to the lines of constant yields ($y^{(1)}$ and $y^{(2)}$ respectively in Figure 9.5). We know the direction $\hat{\beta}_1 / \hat{\beta}_2$ from (9.20), but not the step size. We intuitively choose a step size, which takes us to 'area 2' in Figure 9.5.

(4) We repeat (1)–(3) until a local first-order model is no longer adequate. The literature often uses the significance of the estimated regression parameters as a criterion: if $\hat{\beta}_1$ and $\hat{\beta}_2$ are not significant, then the first-order model is inadequate. However, we can also test the validity of the model in the way explained in the previous chapter. An inadequate first-order model implies that we are close to an optimum: (9.20) can model a hill side, not a hill top. This leads to the next step.

(5) Near the optimum we use the second-order approximation

$$\hat{y} = \hat{\beta}_0 + \hat{\beta}_1 x_1 + \hat{\beta}_2 x_2 + \hat{\beta}_{12} x_1 x_2 + \hat{\beta}_{11} x_1^2 + \hat{\beta}_{22} x_2^2. \quad (9.21)$$

Comparison of the first-order and second-order approximations shows that now we must estimate more parameters. So we have to simulate more factor combinations: in general, $n \geqslant 1 + k + k(k-1)/2 + k$. There are special RSM designs. Figure 9.6 shows such a design for $k = 2$. The six parameters of (9.21) are estimated from nine observations. Because we want to estimate the quadratic effects β_{11} and β_{22}, the factors must have more than two levels (with two levels we would have: $x_0 = x_1^2 = x_2^2$). Actually in this type of design there are five levels: $-a$, $-1, 0, 1$, and a with $a \neq 1$ and $a \neq 0$.

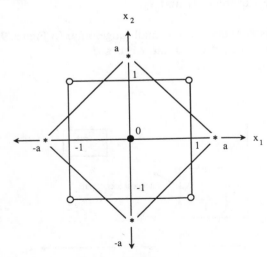

Figure 9.6 Experimental design for two factors with interaction and quadratic effects. ○ 2^k design, * star design, ● central point

In the general case with k factors, the star design of Figure 9.6 consists of $2k$ combinations. In each of these combinations, all factors are zero, except for one factor (the star design is a one factor at a time design). So the star design is specified by the following $2k$ rows where each row has $k-1$ zeros:

$$
\left\{
\begin{array}{l}
-a, 0, \ldots, 0 \\
+a, 0, \ldots, 0 \\
0, -a, \ldots, 0 \\
0, +a, \ldots, 0 \\
\quad\vdots \\
0, \ldots, 0, -a \\
0, \ldots, 0, +a
\end{array}
\right.
$$

The 2^k design of Figure 9.6 becomes a 2^{k-p} design with p so high that all k main effects and $k(k-1)/2$ two-factor interactions are still estimable (such a design is called a 'resolution V' design; Kleijnen (1987, p. 309) lists them for $k = 5, \ldots, 11$).

(6) Finally we differentiate the estimated local second-order model for the inputs, and solve the resulting system of linear equations for these inputs:

$$
\left.
\begin{array}{l}
\dfrac{\partial \hat{y}}{\partial x_1} = \hat{\beta}_1 + \hat{\beta}_{12} x_2 + 2 \hat{\beta}_{11} x_1 = 0 \\[2ex]
\dfrac{\partial \hat{y}}{\partial x_2} = \hat{\beta}_2 + \hat{\beta}_{12} x_1 + 2 \hat{\beta}_{22} x_2 = 0.
\end{array}
\right\}
\tag{9.22}
$$

The resulting values are the estimated optimum values $(\hat{x}_1^*, \hat{x}_2^*)$.

It is possible that we have not estimated the optimum but either a saddle point or a ridge (an infinite number of optimum solutions). Furthermore, we may get stuck on a local optimum. For more details on RSM we refer to the textbooks of Box and Draper (1987), and Box, Hunter, and Hunter (1978), and also to Donohue, Houck, and Myers (1992), and Kleijnen (1987, pp. 202–6, 214–16, 312–16).

9.3.1 Case Study: Production Planning

Kleijnen (1992) discusses the optimization of a simulated production planning system (PPS). This PPS has 14 controllable variables: z_j with $j = 1, \ldots, 14$. Initially, a local first-order model is estimated from the 2^{14-10} design of Table 9.9. RSM has scaling effects; heuristically a scale is selected such that changing the standardized variable x_j from -1 to $+1$ means a 20% increase of the original variable z_j. Furthermore, not one but two response variables are of interest, namely the number of productive hours y (excluding idle times of and switchover times among machines) and the lead time it takes to deliver products, w. Productive hours are to be maximized, subject to a given upper limit for lead time. Simulating the 16 input combinations corresponding to Table 9.9 and analysing the results yields the estimated local effects of the 14 inputs on the two responses: see Table 9.10 (columns $\hat{\beta}_j$ and $\hat{\gamma}_j$). Because each input has its own scale and range, this table also displays the estimated unit effects ($\hat{\beta}_j$ and $\hat{\gamma}_j$) multiplied by the values of the inputs in the base combination, which corresponds with run 1 of Table 9.9.

Table 9.9 2^{14-10} experimental design

Combina-tion	1	2	3	4	5=1·2	6=1·3	7=1·4	8=2·3	9=2·4	10=3·4	11=1·2·3	12=1·2·4	13=1·3·4	14=2·3·4
1	+	+	+	+	+	+	+	+	+	+	+	+	+	+
2	−	+	+	+	−	−	−	+	+	+	−	−	−	+
3	+	−	+	+	−	+	+	−	−	+	−	−	+	−
4	−	−	+	+	+	−	−	−	−	+	+	+	−	−
5	+	+	−	+	+	−	+	−	+	−	−	+	−	−
6	−	+	−	+	−	+	−	−	+	−	+	−	+	−
7	+	−	−	+	−	−	+	+	−	−	+	−	−	+
8	−	−	−	+	+	+	−	+	−	−	−	+	+	+
9	+	+	+	−	+	+	−	+	−	+	−	−	−	−
10	−	+	+	−	−	−	+	+	−	−	−	+	+	−
11	+	−	+	−	−	+	−	−	+	−	−	+	−	+
12	−	−	+	−	+	−	+	−	+	−	+	−	+	+
13	+	+	−	−	+	−	−	−	−	+	−	−	+	+
14	−	+	−	−	−	+	+	−	−	+	+	+	−	+
15	+	−	−	−	−	−	−	+	+	+	+	+	+	−
16	−	−	−	−	+	+	+	+	+	+				

+ means +1, − means −1

Table 9.10 Local sensitivity estimates

Input # j	Effect on productive hours $\hat{\beta}_j$	$\hat{\beta}_j z_j^b$	Effect on lead time $\hat{\gamma}_j$	$\hat{\gamma}_j z_j^b$
1	0.52	62.40	− 0.054	− 6.48
2	− 39.30	− 117.90	− 1.504	− 4.51
3	0.65	78.00	0.072	8.64
4	− 18.07	− 0.90	150.583	7.53
5	− 128.96	− 64.48	− 16.519	− 8.26
6	0.00	0.00	− 0.102	− 29.38
7	− 0.22	− 132.00	− 0.006	− 3.60
8	13.88	20.82	2.963	4.44
9	− 1.53	− 38.25	1.311	32.78
10	1.39	139.00	0.072	7.20
11	0.03	9.00	0.037	11.10
12	527.23	158.17	8.485	2.55
13	− 9.27	− 46.35	− 6.351	− 31.76
14	− 0.46	− 55.20	− 0.145	− 17.40

z_j^b denotes the value of input j in the base combination ($=$ combination 1)

Kleijnen (1992) tries the following two mutually related heuristics for determining the step size.

(1) Select a step size such that one input is (roughly) doubled while the other inputs are less than doubled: in Table 9.11 z_{12} increases from 0.33 to 0.5936.
(2) Fix the inputs as in (1), but further increase the step size such that another input becomes (roughly) halved: z_4 and z_5 are halved.

As Figure 9.5 suggested, a second experiment is executed next. This experiment is again determined by a 2^{14-10} design. The standardized design has already been displayed

Table 9.11 Inputs z_j in base combination and along steepest ascent path

Input z_j j	Unit effect $\hat{\beta}_j$	Base combination	Value of input j in:	
			Heuristic (1)	Heuristic (2)
1	0.52	132	132.0003	132.0001
2	−39.30	3.3	3.28035	3.2214
3	0.65	132	132.0003	132.0001
4	−18.07	0.075	0.065965	0.03886
5	−128.96	0.55	0.48552	0.29208
6	0.00	316.8	316.8	316.8
7	−0.22	660	659.9999	659.996
8	13.88	1.65	1.65694	1.6778
9	−1.53	27.5	27.44992	27.4469
10	1.39	110	110.0007	110.003
11	0.03	330	330	330
12	527.23	0.33	0.5936	0.6
13	−9.27	5.5	5.4954	5.4815
14	−0.46	132	131.9998	131.9991

in Table 9.9. Table 9.11, however, shows that $x_{12} = +1$ corresponds not with 0.33 but with 0.6; similar remarks hold for the other inputs. Unfortunately the improvements of productive hours y in the second experiment are rather small. For further details we refer to Kleijnen (1992).

Exercise 9.12: Apply RSM to estimate the optimal input values of a simulation model. You might use an actual simulation model such as the inventory model of Chapter 5, which requires optimization of the reorder point and the order quantity. However, it is convenient (see also Exercise 9.9) to use

$$y = \gamma_0 + \gamma_1 z_1 + \gamma_2 z_2 + \gamma_{12} z_1 z_2 + \gamma_{11} z_1^2 + \gamma_{22} z_2^2 + \underline{\epsilon},$$

where $\gamma_0 = -669\,046$, $\gamma_1 = 1724$, $\gamma_2 = 1344$, $\gamma_{12} = -1$, $\gamma_{11} = -3$, $\gamma_{22} = -0.5$; $\underline{\epsilon} \sim NID(0, \sigma^2)$ and $\sigma = 1$; the total experimental area is defined by $0 \leqslant z_1 \leqslant 100$ and $100 \leqslant z_2 \leqslant 2000$. Start your search from a corner of the experimental area; determine by chance which corner that will be. Once you have computed the estimated optimum values of y, z_1, and z_2, check your result against the analytical solution, ignoring the noise $\underline{\epsilon}$.

REFERENCES

Bettonvil B. (1990) *Detection of Important Factors by Sequential Bifurcation*, Tilburg University Press, Tilburg.

Bettonvil B. and J. P. C. Kleijnen (1990) Measurement scales and resolution IV designs, *American Journal of Mathematical and Management Sciences*, **10**, 309–22.

Bettonvil B. and J. P. C. Kleijnen (1992) *Identifying the Important Factors in Simulation Models with many Factors*, Tilburg University, Tilburg.

Box G. E. P. and N. R. Draper (1987) *Empirical Model Building and Response Surfaces*, Wiley, New York.

Box G. E. P., W. G. Hunter, and J. S. Hunter (1978) *Statistics for Experimenters*, Wiley, New York.

Donohue J. M., E. C. Houck, and R. H. Myers (1992) Simulation designs for quadratic response surface models in the presence of model misspecification, *Management Science* (accepted).

Ghosh S. (1987) Influential nonnegligible parameters under the search linear model. *Communications in Statistics, Theory and Methods*, 16(4), 1013–25.

Ho Y. and X. Cao (1991) *Perturbation Analysis of Discrete Event Dynamic Systems*, Kluwer, Dordrecht.

Kleijnen J. P. C. (1975) *Statistical Techniques in Simulation*, Part II, Marcel Dekker, New York.

Kleijnen J. P. C. (1987) *Statistical Tools for Simulation Practitioners*, Marcel Dekker, New York.

Kleijnen J. P. C. (1992) Simulation and Optimization in Production Planning: A Case Study, *Decision Support Systems*, 8.

Kleijnen J. P. C. and C. R. Standridge (1988) Experimental design and regression analysis in simulation: an FMS case study, *European Journal of Operational Research*, 33, 257–61.

Morris M. D. (1991) Factorial sampling plans for preliminary computational experiments, *Technometrics*, 22(2), 161–74.

Rubinstein R. (1989) Monte Carlo methods for performance evaluation, sensitivity analysis and optimization of stochastic systems. In *Encyclopedia of Computer Science and Technology*, 20(5), J. Belzer, A. G. Holzman, and A. Kent (executive eds), Marcel Dekker, New York.

Sargent R. G. and T. K. Som (1992) Current issues in frequency domain experimentation, *Management Science*, 38(5), 667–87.

Schruben L. W. and V. J. Cogliano (1987) An experimental procedure for simulation response surface model identification, *Communications ACM*, 30(8), 716–30.

Srivastava J. N. (1975) Designs for searching nonnegligible effects. In J. N. Srivastava (ed.), *A Survey of Statistical Design and Linear Models*, North-Holland Publishing Company, Amsterdam, 507–19.

Suri R. (1989) Perturbation analysis: the state of the art and research issues explained via the GI/G/1 queue, *Proceedings of the IEEE*, 77, 114–37.

Chapter 10

Tactical Aspects

In the previous chapter we discussed questions such as 'which priority rule is best?' and 'how many servers are necessary?' Those questions refer to so-called strategic aspects. Now we discuss tactical aspects, in particular the following two questions: 'How long should a simulation run be?' and 'Can the variance of the run's response be reduced?' Tactical aspects concern problems that must be solved by the simulation specialist; they do not necessarily interest the user.

EXAMPLE 10.1

A bank's management is interested in the waiting times of clients. In the simulation of this queuing problem the analyst studied the average waiting time in the long run or steady state. That steady state was reached after approximately 36 hours of simulated time ('wall clock time'). But this approach means that the analyst overlooked the fact that the bank is open only between 9 a.m. and 4 p.m. In other words, the steady state is not relevant in this situation.

In many practical problems there is an event that stops the simulation run. In the above example, that event is the 'arrival' of a specific point of time, namely 4 p.m. Such models are known as *terminating* models. Other examples are provided by the analysis of peak hours in queuing systems such as traffic intersections and telephone exchanges: these simulations start before the peak and finish immediately after the rush hour. One more example is the simulation of the life of a machine: the simulation begins with the installation of the machine and ends when the machine is scrapped.

In some situations, however, we are interested in the *steady state*. An example is the simulation of the long-term effects of the installation of a flexible manufacturing system (FMS). Furthermore, most theoretical studies of queuing systems consider 'non-terminating' models, because it is only in the steady state that the analysis is relatively simple and asymptotic results apply.

Whether a simulation is terminating or not, the most important tactical question concerns the *run length*: when can we stop the simulation?

This chapter is organized as follows.

—10.1 Terminating models

It is simple to analyse terminating models, since each simulation run gives one independent observation. To compute a $1 - \alpha$ confidence interval we can use basic statistics such as the t statistic. We can also derive the number of simulation runs needed to estimate the simulation response with prefixed accuracy.

—10.2 Non-terminating, steady-state models

In steady-state simulations we often use a single long run. The individual responses within that run are dependent; they form a time series. A simple approach divides the long run into subruns or batches of fixed length, and tests if the batch averages have non-significant correlations. (A more sophisticated approach uses renewal analysis.)

—10.3 Proportions and quantiles

In practice we are often interested not in the expected value but in the probability of a stochastic variable (such as waiting time) exceeding a given value: proportion. A related response is the value that is not exceeded by (say) 90% of the observations on the variable: a quantile.

—10.4 Variance reduction techniques

We limit ourselves to a few simple techniques. Common random numbers can be used when comparing different systems. Antithetic random numbers may decrease the variance of the response averaged over a number of simulation replications of the same system. Control variates correct the response for the deviation between the sampled average input value and the true mean input value; optimal correction factors are estimated by regression analysis.

—10.5 Jackknifing

We discuss a simple computer-intensive technique for reducing possible bias of an estimator and for constructing a robust confidence interval, which also holds for nonnormal distributions.

10.1 TERMINATING MODELS

The analysis of terminating models is very simple from a statistical viewpoint. After all, each replication or run of a simulation experiment provides one independently and identically distributed (i.i.d.) response. For example, in the introduction of this chapter we saw that each simulated day yields one average waiting time of customers arriving between 9 a.m. and 4 p.m. For each replication we reinitialize all state variables; for example, the number of customers waiting is set to zero. All parameters and exogenous variables remain the same; for example, the arrival rate λ and the number of servers s do not change. We use a new sequence of pseudorandom numbers; otherwise we would get identical results (how to get a different sequence of pseudorandom numbers was shown in Chapter 2). Now we examine how to analyse replications statistically.

Suppose we simulate a queuing problem in a bank, and we are interested in the average waiting time per day, say, $\overline{w}$. We wish to derive a $1 - \alpha$ confidence interval for $E(\overline{w}) = \mu$, the expectation of the average waiting time per day. The number of simulated days is m with $m \geqslant 2$. Each simulated day uses a different sequence of pseudorandom numbers. The number of customers on day i is the random variable $\underline{N}_i$. These $\underline{N}_i$ are i.i.d., because all days are governed by the same statistical laws and all days use independent random numbers. So we estimate the standard deviation of the daily average $\overline{w}$ (not an individual time $\underline{w}$) from the m days:

$$S_{\bar{w}} = \sqrt{\left[\frac{\sum\limits_{i=1}^{m}(\bar{w}_i - \bar{\bar{w}}^2)}{m-1}\right]}, \tag{10.1}$$

with average waiting time on day i

$$\bar{w}_i = \frac{1}{N_i}\sum_{t=1}^{N_i} w_{it}, \tag{10.2}$$

and 'overall' average

$$\bar{\bar{w}} = \frac{1}{m}\sum_{i=1}^{m}\bar{w}_i. \tag{10.3}$$

To determine a $(1-\alpha)$ confidence interval, we assume that $\bar{w}$ is normally distributed ($\bar{w}$ is an average; there is a limit theorem that is analogous to the central limit theorem; the latter theorem holds only for independent variables, as we saw in Section 3.5.1). The $\bar{w}_i$ are i.i.d. for the same reasons that apply to N_i. Then the following $1-\alpha$ confidence interval holds:

$$P\left(\bar{\bar{w}} - t_{m-1}^{\alpha/2}\frac{S_{\bar{w}}}{\sqrt{m}} \leqslant E(\bar{w}_i) \leqslant \bar{\bar{w}} + t_{m-1}^{\alpha/2}\frac{S_{\bar{w}}}{\sqrt{m}}\right) = 1-\alpha. \tag{10.4}$$

Exercise 10.1: The t statistic in (10.4) assumes that 'the' responses are NID (normally, independently distributed).
(a) Which responses are meant in (10.4): w, $\bar{w}$, or $\bar{\bar{w}}$?
(b) Why are these responses distributed independently and identically?

Exercise 10.2: Which effects has m in (10.4)?

EXAMPLE 10.2

We construct an 'academic' terminating system: an M/M/1 system that starts in the empty state, and we compute the average waiting time of the first 500 and the first 3000 customers respectively. We repeat the experiment 10 times: $m = 10$ macroreplications. Traffic rate λ is 1.0 and traffic load ρ is 0.7. Given our random numbers, the asymptotically correct 95% confidence intervals for $E(\sum_{i=1}^{N} w_i/N)$ is (1.22, 1.71) for $N = 500$, and (1.43, 1.69) for $N = 3000$. Note that the first customer does not wait. It can be proved that $E(w_i)$ increases with i until the steady state is reached: $E(w_i) = \mu_w$ for $i\uparrow\infty$; here $\mu_w = 1.63$ (see Chapter 5). The confidence interval for $N = 500$ is centred around a smaller mean, and it is longer.

Exercise 10.3: Repeat this example with your own pseudorandom number stream.

After we have computed the $1-\alpha$ confidence interval of (10.4), we might proceed as follows. If we find the interval *too wide*, we increase the number of simulated days.

Suppose that the desired length of the interval is $2c$, so the interval has a length of c to the left and to the right of the average $\overline{\overline{w}}$. We call c the half-width of the confidence interval. Then (10.4) gives

$$t_{m-1}^{\alpha/2}\, \frac{s_{\overline{w}}}{\sqrt{m}} = c. \tag{10.5}$$

Solving this equation for m gives $\underline{m}_c$, the desired number of simulated days:

$$\underline{m}_c = \left(t_{m_c-1}^{\alpha/2}\, \frac{s_{\overline{w}}}{c} \right)^2. \tag{10.6}$$

Unfortunately, this $\underline{m}_c$ is a random variable, whereas m in (10.5) was not. Fortunately, it can be proved that (10.6) leads to acceptable results, provided the average waiting time $\overline{w}$ is indeed normally and independently distributed. If this condition is not met well enough, then the constructed confidence interval covers the expected value $E(\overline{w})$ with a probability not equal to $1 - \alpha$. Unfortunately, the *coverage* probability is then usually smaller than $1 - \alpha$. If $\overline{w}$ has an asymmetric distribution, then Johnson's (1978) modified t test may provide a valid confidence interval. Johnson's test includes an estimate for the skewness of the distribution of $\overline{w}$; see Kleijnen, Kloppenburg, and Meeuwsen (1986).

There are a number of variations on (10.6). We may first compute $s_{\overline{w}}$ from an initial sample of size (say) m_0. So in (10.1) and (10.6) we replace m by m_0. If the resulting $s_{\overline{w}}$ yields $m_c \leqslant m_0$ then we stop: we have an acceptable confidence interval (with a length $\leqslant c$). If, however, $m_c > m_0$ we take $m_c - m_0$ additional observations on $\overline{w}$. From the total sample of size m_c we compute $\overline{\overline{w}}$. We compute the $1 - \alpha$ confidence interval (10.4) from $s_{\overline{w}}^2$ (computed from the first m_0 observations) and use a t statistic with $m_0 - 1$ degrees of freedom. A variation on this two-stage approach is purely sequential: after each observation i with $i \geqslant 2$ we update $\overline{\overline{w}}$ and $s_{\overline{w}}$ until (10.6) holds. For details on these variations we refer to Kleijnen (1987, pp. 47–50).

Exercise 10.4: Return to Exercise 10.3, and determine m such that the true mean is estimated within 0.1 units, with 95% probability. Use a two-stage approach.

10.2 NON-TERMINATING, STEADY-STATE MODELS

To non-terminating models we could apply the technique of the preceding section, which is based on independent replications. Now, however, the steady state is of interest, and this state is reached only after a very long run. So the approach of the previous section becomes expensive, because it seems natural to eliminate the transient phase when evaluating the steady state; but with m runs we must eliminate the transient phase m times. In practice, the transient phase is indeed often thrown away. However, there are some arguments against eliminating the transient phase.

(1) It is not known when exactly the transient phase is over.
(2) For simple queuing models it can be proved that the use of *all* observations minimizes the mean squared error (*MSE*). The *MSE* is defined as

$$MSE = E(\underline{x}-\mu)^2 = \text{var}(\underline{x}) + \{E(\underline{x})-\mu\}^2. \tag{10.7}$$

Note that an unbiased estimator means $E(\underline{x})=\mu$, so *MSE* reduces to var($\underline{x}$). An argument against (2) is that a minimal *MSE* does not guarantee that the confidence interval has the right coverage probability $(1-\alpha)$. (Also see Whitt, 1991.)

There are several approaches to the construction of confidence intervals in non-terminating simulations. For the remainder of this section we assume that we have a single long run instead of several replicated runs. In general, the individual waiting times $\underline{w}_t$ are correlated positively: if customer t must wait long, then the next customer $t+1$ must probably wait long too. We assume that the series of individual waiting times $(\underline{w}_t)$ forms a *wide-stationary process* (see Section 3.9):

$$E(\underline{w}_t)=\mu, \quad \text{corr}(\underline{w}_t, \underline{w}_{t+j})=\rho_j \quad \text{and} \quad \text{var}(\underline{w}_t)=\sigma_w^2 \quad \text{with } t=1,2,\ldots. \tag{10.8}$$

Let $\overline{w}$ now denote the average of m observations $\underline{w}_t$ (contrary to equation (10.2)). Then this average has the variance

$$\text{var}(\overline{w}) = \frac{\sigma_w^2}{m}\left\{1 + 2\sum_{t=1}^{m-1}\left(1-\frac{t}{m}\right)\rho_t\right\}. \tag{10.9}$$

Exercise 10.5: Prove (10.9).

If the observations $\underline{w}_t$ were independent, this formula would reduce to a well-known expression: $\rho_t=0$ yields var($\overline{w}$)$=\sigma_w^2/m$. Consider the traditional formula

$$s_{\overline{w}}^2 = \frac{\sum_{t=1}^{m}(\underline{w}_t - \overline{w}^2)}{(m-1)m}. \tag{10.10}$$

It can be proved that

$$E(\underline{s}_{\overline{w}}^2) = \frac{\sigma_w^2}{m}\left\{1 - \frac{2}{m-1}\sum_{t=1}^{m-1}\left(1-\frac{t}{m}\right)\rho_t\right\}. \tag{10.11}$$

So $\underline{s}_{\overline{w}}^2$ underestimates σ_w^2/m (still assuming positive autocorrelations). For large sample sizes m, this bias may be ignored. However, σ_w^2/m is usually much smaller than var($\overline{w}$), because of the factor in curly brackets in (10.9). So the traditional formula (10.10) leads to erroneous conclusions. For an M/M/1 model and a utilization rate of 0.5 the error amounts to a factor 10; for a 0.9 rate this factor becomes 360. Unfortunately, in practice the incorrect formula is often applied! Also see Kleijnen (1987, pp. 60–2) and Ripley (1987, pp. 143–4).

Exercise 10.6: Simulate an M/M/1 model with a utilization rate of 0.5 and 0.9 respectively, and estimate ρ_1.

In the next subsection we shall discuss batching, which is a simple method that is often applied for the construction of confidence intervals in steady-state simulations. The text on batching is followed by a subsection on renewal analysis, which is more complicated and may be skipped. We do not present the complicated methods of spectral analysis and standardized time series; Kleijnen (1987, p. 79) gives many references for these methods.

10.2.1 Nearly Independent Subruns: Batching

In batching we partition the single long run into nearly independent subruns. Now m denotes the number of subruns, and $\overline{w}_i$ the average of subrun i with $i = 1, 2, \ldots, m$. For example, if we simulate 100 000 customers (besides the customers in the transient phase), we may divide that long run into 10 subruns, each with 10 000 customers. Then the waiting time of customer #10 000 does affect customer #10 001's waiting time, but the waiting time of customer #20 000 is hardly affected by customer #10 000's waiting time. For example, an exponentially decreasing autocorrelation function ρ_t implies that $\rho_{10\,000}$ has decreased to zero, practically speaking (also see Section 3.9). Most individual waiting times within $\overline{w}_2$ (the average of subrun 2) are practically independent of the individual waiting times within $\overline{w}_1$ (the average of the preceding subrun); so $\overline{w}_1$ and $\overline{w}_2$ are virtually independent, provided the subruns are long enough (also see Kleijnen, 1974/75, p. 507). So the most important problem in batching is the choice of the subrun length: if the subruns are too short, the subrun averages $\overline{w}_i$ remain dependent and this results in a serious underestimation of the variance, as (10.9) showed. If the subruns are too long, there are only a few subruns to estimate confidence intervals such as (10.4). To solve this problem we may proceed as follows.

To test the independence of the subrun averages $\overline{w}_i$, we recommend the von Neumann statistic

$$\frac{\sum\limits_{i=2}^{m} (\overline{w}_i - \overline{w}_{i-1})^2}{\sum\limits_{i=1}^{m} (\overline{w}_i - \overline{\overline{w}})^2} \sim N(2, 4(m-2)/(m^2-1)), \qquad (10.12)$$

where the right-hand side assumes normally and independently distributed variables $\overline{w}$. A disadvantage of this test is that we need at least 100 subruns, if we want to have a reasonable chance of detecting dependence: for $m < 100$ the test has low power (high β or type II error). Obviously, when the von Neumann statistic is significant, we make the subruns longer. And so on. After we have used $m \geqslant 100$ subruns in (10.12) and found no dependence, we can follow Schmeiser's (1982) recommendation and combine those m subruns into only 10 or 20 longer subruns. Finally, the t statistic applied to these longer subruns gives a confidence interval for the mean analogous to (10.4). Subruns are further discussed in Kleijnen (1987, pp. 65–9) and Ripley (1987, pp. 150–5); the former reference includes many more references.

Exercise 10.7: Apply batching to an M/M/1 simulation with traffic load $\rho = 0.5$ and $\rho = 0.9$ respectively.

*10.2.2 Renewal Analysis

This subsection is more complicated in that it requires more knowledge of stochastic systems and mathematical statistics. Renewal or regenerative analysis uses the knowledge that some stochastic systems return to a special state that implies that the subsequent events are independent of the preceding history. For example, in a queuing model the queue becomes idle sometimes (hence waiting time is zero); an independent cycle starts as soon as a customer arrives at the idle system, provided the arrival process is Poisson. Figure 10.1 shows an example.

We emphasize that the *transient* phase does not create any problems in this analysis, because this phase is part of the first cycle. Moreover, it is not necessary to take the idle state as the renewal state; for example, the state '5 customers are waiting' is also a renewal state, provided the system is Markovian. A practical problem is that, if the utilization rate is high, then it may take a long time before the empty state occurs. If there are very many states—as may be the case in M/M/s and in network models—then it may take a long time before a specific state occurs again. We might then use 'nearly renewal' states; for example, besides the state 'zero customers waiting' we also define the state 'one customer waiting' as 'idle'.

From a statistical viewpoint, renewal analysis is interesting, because the analysis uses *ratio* estimators. For example, suppose we wish to estimate the expected steady state waiting time μ_w in an M/M/1 model. A cycle is a subrun with a stochastic length $\underline{L}$ determined by two successive entries into the renewal state. The average waiting time per cycle is

$$\underline{\overline{w}}_i = \frac{1}{\underline{L}_i} \sum_{t=1}^{\underline{L}_i} \underline{w}_{it} \qquad \text{with } i = 1, \ldots, m. \tag{10.13}$$

The traditional estimator for μ_w is

$$\underline{\overline{w}} = \frac{1}{\underline{N}} \sum_{t=1}^{N} \underline{w}_t \qquad \text{with } \underline{N} = \sum_{i=1}^{m} \underline{L}_i. \tag{10.14}$$

Waiting time of customer t

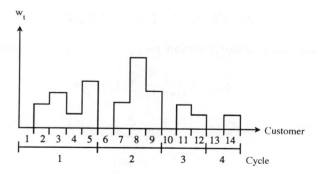

Figure 10.1 Renewal analysis

Combining both equations shows that the traditional estimator $\overline{\underline{w}}$ is identical to the weighted average of the cycle averages $\overline{\underline{w}}_i$ with weights equal to the relative cycle lengths $\underline{L}_i/\underline{N}$:

$$\overline{\underline{w}} = \frac{\sum\limits_{i=1}^{m} \sum\limits_{t=1}^{L_i} \underline{w}_{it}}{\sum\limits_{i=1}^{m} \underline{L}_i} = \frac{\sum\limits_{i=1}^{m} \underline{L}_i \overline{\underline{w}}_i}{\underline{N}}. \tag{10.15}$$

Now we define the sum of waiting times in cycle i:

$$\underline{y}_i = \sum\limits_{t=1}^{L_i} \underline{w}_{it}. \tag{10.16}$$

Combining this equation with (10.13) shows that $\underline{y}_i = \underline{L}_i \overline{\underline{w}}_i$. Obviously the average 'sum' is

$$\overline{\underline{y}} = \frac{1}{m} \sum\limits_{i=1}^{m} \underline{y}_i, \tag{10.17}$$

and the average cycle length is

$$\overline{\underline{L}} = \frac{1}{m} \sum\limits_{i=1}^{m} \underline{L}_i = \underline{N}/m. \tag{10.18}$$

So we can rewrite the traditional estimator (10.15) as

$$\overline{\underline{w}} = \overline{\underline{y}}/\overline{\underline{L}}. \tag{10.19}$$

Crane and Lemoine (1977, pp. 39–46) prove that the central limit theorem yields the asymptotic $(1-\alpha)$ confidence interval for μ_w

$$P\left\{ \left(\overline{\underline{w}} - z^{1-\alpha/2} \frac{\hat{\underline{\sigma}}/\sqrt{m}}{\overline{\underline{L}}} \right) \leqslant \mu_w \leqslant \overline{\underline{w}} + z^{1-\alpha/2} \frac{\hat{\underline{\sigma}}/\sqrt{m}}{\overline{\underline{L}}} \right\} = 1 - \alpha, \tag{10.20}$$

where $\hat{\underline{\sigma}}^2$ is defined by

$$\hat{\underline{\sigma}}^2 = \widehat{\text{var}}(\underline{y}) + \overline{\underline{w}}^2 \, \widehat{\text{var}}(\underline{L}) - 2\overline{\underline{w}} \, \widehat{\text{cov}}(\underline{y}, \underline{L}), \tag{10.21}$$

which is based on the transformation $\underline{y} - \mu_w \underline{L}$, and uses the traditional estimators

$$\widehat{\text{var}}(\underline{y}) = \frac{1}{(m-1)} \sum\limits_{i=1}^{m} (\underline{y}_i - \overline{\underline{y}})^2, \tag{10.22}$$

$$\widehat{\text{var}}(\underline{L}) = \frac{1}{(m-1)} \sum\limits_{i=1}^{m} (\underline{L}_i - \overline{\underline{L}})^2, \tag{10.23}$$

$$\widehat{\text{cov}}(\underline{y}, \underline{L}) = \frac{1}{(m-1)} \sum\limits_{i=1}^{m} (\underline{y}_i - \overline{\underline{y}})(\underline{L}_i - \overline{\underline{L}}). \tag{10.24}$$

So the confidence interval in (10.20) becomes smaller if

(1) we accept a larger α error, so $z^{1-\alpha/2}$ decreases;
(2) the estimated variances of $\underline{y}$ and $\underline{L}$ become smaller, or their covariance becomes larger;
(3) the number of subruns m increases;
(4) the mean number of customers per subrun $\underline{L}$ increases.

Exercise 10.8: Apply renewal analysis to an M/M/1 system with utilization $\rho = 0.5$ and $\rho = 0.9$ respectively.

10.3 PROPORTIONS AND QUANTILES

In practice we are often not interested in the mean μ_w but in *proportion*

$$P(\underline{w} \leqslant c) = p_c. \qquad (10.25)$$

So there is a density function of waiting times $\underline{w}$, and we wish to estimate the fraction or proportion of customers with a waiting time of at most c (c is expressed in time units). To estimate this proportion we introduce the binary variable

$$\underline{y} = \begin{cases} 0 & \text{if } \underline{w} > c; \\ 1 & \text{if } \underline{w} \leqslant c. \end{cases} \qquad (10.26)$$

An unbiased estimator of p_c is the average

$$\hat{\underline{p}}_c = \frac{1}{n} \sum_{t=1}^{n} \underline{y}_t, \qquad (10.27)$$

where n represents the number of observations on $\underline{w}$ and hence on $\underline{y}$. These observations may be dependent, as they are indeed if $\underline{w}_t$ denotes the waiting time of customer t in a queuing model.

Exercise 10.9: Prove that $E(\hat{\underline{p}}_c) = p_c$.

Exercise 10.10: If the $\underline{y}_t$ in (10.27) are independent, what is the distribution of $\hat{\underline{p}}$? What is its variance?

Exercise 10.11: Take n independent samples from the standard normal distribution: $\underline{z} \sim \text{NID}(0,1)$. Estimate the probability that $\underline{z}$ exceeds 1.28; include an 80% confidence interval. Does the true probability ($p = 0.10$) fall within the 80% confidence interval? Repeat the exercise 100 times: do 20 repetitions fail to give a confidence interval that covers $p = 0.10$?

In the terminating queuing example of this chapter, each simulated day gives an estimator $\hat{\underline{p}}_c$ of the probability of a customer having to wait at most c time units.

In other words, there are $\underline{N}$ customers per day, and we score $\underline{v}_t = 0$ if $\underline{w}_t > c$; see (10.26). The m days give m i.i.d. estimators $\hat{\underline{p}}_c$. To these m estimators we apply (10.4) where we replace $\overline{w}$ by $\hat{p}_c$ (so $\overline{\overline{w}}$ is replaced by $\hat{\overline{p}}_c$, and s_w by s_{pc}, etc.). We assume that the t test is not sensitive to possible nonnormality of $\hat{\underline{p}}_c$ (after all, $\hat{\underline{p}}_c$ is an average, as (10.27) shows).

A related question is: how much time does 95% of the customers have to wait at most? So we wish to guarantee that clients 'usually' (95%) wait no longer than a certain time, namely the 95% *quantile* $w_{0.95}$:

$$P(\underline{w} \leqslant w_{0.95}) = 0.95. \tag{10.28}$$

In general we speak of the $1 - \alpha$ quantile $w_{1-\alpha}$, which is sometimes denoted by $w^{1-\alpha}$ (also see the notation for the critical values of statistics like the t and z statistics). To estimate quantiles we *sort* the n observations w_t with $t = 1, \ldots, n$ in increasing order. This gives realizations of the so-called order statistics $\underline{w}_{(t)}$:

$$\underline{w}_{(1)} \leqslant \cdots \leqslant \underline{w}_{(t)} \leqslant \cdots \leqslant \underline{w}_{(n)} \qquad \text{with } t = 1, 2, \ldots, n. \tag{10.29}$$

The estimator of the p quantile w_p is then

$$\hat{\underline{w}}_p = \hat{\underline{w}}_{(\lfloor pn+1 \rfloor)} \qquad \text{with } 0 \leqslant p \leqslant 1 \tag{10.30}$$

where $\lfloor x \rfloor$ denotes the integral part of x. For example, for $n = 100$ and $p = 0.90$ we rank the 100 observations, and observation 91 is the estimated 90% quantile: 90% of the observations are smaller. It can be proved that this estimator is asymptotically unbiased, even if the observations $\underline{w}_t$ are dependent. If the $\underline{w}_t$ are independent, the $1 - \alpha$ confidence interval is

$$P(\hat{\underline{w}}_{(r)} \leqslant w_p < \hat{\underline{w}}_{(s)}) = 1 - \alpha, \tag{10.31}$$

where the indices r and s of the critical order statistics are

$$\begin{aligned} r &= [pn - z^{1-\alpha/2}\sqrt{(np(1-p))}] + 1 \\ s &= [pn - z^{1-\alpha/2}\sqrt{(np(1-p))}] + 1. \end{aligned} \tag{10.32}$$

In other words, we sort the n independent observations $\underline{w}_t$; the rth observation is the lower limit and the sth observation is the upper limit. Obviously (10.32) implies $r < pn$, so the lower limit is smaller than the point estimator in (10.30).

In practice, we can apply the formulae of this section as follows. In the *Monte Carlo* experiments of Chapter 7 we had M independent observations on, for example, $\underline{t}_v = (\hat{\underline{\beta}}_h - \beta_h)/\widehat{\text{var}}(\hat{\underline{\beta}}_h)^{1/2}$. We can sort these observations and estimate the $1 - \alpha$ quantile (the goal of the experiment was to compare this estimated $1 - \alpha$ quantile with the tabulated $1 - \alpha$ quantile of the Student statistic).

Exercise 10.12: Take n independent observations from the standard normal distribution: $\underline{z}_i \sim \text{NID}(0,1)$ with $i = 1, \ldots, n$. Estimate the 90% quantile $z_{0.90}$ from these n observations, including an 80% confidence interval. Does the true value $z_{0.90} = 1.28$ fall within the 80% confidence interval? Repeat the exercise 100 times; do 20 repetitions fail to give a confidence interval that covers $z_{0.90}$? (Also compare Exercise 10.11.)

In the *terminating* queuing example of the present chapter, each simulated day gives an estimator $\hat{w}_p$ of the quantile w_p: there are $\underline{N}$ customers per day, and we sort their waiting times $\underline{w}_t$ ($t = 1, \ldots, \underline{N}$) to estimate the quantile. The m independent simulated days give m i.i.d. estimators of the quantile. To these m estimators we apply not (10.31) but (10.4), where we replace the average $\overline{w}$ by the estimated quantile $\hat{w}_p$, and assume that the t test is not sensitive to non-normality of the quantile estimator.

In *non-terminating* simulations we usually make one long run. We may partition this run into m subruns, and proceed as in the case of terminating simulations. A case study is the simulation of the Europe Container Terminus (ECT) in Rotterdam, which was presented in Chapter 5. For more details on proportions and quantiles we refer to Kleijnen (1987).

10.4 VARIANCE REDUCTION TECHNIQUES

In this section we examine techniques that reduce the variance of the response of a random simulation model. 'Common' and 'antithetic' random numbers imply that pseudorandom numbers are sampled such that the expected value of the estimator does not change, but its variance decreases (see Sections 10.4.1 and 10.4.2). 'Control variates' correct for a too high or a too low value of the sampled input variables (see Section 10.4.3). There are also more complicated techniques, which we do not discuss; a detailed survey is Kleijnen (1974/75, pp. 105–285). Here we discuss only the simplest techniques, which for that reason are indeed used in practice. Actually common random numbers are used routinely.

10.4.1 Common Random Numbers

In many simulation experiments we are interested not in the 'absolute' results of an experiment but in *differences* among results for various values of parameters and exogenous variables (called 'factors' in the previous chapter). Therefore it seems obvious to examine systems under 'equal' conditions. For example, in a queuing simulation we use the same customer arrival times. This implies that we use the same pseudorandom numbers per system variant (factor combination): common random numbers. The responses are then correlated not only within a simulation run but also among runs; therefore this method is also called 'correlated sampling'. Let us consider some statistical details.

The general expression for the variance of the difference between two stochastic variables $\underline{x}$ and $\underline{y}$ is

$$\text{var}(\underline{x} - \underline{y}) = \text{var}(\underline{x}) + \text{var}(\underline{y}) - 2\,\text{cov}(\underline{x}, \underline{y}). \tag{10.33}$$

So if the use of the same pseudorandom numbers gives positive correlation, then the variance of the difference decreases. In more complicated models, however, it may be difficult to realize a strongly positive correlation. To increase the correlation we may use a separate sequence of pseudorandom numbers per 'process'. For example, in an M/M/s system we use one seed for the arrival process, a different seed for the service times at server 1, another seed for server 2, and so on. We may select these various seeds using the computer's internal clock; also see Chapter 2. Kleijnen (1974/75, pp. 200–6) discusses common random numbers in more detail.

Exercise 10.13: (a) Simulate an M/M/1 system for $\rho = 0.5$ and $\rho = 0.9$ respectively. Estimate var($\underline{d}$) where $\underline{d} = \underline{x} - \underline{y}$, and $\underline{x}$ and $\underline{y}$ represent the average waiting time of the first 1000 customers for $\rho = 0.5$ and $\rho = 0.9$ respectively. Estimate var($\underline{d}$) from 25 independent replications, once using common seeds and once using independent seeds.

(b) Simulate two M/M/s systems, namely $s = 1$ and 2 respectively. Use a series of pseudorandom numbers per process, as outlined above. Compare this approach with the following approach: sample a customer's arrival *and* service time, and feed that to a system with one and two servers respectively.

The advantage of a smaller variance comes at a price: the *analysis* of the results becomes more complicated, since the responses are no longer independent. If we analyse the simulation data by regression analysis, this dependence implies that the covariance matrix of the simulation responses is no longer diagonal. We must then use generalized least squares or corrected least squares (see Chapter 8). In practice this complication is often overlooked.

Exercise 10.14: You wish to simulate and compare only two systems (for example, M/M/s with $s = 1$ and 2 respectively). How can you still apply the t test when using common seeds? What are the degrees of freedom of the t test if you run both systems m times?

10.4.2 Antithetic Variables

The variance of the average $\bar{\underline{x}}$ of two random variables $\underline{x}_1$ and $\underline{x}_2$ is

$$\mathrm{var}(\bar{\underline{x}}) = 1/4\{\mathrm{var}(\underline{x}_1) + \mathrm{var}(\underline{x}_1) + 2\,\mathrm{cov}(\underline{x}_1, \underline{x}_2)\}. \tag{10.34}$$

Exercise 10.15: Use (10.34) to derive var($\bar{\underline{x}}$) if the variables $\underline{x}_1$ and $\underline{x}_2$ are identically and independently distributed.

If cov($\underline{x}_1, \underline{x}_2$) in (10.34) is negative, then the variance of the average $\bar{\underline{x}}$ decreases. To realize such a negative covariance we obtain the simulation response $\underline{x}_1$ using the pseudorandom numbers $\underline{r}$, while we obtain $\underline{x}_2$ using the complements or 'antithetics' $1 - \underline{r}$ in the same simulation computer program. As we saw in Chapter 2, $\underline{r}$ and $1 - \underline{r}$ are both distributed uniformly on (0,1). The correlation coefficient for $\underline{r}$ and $1 - \underline{r}$ is -1. The simulation model is a non-linear transformation of a sequence of pseudorandom numbers, and gives $\underline{x}_1$ and $\underline{x}_2$ as result. Hence $\underline{x}_1$ and $\underline{x}_2$ do not have a correlation coefficient of -1. Nevertheless we hope that an outlier in x_1 will be compensated by an opposite outlier in x_2; that is, we assume that $cov(x_1, x_2)$ is negative.

To generate the antithetic values $(1 - r_i)$, the computer does not have to calculate the complements $1 - r_i$ from r_i. Suppose the computer uses the multiplicative congruential generator $n_i = (an_{i-1}) \bmod m$ and $r_i = n_i/m$. All we have to do is replace the seed n_0 by its complement $m - n_0$; the antithetic values $1 - r_i$ are then generated automatically, as Kleijnen (1974/75, p. 254) proved. Also see the many references in Chapter 2.

Exercise 10.16: Simulate an M/M/1 model for 100 customers, with antithetic variables according to the scheme in Table 10.1.

Table 10.1

Arrival time	Service time	
r_1	$\tilde{r}_1$	
r_2	$\tilde{r}_2$	$\bar{w}_1$
$\vdots$	$\vdots$	
r_{100}	$\tilde{r}_{100}$	
$1 - r_1$	$1 - \tilde{r}_1$	
$1 - r_2$	$1 - \tilde{r}_2$	$\bar{w}_2$
$\vdots$	$\vdots$	
$1 - r_{100}$	$1 - \tilde{r}_{100}$	
r_{101}	$\tilde{r}_{201}$	
r_{102}	$\tilde{r}_{202}$	$\bar{w}_3$
$\vdots$	$\vdots$	
r_{200}	$\tilde{r}_{200}$	
$1 - r_{101}$	$1 - \tilde{r}_{101}$	
$1 - r_{102}$	$1 - \tilde{r}_{102}$	$\bar{w}_4$
$\vdots$	$\vdots$	
$1 - r_{200}$	$1 - \tilde{r}_{200}$	

(a) Are the arrival times $\underline{AT}_1 = \dfrac{-1}{\lambda} \ln(\underline{r}_1)$ and $\underline{AT}_2 = \dfrac{-1}{\lambda} \ln(\underline{r}_2)$ dependent or independent?

(b) Are $\underline{AT}_1$ and the service time $\underline{ST}_1 = \dfrac{-1}{\lambda} \ln(\tilde{r}_1)$ dependent or not, assuming $\tilde{r} \neq r$?

(c) Are $\underline{AT}_1$ and $\underline{AT}_{101} = \dfrac{-1}{\lambda} \ln(1 - \underline{r}_1)$ dependent?

(d) Are $\bar{w}_1$ and $\bar{w}_2$ dependent?
(e) Are $\bar{w}_1$ and $\bar{w}_3$ dependent?
(f) Are $(\bar{w}_1 + \bar{w}_2)/2$ and $(\bar{w}_3 + \bar{w}_4)/2$ dependent?
(g) Simulate and calculate a $1 - \alpha$ confidence interval for $E(\bar{w})$ with and without antithetic variables respectively; use 20 replications.

10.4.3 Control Variates or Regression Sampling

Let y be a random input variable, for example, service time exponentially distributed with expectation μ_y ($=1/\lambda$). Let $\bar{y}$ denote the average of T observations on y. Furthermore, $\underline{x}$ is the response variable, with $E(\underline{x}) = \mu_x$. Now we define a new estimator of μ_x, namely the *control variate*

$$\underline{x}_c = \underline{x} + \beta\,(\mu_y - \bar{y}). \tag{10.35}$$

This new estimator remains unbiased:

$$E(\underline{x}_c) = E(\underline{x}) + \beta\mu_y - \beta E(\bar{y}) = E(\underline{x}) = \mu_x. \tag{10.36}$$

The question is whether the new estimator is a better estimator. Equation (10.35) gives

$$\text{var}(\underline{x}_c) = \text{var}(\underline{x}) + \beta^2 \text{var}(\bar{y}) - 2\beta\,\text{cov}(\underline{x}, \bar{y}). \tag{10.37}$$

So the variance of the new estimator is smaller than that of the old estimator, if either

$$0 < \beta < \frac{2\,\text{cov}(\underline{x}, \bar{y})}{\text{var}(\bar{y})} \tag{10.38}$$

or

$$\frac{2\,\text{cov}(\underline{x}, \bar{y})}{\text{var}(\bar{y})} < \beta < 0. \tag{10.39}$$

The optimum value of β, say β_0, follows from differentiating (10.37) and solving for β:

$$\beta_0 = \frac{\text{cov}(\underline{x}, \bar{y})}{\text{var}(\bar{y})}. \tag{10.40}$$

We interpret this mathematical result as follows. Suppose that the output $\underline{x}$ and the input $\bar{y}$ are positively correlated, as is the case if $\underline{x}$ denotes the average waiting time and $\bar{y}$ denotes the average service time. Then a relatively high average service time ($\mu_y - \bar{y} < 0$) means that we correct the waiting time downwards: $\beta(\mu_y - \bar{y}) < 0$; see (10.35) and (10.40).

Exercise 10.17: Let $\underline{x}$ denote average waiting time and y denote interarrival time. Suppose most customer interarrival times are relatively long, that is longer than their expected value. How do (10.35) and (10.40) correct the old estimator $\underline{x}$?

In practice, we do not know $\text{cov}(\underline{x}, \bar{y})$, so we have to estimate this covariance. Consider the following estimator of β_0:

$$\hat{\beta} = \frac{\widehat{\text{cov}}(\underline{x}, \bar{y})}{\widehat{\text{var}}(\bar{y})}. \tag{10.41}$$

This estimator is identical to the ordinary least squares (OLS) estimate $\hat{\beta}$ in the model

$$\hat{x} = \hat{\alpha} + \hat{\beta}\,\bar{y}. \tag{10.42}$$

Therefore the technique of control variates is also called *regression sampling*. Note that $\hat{\beta}$ is estimated from (say) m observations $(\bar{y}_i, x_i)$ with $i = 1, \ldots, m$. For example, we have m simulated days, and day i gives a pair of correlated observations $(\bar{y}_i, \underline{x}_i)$ that is independent of the pairs for the other days. OLS is applied to estimate the line that passes through these m pairs, with the explanatory variable $\bar{y}$ and the explained variable x. OLS implies that this line passes through the 'centre of gravity' $(\bar{y}, \bar{x})$. This yields the estimated control variate

$$\hat{x}_c = \hat{x} + \underline{\beta}\mu_y$$
$$= \bar{x} + \underline{\beta}(\mu_y - \bar{y}). \tag{10.43}$$

Exercise 10.18: Simulate an M/M/1 model and let $\bar{w}$ be the average of the first 1000 customers. Take 10 macroreplications, and use as control variates

    (a) the average service time $\overline{ST}$ per replication;
    (b) the average arrival time $\overline{AT}$ per replication;
    (c) the average service time and the average arrival time per replication (hint: derive the multiple regression equivalent of (10.42));
    (d) the estimated utilization rate $\hat{\rho} = \overline{ST}/\overline{AT}$ per replication.

A problem is that substitution of the estimator $\hat{\beta}$ into (10.35) leads to a biased control variate. Moreover, the construction of a confidence interval becomes problematic. These problems can be solved if we assume a bivariate normal distribution for the pairs $(\underline{x}, \bar{y})$. A robust solution uses jackknifing, which we shall discuss in the next section. Control variates are also discussed by Kleijnen et al. (1989) in an auditing context.

10.5 JACKKNIFING

Jackknifing is a computer-intensive 'trick' that has the following two objectives:

(1) reduce possible *bias* of an estimator,
(2) calculate a *'robust' confidence interval*, that is, an interval that also holds if the original observations are mutually dependent or nonnormal.

Miller (1974) gives the classic review of jackknifing. We present the basics.

Suppose we have m observations x_j ($j = 1, 2, \ldots, m$) that yield an estimator $\hat{\vartheta}$; for example, $\hat{\vartheta}$ is the average $\Sigma_{j=1}^{m} x_j/m$. We partition those m observations into N groups of equal size M ($= m/N$); N may be equal to m (so $M = 1$). We eliminate one group of observations, and we calculate the same estimator from the remaining $(N-1)M$ observations (this is analogous to cross-validation in Section 8.4.1). For example, we compute $\hat{\vartheta}_1 = \Sigma_{j=M+1}^{m} x_j/\{(N-1)M\}$. Each time we eliminate another group, so that we get N estimators $\hat{\vartheta}_i$ ($i = 1, 2, \ldots, N$). The *pseudovalue* $\underline{J}_i$ is defined as the following linear combination of the original and the ith estimator:

$$\underline{J}_i = N\hat{\vartheta} - (N-1)\,\hat{\vartheta}_i \qquad \text{with } i = 1, 2, \ldots, N. \tag{10.44}$$

The jackknifed estimator is defined as the average pseudovalue:

$$\bar{J} = \frac{1}{N} \sum_{i=1}^{N} J_i = N\bar{\vartheta} - (N-1)\bar{\bar{\vartheta}}, \tag{10.45}$$

where $\bar{\bar{\vartheta}} = \sum_{i=1}^{N} \bar{\vartheta}_i / N$. It can be proved that if the original estimator $\bar{\vartheta}$ is biased, then the jackknifed estimator $\bar{J}$ has less bias. Obviously, if $\bar{\vartheta}$ is unbiased, then $\bar{\vartheta}_i$ is unbiased and so is $\bar{J}$. Moreover, jackknifing results in a robust confidence interval, if we treat the N pseudovalues J_j as N independently and identically distributed variables, and compute the $1 - \alpha$ confidence interval from the Student statistic with $N-1$ degrees freedom:

$$\underline{t}_{N-1} = \frac{(\bar{J} - \vartheta)}{\underline{s}_J / \sqrt{N}}, \tag{10.46}$$

where $\underline{s}_J$ is the square root of

$$\underline{s}_J^2 = \frac{\sum_{i=1}^{N} (J_i - \bar{J})^2}{N-1}. \tag{10.47}$$

EXAMPLE 10.3: CONTROL VARIATE

In Section 10.4.3 we had m replications; that is, we had the pairs $\bar{y}_j, x_j$ with $j = 1, \ldots, m$. After eliminating pair j, we calculate the control variate $\hat{x}_{c(-j)}$ analogous to (10.43):

$$\hat{x}_{c(-j)} = \bar{x}_{-j} + \hat{\beta}_{-j}(\mu_y - \bar{\bar{y}}_{-j}) \qquad \text{with } j = 1, \ldots, m, \tag{10.48}$$

where $\bar{x}_{-j}$ is the average of the $m-1$ observations on the simulation response x that result after elimination of one observation, namely x_j; analogously $\bar{\bar{y}}_{-j}$ is the average of the $m-1$ observations on the average simulation input $\bar{y}$ that result after elimination of $\bar{y}_j$; finally $\hat{\beta}_{-j}$ is the OLS estimator of β in (10.42) computed from the $m-1$ pairs that result from eliminating the pair $(\bar{y}_j, x_j)$. Those $\hat{x}_{c(-j)}$ give the pseudovalues J_j

$$J_j = m\hat{x}_c - (m-1)\hat{x}_{c(-j)} \qquad \text{with } j = 1, \ldots, n, \tag{10.49}$$

where $\hat{x}_c$ is computed from all m pairs; see (10.43).

Exercise 10.19: Apply jackknifing to the control variate example of Exercise 10.18 (d).

*EXAMPLE 10.4: RENEWAL ANALYSIS

In Section 10.2.2 we may eliminate one cycle at a time, so that (10.19) results in

$$\bar{w}_{-j} = \frac{\bar{y}_{-j}}{\bar{L}_{-j}} \qquad \text{with } j = 1, 2, \ldots, m.$$

And so on.

Exercise 10.20: Apply jackknifing to the renewal example of Exercise 10.8.

EXAMPLE 10.5: ESTIMATED WEIGHTED LEAST SQUARES

In Chapter 7 we introduced estimated weighted least squares (EWLS). We estimated σ_i^2 from m_i replications. To jackknife this estimator, we eliminate one replication per input combination. Then m_i becomes $m_i - 1$; and so on. For details we refer to Kleijnen et al. (1987).

REFERENCES

Crane M. A. and A. J. Lemoine (1977) *An Introduction to the Regenerative Method for Simulation Analysis*, Springer-Verlag, Berlin.

Johnson N. J. (1978) Modified *t* tests and confidence intervals for asymmetric populations, *Journal American Statistical Association*, **73**, 536–44.

Kleijnen J. P. C. (1974/75) *Statistical Techniques in Simulation* (two volumes), Marcel Dekker, New York.

Kleijnen J. P. C. (1987) *Statistical Tools for Simulation Practitioners*, Marcel Dekker, New York.

Kleijnen J. P. C., G. L. J. Kloppenburg, and F. L. Meeuwsen (1986) Testing the mean of an asymmetric population: Johnson's modified *t*-test revisited, *Communications in Statistics, Simulation and Computation*, **15**(3), 715–32.

Kleijnen J. P. C., P. C. A. Karremans, W. K. Oortwijn, and W. J. H. Van Groenendaal (1987) Jackknifing estimated weighted least squares: JEWLS, *Communications in Statistics, Theory and Methods*, **16**(3), 747–64.

Kleijnen J. P. C., J. Kriens, H. Timmermans and H. Van den Wildenberg (1989) Regression sampling in statistical auditing, a practical survey and evaluation, *Statistica Neerlandica*, April, 193–209, 225.

Miller R. G. (1974) The jackknife—a review, *Biometrica*, **61**, 1–15.

Ripley B. D. (1987) *Stochastic Simulation*, Wiley, New York.

Schmeiser B. W. (1982) Batch size effects in the analysis of simulation output, *Operations Research*, **30**(3), 556–68.

Whitt W. (1991) The efficiency of one long run versus independent replications in steady-state simulation, *Management Science*, **37**(6), 645–66.

Verification and Validation

Once we have programmed a simulation model, we must verify that no programming errors have been made. Next we ask if the model is a valid representation of reality. Unfortunately, there are no perfect solutions for the problems of verification and validation. Note that these problems are not confined to simulation models.

Sargent (1991) states

the *conceptual model* is the mathematical/logical/verbal representation (mimic) of the problem entity developed for a particular study; and the *computerized model* is the conceptual model implemented on a computer. The conceptual model is developed through an *analysis and modelling phase*, the computerized model is developed through a *computer programming and implementation phase*, and inferences about the problem entity are obtained by conducting computer experiments on the computerized model in the *experimentation phase*.

Chapter 11 is organized as follows.

—Section 11.1 Verification
   We discuss how to discover programming errors.
—Section 11.2 Validation
   We show how to investigate whether the model is a good representation of reality.
—Section 11.3 Case-study: mine hunting by sonar
   We illustrate several validation problems through a case study.

11.1 VERIFICATION

Once we have programmed the simulation model, we should check whether any mistakes have been made. We may proceed as follows.

(1) We can calculate some results manually, and compare these data with results of the simulation program. Getting all intermediate results from a computer program is called *tracing*. Even if we do not wish to calculate intermediate results by hand, we can still 'eyeball' the program's trace and look for 'bugs'. Simulation software provides tracing facilities and more advanced 'debuggers'; see Pegden et al. (1990, pp. 137–48).

Moreover, we may verify certain *modules* of the simulation program. For example, we might check the pseudorandom number generator, if we had to program it ourselves or if we do not trust the software supplier's expertise (see Section 2.4). GPSS/H automatically computes chi-square statistics to test the hypothesis that the pseudorandom numbers used are uniformly distributed; see Schriber (1991, p. 317). We may compute the average of a sampled input variable such as service time, and compare that average to its expected value. Random deviations between average and expectation can be used to improve the estimated output, as we saw in Section 10.4.3 on control variates. Systematic deviations between the (observed) average and the (theoretical) mean may be tested through the t test. Examples were presented in Chapter 3 (Exercise 3.11 in the Appendix), where we pointed out that the user may mix up the variance and the standard deviation of the normal distribution. The user may further specify the wrong unit of measurement, for example, seconds instead of minutes (so the results are wrong by a factor 60). Instead of testing the mean, we can test the whole distribution through a goodness-of-fit test such as the chi-square test in (2.10).

(2) The final output of the simulation program may result only after (say) a hundred thousand customers have been processed and the steady state has been reached. That result can be verified by running a simplified version of the program with a known *analytical solution*, provided we can find such a version. In the Appendix of Chapter 5 we presented steady-state expectations for several output measures of the $M/M/n$ model. For certain queuing networks we can compute steady-state solutions numerically (see Lavenberg, 1983). In the steady state the system is still stochastic (but the probability law that governs the stochastic process no longer depends on the initial state). So we should use mathematical statistics to test that the expected value of (say) $\bar{x}$, the simulation program's average output, equals the computed steady state expectation μ:

$$H_0 : E(\bar{x}) = \mu. \tag{11.1}$$

To test this hypothesis we may assume normality, and estimate the variance of $\bar{x}$. In the preceding chapter we explained how to estimate this variance. If, for example, we use m subruns to compute the estimated variance $s_{\bar{x}}^2$ of $\bar{x}$, then the test statistic becomes

$$t_{m-1} = \frac{\bar{x} - \mu}{s_{\bar{x}}} = \frac{\bar{x} - \mu}{s_x / \sqrt{m}}. \tag{11.2}$$

If the simulation has multiple responses (as is usually the case), then we can apply Bonferroni's inequality to preserve the overall 'experimentwise' error rate (as we saw in Section 8.4). We shall present an example in Section 11.3. Multivariate techniques are alternatives to the combination of univariate techniques and Bonferroni's inequality; see Balci and Sargent (1984b).

In Monte Carlo studies on the performance of statistical procedures, we often know the analytic solution provided distributions are normal or sample sizes are large. For example, in Section 7.5.1 we showed how to verify parts of a Monte Carlo computer program, applying (11.2). For some models we know the theoretical output, provided the inputs are deterministic. Examples can be found in Chapter 4 on economic models. In that case we can verify the correctness of the simulation program, at least for one set of inputs.

(3) To verify the computer program of a dynamic system we may use *animation*, which we briefly discussed in Section 6.2 on simulation software. So we present the user a moving picture of the simulated system. The user is well qualified to detect certain errors in the simulated behaviour. These errors may be either programming errors or modelling errors; the latter type will be discussed below.

Exercise 11.1: Simulate average waiting time (say)

$$\overline{w} = \sum_{i=1}^{N} \frac{w_i}{N}$$

of the M/M/1 model; start the simulation in the empty state. To verify the simulation program, test the null-hypothesis

$$H_0 : E(\overline{w}) = \mu,$$

where μ denotes the analytically computed steady-state mean waiting time. Study the eight cases that result from combining

(a) 'long' versus 'short' simulation runs (steady-state versus transient simulation);
(b) 'light' versus 'heavy' traffic (short versus long warm-up period);
(c) a 'few' versus 'many' macroreplications (low versus high power of the test).

Simulation programs have special problems and opportunities. Software engineers have developed procedures for writing good computer programs and for verifying software in general: modular programming, chief programmer's approach, structured walk-throughs, correctness proofs, and so on; see Baber (1987), DeMillo et al. (1987), and Whitner and Balci (1989). The book by DeMillo et al. has a comprehensive bibliography.

11.2 VALIDATION

Once we believe that the simulation model is programmed correctly, we ask: is this a *valid* model? By definition, a valid model gives a 'good' representation of reality. This raises several questions. Some of these questions are quite philosophical; for example, do we really know reality or do we have only flickering images of reality (as Plato stated)? Ignoring these philosophical questions, it is obvious that we must make our knowledge of reality 'operational'; that is, we must explicitly formulate the laws that we think govern the simulated system, and we should measure inputs and outputs of the real system (the system concept implies that we subjectively decide on the boundary of the system and on the attributes we want to quantify; see Section 1.2). Sometimes it is difficult or impossible to obtain these measurements. For example, in a simulation of the recovery of the US economy after a nuclear attack, it is (fortunately) impossible to get these data. In simulation we often examine several system variants (in order to select a 'good' variant), but usually we have data only on the existing variant or on a few historical variants. In the military, however, it is usual to conduct field tests in order to obtain data on *future* variants. In Section 11.3 we shall present a case study. Shannon (1975, pp. 231–3) briefly discusses field tests, too. Sometimes simulation is meant to predict not relative responses, which correspond to different system variants, but absolute responses. In the latter case, validation is more difficult; an example will be discussed in the case study of Section 11.3.

To validate the simulation model, we feed it real-life input data in historical order (assuming that those data are indeed available); this is sometimes called 'trace driven' simulation. We run the simulation program, obtain the simulation output, and compare that output to the real-life output of the existing system. So we do not sample the simulation input (from the—raw or smoothed—histogram of real-life input values); instead we use the historical values in historical order: $(x_{-T}, x_{-T+1}, \ldots, x_{-1}, x_0)$ where $T+1$ denotes the size of the historical sample. The further we go back into the past, the more data we get and the more powerful the validation test will be, unless we go so far back that different laws governed the system. For example, in many econometric models we do not use data prior to 1945. The output data of the real system and the simulated system can be plotted such that the horizontal axis denotes time $(t = -T, -T+1, \ldots, -1, 0)$ and the vertical axis denotes the observed and simulated values respectively. We usually 'eyeball' these timepaths to decide whether the simulation model adequately reflects the phenomena of interest. For example, do the simulation data indicate an economic downturn in a business cycle study; do the simulation data show saturation behaviour (such as exploding queue lengths) in a queuing study?

Instead of eyeballing the time series, we can use mathematical statistics. The problem with the statistical analysis of simulation output data is that these data form a time series, whereas elementary statistical procedures assume identically and independently distributed (i.i.d.) observations. As we saw in Chapter 10 on tactical aspects, we can try to derive independent observations. Then we can apply elementary statistical theory. For example, let us denote the *average* waiting time on day i in the simulated and the real system by $\underline{w}_i$ and $\underline{v}_i$ respectively, with $i = 1, \ldots, n$. Suppose further that we use the historical arrival times to drive the simulation model (in the case study of Section 11.3 we shall not be able to use historical inputs). Hence we can define the 'paired' differences $\underline{d}_i = \underline{w}_i - \underline{v}_i$. Then the t statistic is

$$\underline{t}_{n-1} = \frac{\overline{\underline{d}} - \delta}{\underline{s}_d / \sqrt{n}}, \tag{11.3}$$

where $\overline{\underline{d}}$ is the average and $\underline{s}_d$ is the estimated standard deviation of $\underline{d}$ (so $\overline{\underline{d}}$ is the average of the n differences between two average waiting times per day). If for $\delta = 0$ the calculated value of $\underline{t}_{n-1}$ is significant, then we reject the model. If $\delta = 0$ gives a non-significant $\underline{t}_{n-1}$, then we conclude that the simulated and the real means are 'practically' the same so the simulation is 'valid enough'. Strictly speaking, the simulation is only a model (not reality), so a large enough sample size n would show that δ is not exactly zero. When testing the validity of a model through statistics like (11.3), we can make 'type I' and 'type II' errors respectively: we may reject the model while the model is valid, and we may accept the model while the model is not valid, respectively. The type I error may be called the model builder's risk; the type II error is the model user's risk. The power of the statistical test increases as the model specification error δ increases. A significance or 'critical' level α means that the type I error equals α. Obviously the type II or β error increases as α decreases, given a fixed sample size n. To decrease both error probabilities we can increase the sample size n and decrease the variance of the simulated system, var($\underline{w}$), through variance reduction techniques (discussed in Chapter 10). Balci and Sargent (1984b) give a theoretical trade-off analysis among these factors (sample size, and so on).

A most stringent validation test requires not only that the means of the model and the historical observations are identical, but also that if a historical observation exceeds its mean then the corresponding model observation (that is the observation that uses the same inputs as the historical observation did) tends to exceed its mean, too. For example, $\underline{v}$ and $\underline{w}$ should not only have the same mean but also be *positively correlated*. To investigate this correlation we can plot w versus v, as we saw in the chapter on regression analysis. We can formalize this graphical approach using least squares, and we can apply a test if certain statistical assumptions hold and there are enough observations to make the test powerful enough. Testing the hypothesis of positively correlated $\underline{v}$ and $\underline{w}$ is simple if $\underline{v}$ and $\underline{w}$ are bivariate normally distributed (which is a realistic assumption in the example, because of a central limit theorem). It can be proved that a bivariate normal distribution implies

$$E(\underline{w}\,|\,\underline{v}=v)=\beta_0+\beta_1 v. \tag{11.4}$$

So we can plot w as a function of v, and use ordinary least squares to estimate the intercept and slope of the straight line that passes through the 'cloud' of points (v_i, w_i); the formulae were given in Chapter 7. Our stringent test calls the model valid if the following composite hypothesis holds:

$$H_0: \beta_0=0 \qquad \text{and} \qquad \beta_1=1, \tag{11.5}$$

which implies $E(\underline{w})=E(\underline{v})$ (as tested through equation (11.3)). Moreover it can be proved that

$$\beta_1=\rho\,\frac{\sigma_w}{\sigma_v}. \tag{11.6}$$

This equality implies that, if $\beta_1=1$ and $\rho<1$ then $\sigma_w>\sigma_v$, that is, if the model is not perfect, then its variance exceeds the real variance. (If $\beta_1=1$ and $\sigma_w=\sigma_v$ then $\rho=1$, which is an unrealistic case; if $\beta_1=1$ and $\sigma_w<\sigma_v$ then $\rho>1$, which violates the statistical model.) To test the hypothesis of (11.5), we compute the sum of squared errors (SSE) with and without that hypothesis (the 'reduced' and the 'full' model respectively), and compare these two values, as follows. Based on the full model (11.4) we compute

$$\hat{\underline{w}}_i=\hat{\beta}_0+\hat{\beta}_1\,\underline{v}_i, \tag{11.7}$$

which yields

$$\underline{SSE}_{\text{full}}=\sum_1^n (\underline{w}_i-\hat{\underline{w}}_i)^2. \tag{11.8}$$

Next we compute the SSE under the composite hypothesis of (11.5) (obviously a restricted model gives a higher SSE). That hypothesis implies $\hat{w} = v$, so

$$SSE_{\text{reduced}} = \sum_{1}^{n} (\underline{w}_i - \underline{v}_i)^2. \tag{11.9}$$

It can be proved that the following expression is an F statistic with degrees of freedom 2 (the number of parameters in the hypothesis of equation (11.5)) and $n - 2$ (the degrees of freedom of the SSE for the full model, where the factor 2 occurs because two parameters are estimated in that model):

$$\underline{F}_{2, n-2} = \frac{(SSE_{\text{reduced}} - SSE_{\text{full}})/2}{SSE_{\text{full}}/(n - 2)}. \tag{11.10}$$

If the computed F statistic is significantly high, we reject the hypothesis in (11.5) and conclude that the model is not valid. For details on this F test we refer to Kleijnen (1987, pp. 156–7).

We may formulate a less stringent validation requirement: the means are not necessarily equal, but the model and the real responses are positively correlated. This requirement makes sense if the model is used to predict relative responses (as in sensitivity analysis), not absolute responses. To test this hypothesis we formulate the null-hypothesis

$$H_0 : \beta_1 \leqslant 0. \tag{11.11}$$

To test this hypothesis we use the t statistic, as we saw in Chapter 7. This means that we reject the null-hypothesis of (11.11) and accept the model if there is strong evidence that the model and the real-life responses are *positively* correlated.

Note that statistical analyses as in (11.3)–(11.11) require many observations. In validation, however, there are often not many observations on the real system.

In a more sophisticated analysis we estimate the autocorrelation structure from the simulated and the historical time series respectively, and compare these two structures (spectral analysis is the technique developed for the estimation of autocorrelation functions; unfortunately, that analysis is rather sophisticated and requires long time series).

A simple technique is the *Schruben–Turing* test, which runs as follows. We present a mixture of computer output and real-life output to one or more users, and we challenge them to identify the data that was generated by computer. Of course, they may correctly identify some of the data by mere chance; this, however, we can test statistically. Turing introduced this procedure to validate artificial intelligence computer programs: which data is generated by computer, and which is provided by humans? Schruben (1980) applied this concept to the validation of simulation models. He discusses several statistical tests and case studies.

Above we mentioned that going far back into the past may yield historical data that are not representative of the current system; that is, the old system was ruled by different laws. Similarly, a model is adequate only if the values of its input data remain within a certain area. One example we saw in Chapter 8 on metamodelling: a regression model of *first* order is a good approximation of a simulated M/M/1 system only if the traffic load is 'low'. In practice, there are many input variables, and we should use experimental designs combined with regression analysis (or analysis of variance, ANOVA) to detect the important factors. For the important factors we must obtain accurate information on the values that may occur in practice. For example, we applied experimental designs and regression analysis to a model of the greenhouse effect of carbon dioxide (CO_2) and other gases. The computed sensitivity estimates should have the right signs: some factors are known to increase global temperature. The magnitudes of the sensitivity estimates show which factors are important so accurate information must be collected or—if the factors are controllable—their emissions should be restricted. For details see Bettonvil and Kleijnen (1992) and Kleijnen, Rotmans, and Van Ham (1992). We shall return to this issue in the case study of Section 11.3.

Note that if a factor is qualitative, then we can estimate the effects of the quantitative factors *per* scenario. If these estimates do not vary with the scenario, then there are no interactions between the quantitative and the qualitative factors.

Some authors claim that a model should remain valid under 'extreme' conditions; see Banks (1989). We, however, state that a model is valid only within a certain experimental domain. For example, Bettonvil and Kleijnen's (1992) sensitivity analysis shows that the ecological simulation model is valid only if the factors range over a relatively small area. Zeigler (1976, p. 30) emphasizes the concept of *experimental frame*, that is, 'a limited set of circumstances under which the real system is to be observed or experimented with . . . a model may be valid in one experimental frame but invalid in another'.

Sensitivity analysis should be applied to find out which inputs are really important. Collecting information on those inputs is worth the effort. If nevertheless it is impossible or impractical to collect reliable information on those inputs, *risk analysis* may be applied. A probability distribution of inputs is then derived from the users' expert knowledge, which yields a probability distribution of output values; see Section 4.6. The relationship between sensitivity and risk analyses requires more research; see Kleijnen (1990).

Note that model 'calibration' means that a model's parameters are adjusted such that its output resembles the real system's output. Obviously, those latter data can *not* be used to validate the model. We refer back to cross-validation, discussed in Section 8.4.1.

The validation of simulation models is closely related to the validation of other mathematical models, such as models in regression analysis, inventory control, and linear programming. We have already mentioned some typical aspects of simulation models; for example, the time series character of its inputs and outputs (because simulation is dynamic), and the random noise in stochastic simulation and Monte Carlo models. Other models share some of these characteristics with simulation models. For example, an econometric model may also be dynamic and stochastic. Another typical aspect of simulation is that its models are based on common sense or on direct observation of the real-life system; that is, the latter system is not a black box. For example, a simulation model of a queuing system represents intuitive knowledge about the system: a customer arrives, looks for an idle server, and so on. Connecting the modules for system parts gives the total simulation model, which grows in complexity and—hopefully—realism (also see the corporate model in Section 4.5.1). Such a bottom-up approach cannot be followed in other models. Note that animation may help to obtain 'face validity'. In some applications, however, the simulation model is given by the theories of a certain discipline (for example, economics), and these models may then be black-box models.

The validation of black-box models is more difficult, since we can measure input and output data only. The emphasis in validation is then on prediction, not explanation.

The model's validity is determined by its assumptions. Therefore these assumptions should be stated in the model documentation. (Being explicit about one's assumptions is the difference between a scientist and a politician, we think.) In practice, however, many assumptions are left implicit. The importance of documentation is discussed at length by Fossett et al. (1991). They define *assessment* as 'a process by which interested parties (who were not involved in a model's origins, development, and implementation) can determine, with some level of confidence, whether or not a model's result can be used in decision making' (Fossett et al., 1991, p. 711). Important components of assessment are verification and validation. They further define *credibility* as 'the level of confidence in [a simulation's] results' (Fossett et al., 1991, p. 712). They present a framework for assessing the credibility of a simulation; this framework comprises 14 factors (these factors are also discussed in this chapter, explicitly or implicitly). They apply this framework to three military weapon simulations (in Section 11.3 we shall present another military case study). Gass (1984) proposes to produce four manuals, namely for analysts, users, programmers, and managers respectively.

Validation and verification are further discussed in Banks and Carson (1984), Law and Kelton (1991, pp. 298–324), and Pegden, Shannon, and Sadowski (1990, pp. 133–62). These textbooks give many additional references. We also refer to the production-planning case study in Kleijnen (1992) and the cigarette fabrication case study in Carson (1989). Dekker, Groenendijk, and Sliggers (1990) discuss the verification and validation of models that are used to compute air pollution; these models are needed to issue permits for building new factories and the like. Validation of system dynamics models is discussed in Kleijnen (1980, p. 137) and Wolstenhome (1990, pp. 58–60). Banks (1989) proposes control charts, which are used in quality control. Reckhow (1989) discusses several more statistical techniques. Balci and Sargent (1984a) give a detailed bibliography.

Models resemble information systems. Actually, models are a key element in some types of information systems, namely decision support systems (DSSs). The problems of developing 'good' information systems are notorious; see Davis and Olson (1985).

This book demonstrates the importance of mathematical statistics in simulation. Nevertheless we believe that the developers and users of a simulation model should be convinced of its validity, not only by statistics but also in many other ways, some of which have been presented above. In conclusion, modelling—including simulation—has elements of art as well as science.

11.3 CASE STUDY: MINE HUNTING BY SONAR

In Section 11.3.1 we give the conceptual model of mine hunting at sea by means of sonar. In Section 11.3.2 we validate the resulting simulation model. First we perform sensitivity analysis for some modules that give intermediate simulated results. Next we compare simulated detection probabilities resulting from the model as a whole, with real-life probabilities; we test if simulated and real probabilities are equal. We emphasize the importance of measuring the environment or scenario that drives the simulation and the field test respectively. We further test whether the estimated simulation and real detection probabilities are positively correlated (not necessarily equal). In Section 11.3.3 we discuss future research. Some factors have been modelled rather poorly as qualitative factors. And 'false' detections may be counted as detections: measurement errors. We do not give many data since most data are confidential or not available.

11.3.1 Conceptual Model of Mine Hunting

Conceptually, a sonar installation may be viewed as a torchlight; that is, in the 'dark' a certain area becomes 'lighted' so objects within that area can become visible. As the ship's sonar moves, new areas become visible, while old areas become invisible again. Mines can be detected only when they are within the area 'lighted' by the sonar. The following discussion gives some information on the model presented in Figure 11.1.

As the name 'sonar' suggests, sonar performance depends on sound velocity, which varies with water temperature and salinity. Obviously these characteristics vary with the water depth. The *sound velocity profile* (SVP) maps sound velocity as a function of depth. In the model the SVP is a simple piecewise-linear function that is kept constant during the whole simulation run. In practice, the SVP varies from place to place. And at another time, the SVP at the same place will be different, because of seasonal and daily variations.

When an object is 'lighted' by the sonar, its echo appears on the sonar screen with a certain *contrast*. This contrast depends deterministically on, for example, the 'aspect' angle at which the sonar beam hits the object. Harmless objects may look like mines because there is acoustic noise, which generates 'spurious' contrasts. Mines may be hidden behind hills on the sea bottom: the bottom profile may be important.

A contrast may be missed by the *human operator*. Human behaviour shows noise and is therefore represented by statistical distribution functions, called 'operator curves'. An object is visible only during a certain time, which depends on the sonar 'search window' (like the light circle of a torch) and the position of the object relative to the ship's course. The longer an object is visible, the higher its detection probability. When the object becomes invisible or the operator is busy, the detection probability drops to zero. The operator must classify the observed contrast as either a mine or a harmless object. That classification may be true or false. The model, however, does not cover this classification stage nor any other follow-up operations such as sending an unmanned minisubmarine to identify a classified object or to neutralize or destroy the mine.

The laws of physics that govern sonar performance are represented by deterministic relationships. The environment, however, is not well known: the SVP and sea bottom profile are uncertain. So, even if the model were perfect, it would give the wrong answer when fed with the wrong inputs. This type of uncertainty must be distinguished from random noise in the operator module; see also Kleijnen (1990).

Another problem is the continuous character of time in many physics laws (see also Chapters 4 and 5). The simulation model, however, is programmed with time sliced into periods of fixed length: differential equations are approximated by difference equations. If the ship's speed is two metres per second, a time slice of three seconds gives acceptable numerical accuracy.

The model is 'calibrated', that is, a parameter is used to correct the computed contrasts such that the model's outputs are closer to the real outputs; this parameter has no physical interpretation.

The model is used for different *purposes*. In sensitivity analysis, different tactics for mine hunting are compared; for example, the angle of the sonar may be changed. Moreover, a given tactic may give different results depending on the environment; therefore the non-controllable factors should also be investigated. Absolute predictions are needed to determine the 'huntability' of the minefield.

Altogether the simulation model has nearly 40 factors; some were mentioned above. Figure 11.1 shows the various modules of the model. There are actually several variants of the model. For example, the SVP may be either input to the model or it may be calculated as a function of salinity and temperature; so in the figure SVP is displayed

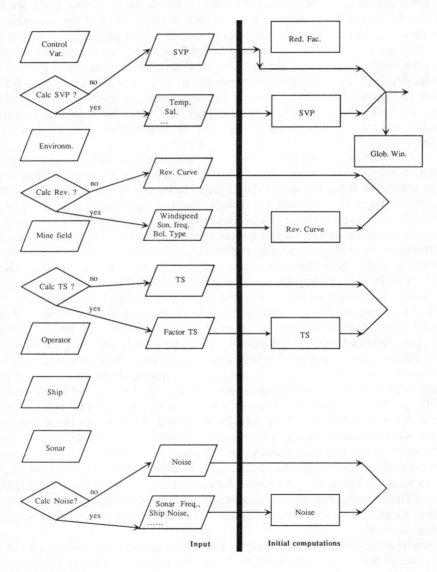

Figure 11.1 Mine-hunting model

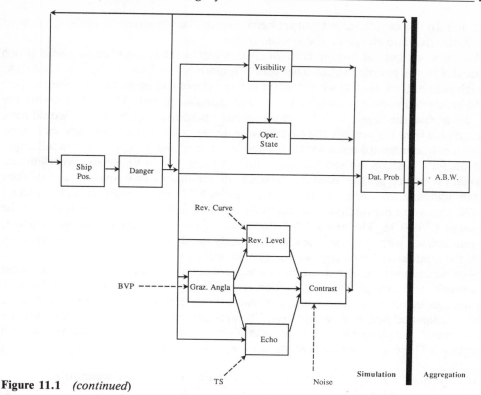

Figure 11.1 *(continued)*

not at the extreme left (input), but more to the right (initial computations).

11.3.2 Validation of Mine-hunting Model

Some modules give *intermediate* outputs that are impossible or hard to validate. We then apply sensitivity analysis per module. Because of time constraints we examine only the 'sonar window' module and the 'visibility' module.

The response variables of the *sonar window* module are the maximum and the minimum distance of the sonar beam on the sea bottom. First we consider the minimum distance. We investigate three factors: SVP or x_1, average water depth or x_2, and the sonar downward angle (relative to the ship's keel) or x_3. The response depends deterministically on these factors. Our regression metamodel is a second-order approximation in x_2 and x_3. It gives a multiple correlation coefficient R^2 between 0.96 and 0.98, for four different SVPs (we could also have used cross-validation; see Section 8.4.1). Qualitative knowledge about the simulated module suggests that the regression coefficients should have specific signs: $\beta_2 > 0$, $\beta_3 < 0$, and $\beta_{23} < 0$. The estimates turn out to have the right signs; the pure quadratic effects are not significantly different from zero. For the second response, maximum distance, similar results hold, except for one SVP that results in an R^2 of only 0.68 and a non-significant β_2. We trust the underlying simulation module more if the estimated regression coefficients have the right signs, provided of course that the metamodel fits reasonably well so the coefficients have some meaning. In this case the input/output behaviour of the simulation module agrees with the qualitative knowledge of the system analysts.

An object on the sea bottom is *visible* if it is within the sonar window and it is not concealed by the bottom profile. That profile is modelled by a simple geometric pattern, namely hills of fixed heights with constant upward slopes and uniform downward slopes. A fixed bottom profile is used within a single simulation run. The response variable is the time that the object is visible, expressed as a percentage of the time it would have been visible were the bottom flat (so no concealment could occur). We vary six inputs: water depth, downward sonar angle, hill height, upward hill slope, downward hill slope, and object's position on the hill slope (top, bottom, or in between). We eliminate navigation error, so the module becomes deterministic. We specify a quadratic metamodel, and use a central composite design with 77 input combinations to estimate the 28 regression parameters. The multiple correlation coefficient R^2 is 0.86 and the adjusted R^2 is 0.78. The upward hill slope has no significant effects (no main effect, no interactions with the other factors, no purely quadratic effect); these results agree with the qualitative knowledge of the system analysts.

Next we compare simulated mine detection probabilities, which result from the model as a whole, with real probabilities, which are estimated from field tests. Let M denote the number of mines in the minefield (simulated or real); R and K denote the number of simulation and field runs respectively. The simulated and the real probabilities depend on uncertain but deterministic inputs like SVP and mine location, together called a 'scenario'. There are numerous scenarios (say) S_h with $h = 1, 2, \ldots$. So we define

$$\underline{x}_{ijh} = 1 \text{ if mine } i \text{ is detected in simulation run } j \text{ under scenario } h,$$
$$\text{where } i = 1, \ldots, M \text{ and } j = 1, \ldots, R \text{ and } h = 1, 2, \ldots \tag{11.12}$$

Obviously $\underline{x}_{ijh} = 0$ if that mine is *not* detected. This leads to the conditional probabilities

$$P(\underline{x}_{ij} = 1 \,|\, S_h) = p_{ih}. \tag{11.13}$$

For the field runs we replace x by y, j by k (with $k = 1, \ldots, K$), and p by q in (11.12) and (11.13). To estimate p_{ih} from R simulation runs, we keep the scenario fixed at S_h and use pseudorandom numbers to sample navigation errors, spurious contrasts, and human operator performance. Now consider

$$p_i = \sum_h P(\underline{x}_{ij} = 1 \,|\, S_h) P(S_h) \neq P(\underline{x}_{ij} = 1 \,|\, E(S)). \tag{11.14}$$

To estimate p_i (the average detection probability of mine i over all scenarios) we must sample scenarios too. The average scenario $E(S)$ may be an impossible scenario, that is, a scenario that can never occur. We claim that the validation procedure should test, not the unconditional probabilities p_i and q_i, but the conditional probabilities p_{ih} and q_{ih}. Figure 11.2 illustrates how the detection probabilities (simulated or real) may depend on the scenario; it includes confidence intervals for the estimators of these probabilities. At scenario S_1 the model is not valid; at S_2 it is valid, and at S_3 it may be considered acceptable. If, however, the model is run with scenario S_2 whereas the field test uses scenario S_1, then the model might be (incorrectly) rejected. So we must estimate whether the simulated and the real detection probabilities respond to the

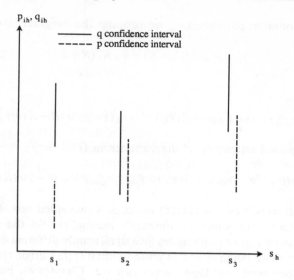

Figure 11.2 Sensitivity of detection probability to scenario h for mine i

scenario. If the detection probabilities are found to be sensitive to the scenario, then scenarios must be measured accurately; otherwise only extremely weak validation tests are possible. As the figure illustrates, the estimated simulated probabilities $\hat{p}_{ih}$ may lie within the range of estimated field results $\hat{q}_{ih}$, so without measurement of the scenario the model cannot be rejected. (A queuing situation provides an analogy: the traffic load replaces the scenario and the average waiting time replaces the estimated detection probabilities: if the traffic load is not measured, it is virtually impossible to validate the model.) Note that the Netherlands Navy plans to acquire a real-time measurement device to monitor SVPs.

We specify the hypothesis that, for each mine, the model and the real system give the same detection probability under scenario h:

$$H_0 : p_{ih} = q_{ih}. \tag{11.15}$$

The estimated detection probability (of mine i under scenario h) in simulation is denoted by $\hat{p}_{ih}$. This estimator is binomially distributed, so

$$\operatorname{var}(\underline{\hat{p}}_{ih}) = p_{ih}(1 - p_{ih})/R. \tag{11.16}$$

The field runs give binomial variables $\hat{q}_{ih}$ with parameters q_{ih} and K. The estimators $\hat{p}_{ih}$ and $\hat{q}_{ih}$ are independent, because the simulation outputs depend on pseudorandom numbers whereas the real outputs depend on other random events. The variance of $\hat{p}_{ih} - \hat{q}_{ih}$ under the hypothesis that the simulated and the real probabilities are equal to (say) r_{ih}, is:

$$\operatorname{var}(\underline{\hat{p}}_{ih} - \underline{\hat{q}}_{ih} \mid p_{ih} = q_{ih} = r_{ih}) = r_{ih}(1 - r_{ih})/R + r_{ih}(1 - r_{ih})/K$$
$$= r_{ih}(1 - r_{ih})(K + R)/(RK). \tag{11.17}$$

To estimate the common parameter r_{ih} we propose the weighted average

$$\hat{\underline{r}}_{ih} = \hat{\underline{p}}_{ih} R/(R+K) + \hat{\underline{q}}_{ih} K/(R+K). \tag{11.18}$$

Using

$$E(\underline{r}_{ih}^2) = \text{var}(\hat{\underline{r}}_{ih}) + [E(\hat{\underline{r}}_{ih})]^2 = r_{ih}(1-r_{ih})/(R+K) + r_{ih}^2, \tag{11.19}$$

we derive the unbiased estimator of the variance in (11.17):

$$\widehat{\text{var}}(\hat{\underline{p}}_{ih} - \hat{\underline{q}}_{ih} \mid p_{ih} = q_{ih} = r_{ih}) = \hat{\underline{r}}_{ih}(1 - \hat{\underline{r}}_{ih})(K+R-1)/(RK). \tag{11.20}$$

Obviously the null-hypothesis in (11.15) requires a two-sided test. Because there are several mines ($M>1$), we apply Bonferroni's inequality. So the (composite) null-hypothesis is rejected if one or more mines give significantly different estimated detection probabilities, each mine being tested at an individual type I error rate of α/M, where α denotes the 'experimentwise' type I error rate (see Chapter 8). For convenience we use the Gaussian distribution to approximate the distribution of the difference between two binomial variables. Its estimated mean is

$$\hat{\underline{p}}_{ih} - \hat{\underline{q}}_{ih} = \sum_{j=1}^{R} \underline{x}_{ijh}/R - \sum_{k=1}^{K} \underline{y}_{ikh}/K. \tag{11.21}$$

Its estimated variance was given in (11.20). So if $z_{1-\alpha}$ denotes the 'upper α point' or $1-\alpha$ quantile of the standard normal distribution, we reject the null-hypothesis if

$$\max_i [\, |\hat{\underline{p}}_{ih} - \hat{\underline{q}}_{ih}| / \sqrt{\widehat{\text{var}}(\hat{\underline{p}}_{ih} - \hat{\underline{q}}_{ih} \mid p_{ih} = q_{ih} = r_{ih})}\,] > z_{1-\alpha/M}. \tag{11.22}$$

We emphasize that Bonferroni's inequality also applies if the M estimated probabilities within a given run are dependent. Indeed, if the operator is busy with one mine then the detection probability of the next mine may be affected.

When testing the validity of a model through (11.22), we can make type I and type II errors, as we saw in Section 11.2 (see the discussion of equation (11.3)). Now the power of the test increases as the model specification error $\delta_{ih} = |p_{ih} - q_{ih}|$ increases. Bonferroni's inequality implies that the 'experimentwise' type I error rate is α. Obviously the power decreases as α decreases, given fixed sample sizes. A classical value for the experimentwise error rate α is 0.20 (this means that the per comparison error rates are α/M). To decrease both error probabilities we can increase the sample size of the simulation; the sample size of the field test is usually given.

As we saw in Section 11.2 we may formulate a *less stringent* validation requirement: the estimated simulation and real detection probabilities do not necessarily have equal means, but they are *positively correlated*. So if a particular mine has a relatively high estimated detection probability in reality, then its estimated simulation probability should also be relatively high. To test this hypothesis we formulate the regression model

$$\hat{\underline{p}}_{ih} = \beta_{0h} + \beta_{1h} \hat{\underline{q}}_{ih} + \underline{\epsilon}_{ih}, \tag{11.23}$$

where $\underline{\epsilon}_{ih}$ is assumed to be normally independently distributed with mean zero and variance σ_h^2. So if the scenarios in the field test and in the simulation are measured, we can plot $\hat{p}_{ih}$ as a function of $\hat{q}_{ih}$ for a fixed h. We use ordinary least squares to estimate the intercept and slope of the straight line through the 'cloud' of points. The null-hypothesis is

$$H_0 : \beta_{ih} \leqslant 0. \tag{11.24}$$

To test this hypothesis we use the classic t statistic; see Chapter 7. So we reject the null-hypothesis in (11.24) and accept the simulation model if there is strong evidence that estimated simulation and real detection probabilities are positively correlated. The number of points in the 'cloud' would be M if the scenario could be kept constant during the whole field test. Several field tests may be combined to get more observations, provided the scenarios are measured. If scenarios are not measured, then collecting all data in a single diagram creates extra noise; technically it means that the index h is deleted in (11.23) and (11.24). The weaker validation requirement makes sense if the model is used to predict relative responses (as in sensitivity analysis of tactics and sonar design), not absolute responses (needed to gauge the 'huntability' of a minefield).

11.3.3 Future Research in Mine Hunting

We applied sensitivity analysis to only two modules. So not all 40 factors of the total model have been investigated systematically. *Screening* so many factors can be done through sequential bifurcation, mentioned in Section 9.2.

A factor that certainly requires more research is the *SVP*. In the model it is treated as a qualitative factor. Such a nominal scale indicates lack of knowledge (see Kleijnen, 1987, pp. 138–42). Moreover, the model uses a single *SVP* in the whole simulation run. (An analytical model has been developed that considers multiple *SVP*s.) One challenge is to find 'robust' tactical procedures, that is, procedures that are not sensitive to the specific *SVP*. It would also be useful to develop a real-time measurement device installed on board the ship. Its measurements provide time- and space-dependent input to the simulation model, which then becomes a decision support system (DSS).

Bottom profile is also a qualitative factor. In the model a simple geometric pattern is used. Moreover bottom type (sand, rock, etc.) is modelled too crudely: it is scaled from one to four, whereas it is actually a qualitative factor.

Improvements of the current model should make it possible to eliminate the artificial calibration parameter.

A complication is caused by the *measurement errors* in the field tests. In these tests a circle with a given radius is drawn around the 'true' location of the mine, assuming that location is exactly known. If and only if the operator records a contrast within that circle, the mine is supposed to be detected. So the operator may see a false contrast (minelike object or noise) that falls within the circle; that echo is counted as a detection. Several more types of response variable are discussed in Kleijnen and Alink (1992).

REFERENCES

Baber R. (1987) *The Spine of Software; Designing Provable Correct Software: Theory and Practice*, Wiley, Chichester.

Balci O. and R. G. Sargent (1984a) A bibliography on the credibility, assessment and validation of simulation and mathematical models, *Simuletter*, **15**(3), 15–27.

Balci O. and R. G. Sargent (1984b) Validation of simulation models via simultaneous confidence intervals, *American Journal of Mathematical and Management Science*, **4**(3 and 4), 375–406.

Banks J. (1989) Testing, understanding and validating complex simulation models, *Proceedings of the 1989 Winter Simulation Conference*, New York.

Banks J. and J. S. Carson (1984) *Discrete-event System Simulation*, Prentice-Hall, Englewood Cliffs, New Jersey.

Bettonvil B. and J. P. C. Kleijnen (1992) *Identifying the Important Factors in Simulation Models with Many Factors*, Tilburg University.

Carson J. S. (1989) Verification and validation: a consultant's perspective, *Proceedings of the 1989 Winter Simulation Conference*, New York.

Davis G. B. and M. H. Olson (1985) *Management Information Systems: Conceptual Foundations, Structure and Development*, McGraw-Hill, New York.

Dekker C. M., A. Groenendijk, and C. J. Sliggers (1990) *Kwaliteitscriteria voor modellen om luchtverontreiniging te berekenen* (*Quality criteria for models to compute air pollution*), Report 90, VROM, Leidschendam.

DeMillo R. A., W. M. McCracken, R. J. Martin, and J. F. Passafiume (1987) *Software Testing and Evaluation*, Benjamin/Cummings, Menlo Park, California.

Fossett C. A., D. Harrison, H. Weintrob, and S. I. Gass (1991) An assessment procedure for simulation models: a case study, *Operations Research*, **39**(5), 710–23.

Gass S. I. (1984) Documenting a computer-based model, *Interfaces*, **14**(3), 84–93.

Kleijnen J. P. C. (1980) *Computers and Profits: Quantifying Financial Benefits of Information*, Addison-Wesley, Reading, Massachusetts.

Kleijnen J. P. C. (1987) *Statistical Tools for Simulation Practitioners*, Marcel Dekker, New York.

Kleijnen J. P. C. (1990) Statistics and deterministic simulation models: Why not?, *Proceedings of the 1990 Winter Simulation Conference*, New York.

Kleijnen J. P. C. (1992) Simulation and Optimization in Production Planning: a Case Study, *Decision Support Systems*, **8**.

Kleijnen J. P. C. and G. A. Alink (1992) *Validation of Simulation Models: Mine-hunting Case Study*, Tilburg University.

Kleijnen J. P. C., J. Rotmans, and G. van Ham (1992) Techniques for Sensitivity Analysis of Simulation Models: a Case Study of the CO_2 Greenhouse Effect, *Simulation* (in press).

Lavenberg S. S. (1983) *Computer Performance Modeling Handbook*, Academic Press, New York.

Law A. M. and W. D. Kelton (1991) *Simulation Modeling and Analysis* (2nd edn), McGraw-Hill, New York.

Pegden C. P., R. E. Shannon, and R. P. Sadowski (1990) *Introduction to Simulation using SIMAN*, McGraw-Hill, New York.

Reckhow K. H. (1989) Validation of simulation models: philosophical and statistical methods of confirmation. In M. D. Singh (ed.) *Systems & Control Encyclopedia*, Pergamon Press.

Sargent R. G. (1991) Simulation model verification and validation, *Proceedings of the 1991 Winter Simulation Conference*, New York.

Schriber T. J. (1991) *An Introduction to Simulation Using GPSS/H*, Wiley, New York.

Schruben L. W. (1980) Establishing the credibility of simulations, *Simulation*, **34**(3), 101–5.

Shannon R. E. (1975) *Systems Simulation: the Art and Science*, Prentice-Hall, Englewood Cliffs, New Jersey.

Whitner R. B. and O. Balci (1989) Guidelines for selecting and using simulation model verification techniques, *Proceedings of the 1989 Winter Simulation Conference*, New York.

Wolstenhome E. F. (1990) *Systems Enquiry: A System Dynamics Approach*, Wiley, Chichester.

Zeigler B. (1976) *Theory of Modelling and Simulation*, Wiley Interscience, New York.

Chapter 12

Epilogue

There are too many textbooks on simulation to name all of them. Each university library has some books on simulation. We have already mentioned a few classical books: the standard work of Naylor et al. (1966) and the more recent texts by Bratley, Fox, and Schrage (1983), Fishman (1973, 1978), Law and Kelton (1991), and Shannon (1975). Textbooks with a simulation language 'bias' are Pegden, Shannon, and Sadowski (1990), Pritsker (1986), and Schriber (1991).

The latest developments in simulation are documented in the journals *Management Science, Operations Research*, and *Communications of the Association for Computing Machinery*, and also in *European Journal of Operational Research* and *Decision Sciences*. Simple articles are published in *Simulation*, which concentrates on simulation (be it discrete or continuous models). Moreover, simulation applications appear in all journals that publish quantitative models, from astronomy to sociology.

International associations for simulationists are the *Society for Computer Simulation* (SCS), and the special interest groups of *The Institute of Management Sciences* (TIMS) and the *Association for Computing Machinery* (ACM). Most European countries and Japan have their own professional organizations for simulationists. Developments in Europe are reported in EUROSIM—Simulation News in Europe.

REFERENCES

Bratley P., B. L. Fox, and L. E. Schrage (1983) *A Guide to Simulation*, Springer-Verlag, New York.

Fishman G. S. (1973) *Concepts and Methods in Discrete Event Digital Simulation*, Wiley, New York.

Fishman G. S. (1978) *Principles of Discrete Event Simulation*, Wiley, New York.

Law A. M. and W. S. Kelton (1991) *Simulation Modeling and Analysis* (2nd edn), McGraw-Hill, New York.

Naylor T. H., J. L. Balintfy, D. S. Burdick, and Kong Chu (1966) *Computer Simulation Techniques*, Wiley, New York.

Pegden C. P., R. E. Shannon, and R. P. Sadowski (1990) *Introduction to Simulation using SIMAN*, McGraw-Hill, New York.

Pritsker A. A. B. (1986) *Introduction to Simulation and SLAM II* (3rd edn), Halsted Press, New York.

Schriber T. J. (1991) *An Introduction to Simulation Using GPSS/H*, Wiley, New York.

Shannon R. E. (1975) *Systems Simulation: the Art and Science*, Prentice-Hall, Englewood Cliffs, New Jersey.

Solutions to Exercises

CHAPTER 1

1. Cost must increase, not decrease, as stockouts increase.
2. No back-ordering allowed.
3. Physical inventory.
4. If H_0 holds, then $\sigma_{\hat{\alpha}}^2 = (0.05)(0.95)/1000 = 0.0000475$. The normal approximation yields $z = (\hat{\alpha} - \alpha)/\sigma_{\hat{\alpha}} = (40/1000 - 0.05)/0.007 = -0.01/0.007 = -1.45$. Not significant: do not reject H_0.
5. Sample the first quadrant only; that is, estimate $\pi/4$. So $x_1 := RANDOM$ and $x_2 := RANDOM$; area := count/number.
   So x_1 and x_2 are defined such that computer time is saved.

CHAPTER 2

1. Modulo m yields a number in the range $[0, m-1]$. Hence (2.5) yields $[0, (m-1)/m = 1 - 1/m]$.
2. $n_1 = an_0 + b - k_1 m$
   $n_2 = an_1 + b - k_2 m = a^2 n_0 + ab - ak_1 m + b - k_2 m = a^2 n_0 + b(a+1) - m(k_2 + ak_1)$
   $$\vdots$$
   $$n_i = a^i n_0 + b(a^{i-1} + a^{i-2} + \cdots + a + 1) - m(k_i + ak_{i-1} + \cdots + a^{i-1} k_1)$$
   $$= \left(a^i n_0 + \frac{b(a^i - 1)}{(a-1)} \right) \bmod m.$$
3. See disk.
4. Every r_i occurs in two successive pairs, except for r_0 and r_n.

CHAPTER 3

1. $P(\underline{x} = 5) = P(0 \leqslant r < 0.1) = \int_0^{0.1} 1 \, dr = 0.1$.
2. $P(1 - \underline{r} \leqslant r) = P(-\underline{r} \leqslant r - 1) = P(\underline{r} \geqslant 1 - r) = 1 - P(\underline{r} < 1 - r) = 1 - (1 - r) = r$.
3. See disk.
4. Normal and gamma distributions have no explicit distribution functions.
5. Log is a slow computer subroutine. Now we have only one log instead of k logs.
6. $\underline{k} = 4$ and 3 respectively.

7. See disk.
8. $L = (1,1)$ and $\Omega_2 = \begin{bmatrix} \sigma_1^2 & \sigma_{12} \\ \sigma_{12} & \sigma_2^2 \end{bmatrix}$; so $\text{var}(\underline{z}_1 + \underline{z}_2) = (1,1) \begin{bmatrix} \sigma_1^2 & \sigma_{12} \\ \sigma_{12} & \sigma_2^2 \end{bmatrix} \begin{bmatrix} 1 \\ 1 \end{bmatrix}$
   $= \sigma_1^2 + 2\sigma_{12} + \sigma_2^2$.
9. See disk.
10. Because $E(\underline{y}_t) = 0$ we have $\text{cov}(\underline{y}_t, \underline{y}_{t+k}) = E(\underline{y}_t \underline{y}_{t+k})$.
    Now $\underline{y}_{t+k} = [\lambda^k \underline{y}_t + \lambda^{k-1} \underline{x}_{t+1}] + \lambda^{k-2} \underline{x}_{t+2} + \cdots + \lambda^0 \underline{x}_{t+k}$.
    Multiply left- and right-hand sides by $\underline{y}_t$ and take expectations:
    $$E[\underline{y}_t \underline{y}_{t+k}] = E[\lambda^k \underline{y}_t^2] + E[\lambda^{k-1} \underline{y}_t \underline{x}_{t+1}] + E[\lambda^{k-2} \underline{y}_t \underline{x}_{t+2}] + \cdots$$
    $$+ E[\underline{y}_t \underline{x}_{t+k}] = \lambda^k \text{var}(\underline{y}_t),$$
    because $\underline{y}_t$ and $\underline{x}_{t+i}$ with $i > 0$ are independent.
11. See disk.

CHAPTER 4

1. Substitution of (4.14) and (4.15) into (4.16) gives
   $a_1 \underline{P}_t + b_1 \underline{P}_{t-1} = a_0 - b_0 + (\underline{\epsilon}_t - \underline{\xi}_t - \underline{\eta}_t)$. In the equilibrium state we have $E(\underline{P}_t) = E(\underline{P}_{t-1}) = P_e$, which yields (4.17).

2. $a_1 \underline{P}_t + b_1 \underline{P}_{t-1} - (a_0 - b_0) = (\underline{\epsilon}_t - \underline{\xi}_t - \underline{\eta}_t)$ $\Leftrightarrow$

   $a_1 \underline{P}_t + b_1 \underline{P}_{t-1} - (a_0 - b_0) \left[\dfrac{a_1 + b_1}{a_1 + b_1} \right] = (\underline{\epsilon}_t - \underline{\xi}_t - \underline{\eta}_t)$ $\Leftrightarrow$

   $a_1 \underline{P}_t + b_1 \underline{P}_{t-1} - (a_1 + b_1) P_e = (\underline{\epsilon}_t - \underline{\xi}_t - \underline{\eta}_t)$ $\Leftrightarrow$

   $a_1(\underline{P}_t - P_e) + b_1(\underline{P}_{t-1} - P_e) = (\underline{\epsilon}_t - \underline{\xi}_t - \underline{\eta}_t)$ $\Leftrightarrow$

   $\underline{p}_t = -(b_1/a_1)\underline{p}_{t-1} + (\underline{\epsilon}_t - \underline{\xi}_t - \underline{\eta}_t)$ $\Leftrightarrow$

   $\underline{p}_t = -(b_1/a_1)\{-(b_1/a_1)\underline{p}_{t-2} + (\underline{\epsilon}_{t-1} - \underline{\xi}_{t-1} - \underline{\eta}_{t-1})/a_1\}$
   $\qquad\qquad\qquad + (\underline{\epsilon}_t - \underline{\xi}_t - \underline{\eta}_t)/a_1$ $\Leftrightarrow$

   $$\underline{p}_t = \frac{1}{a_1} \sum_{j=0}^{\infty} (-1)^j \left[\frac{b_1}{a_1} \right]^j (\underline{\epsilon}_{t-j} - \underline{\xi}_{t-j} - \underline{\eta}_{t-j}).$$

3. $\text{var}(\underline{p}_t) = \text{var} \left\{ \dfrac{1}{a} \displaystyle\sum_{j=0}^{\infty} (-1)^j \left[\dfrac{b_1}{a_1} \right]^j (\underline{\epsilon}_{t-j} - \underline{\xi}_{t-j} - \underline{\eta}_{t-j}) \right\}$.

   Assuming no cross-correlation and no autocorrelation for the errors, we get

   $$\text{var}(\underline{p}_t) = (a_1)^{-2} E \left\{ \sum_{j=0}^{\infty} \left[\frac{b_1}{a_1} \right]^{2j} (\underline{\epsilon}_{t-j}^2 - \underline{\xi}_{t-j}^2 - \underline{\eta}_{t-j}^2) \right\}$$

   $$= (a_1)^{-2} \sum_{j=0}^{\infty} \left[\frac{b_1}{a_1} \right]^{2j} E(\underline{\epsilon}_{t-j}^2 - \underline{\xi}_{t-j}^2 - \underline{\eta}_{t-j}^2)$$

   $$= (a_1)^{-2} (\sigma_\epsilon^2 - \sigma_\xi^2 - \sigma_\eta^2) \sum_{j=0}^{\infty} \left[\frac{b_1}{a_1} \right]^{2j}$$

   $$= \left[\frac{1}{a_1^2 - b_1^2} \right] (\sigma_\epsilon^2 - \sigma_\xi^2 - \sigma_\eta^2).$$

4. See disk.
5. See disk.
6. See disk.
7. $LEVEL1.K$ $= LEVEL1.J + DT(IN.JK - OUT1.JK)$
    $OUT1.KL$ $= LEVEL1.L/(DELAY/3)$
    $LEVEL2.K$ $= LEVEL2.J + DT(OUT1.JK - OUT2.JK)$
    $OUT2.KL$ $= LEVEL2.K/(DELAY/3)$
    $LEVEL3.K$ $= LEVEL3.J + DT(OUT2.JK - OUT3.JK)$
    $OUT3.KL$ $= LEVEL3.K/(DELAY/3)$

    $LEVEL.K$ $= LEVEL1.K + LEVEL2.K + LEVEL3.K$
8. $LEVELy.K$ $= LEVELy.J + DT(RATEy.JK)$
    $RATEy.KL$ $= (H - LEVELy.K)/DEL1$
    $LEVELx.K$ $= LEVELx.J + DT(RATEx.JK)$
    $RATEx.KL$ $= (LEVELy.K - LEVELx.K)/DEL2$
9. $OILRATE.JK$ $= (-TEMP.J + DESTEMP.J)/DELAY$ if $TEMP.J < DESTEMP.J$
                $= 0$ else.

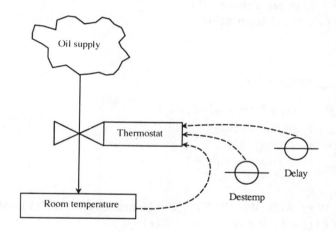

CHAPTER 5

1. Negative inventory increases (not decreases) out-of-stock costs.
2. No back-orders. If there are stockouts ($stock < 0$), then the instruction '$stock := 0$' follows in Figure 5.2.
3. Technical inventory.
4. (a) *EOQ* would then have the value computed one day ago, not a lead time ago when that order was actually placed. (b) Actual lead time is not known until actual delivery.
5. See disk.
6. —
7. Sample arrival time of first customer, which exceeds zero with probability one.
8. See disk.
9. Average queue length $= \Sigma_{t=1}^{T}$ (queue length at time t)/$TIME = TWT/TIME$.

10. See disk.
11. See disk.
12. $JMIN = WR(I)$; do not rearrange $WR(H)$.
13. See disk.
14. $AT_1 = 0$; $WT_1^1 = 0$, $WT_2^1 = 0$, ..., $WT_n^1 = 0$; $IT_1 = 0$, $IT_2 = ST_1^1$, ..., $IT_n = \Sigma_{h=1}^{n-1} ST_h^1$.
15. See disk.
16. See disk.
17. See disk.

CHAPTER 6

1. $SV = ST$ with $ST =$ service time.
2. $SV = TLS$ and for newly arrived transactions $TLS = -1/TAT$. Other implementations are possible!
3. Transaction in state 6 means a setdown, which ends in state 1. Hence the server goes from 1 to 0; see Table 6.1(b).
4. See Table 6.4, line 2 from below.
5. See disk.

CHAPTER 7

1. See Figure 1.7: end as follows:
      chi $= (n-1)vx/(1/12)$
   If chi $> \chi_{n-1}^2$ then $count = count + 1$
   END.
2. $m_1 = 4$, $m_2 = 4$.
3. $E(\hat{\beta}) = E(\mathbf{W} \mathbf{y})$ with $\mathbf{W} = (\mathbf{X}' \mathbf{X})^{-1} \mathbf{X}'$. Hence $E(\hat{\beta}) = \mathbf{W} E(\mathbf{y}) = \mathbf{W} E(\mathbf{X}\beta + \epsilon) = \mathbf{W}\mathbf{X}\beta + \mathbf{W}E(\epsilon) = \beta + \mathbf{W}E(\epsilon) = \beta$ since $E(\epsilon) = 0$.
4. $\mathbf{cov}(\hat{\beta}) = \mathbf{L}\, \mathbf{cov}(\mathbf{y})\, \mathbf{L}' = \sigma^2 \mathbf{L}\mathbf{L}' = \sigma^2 [(\mathbf{X}'\mathbf{X})^{-1}\mathbf{X}'][\mathbf{X}(\mathbf{X}'\mathbf{X})^{-1}]$ since $\mathbf{X}'\mathbf{X}$ is symmetric. So $\mathbf{cov}(\hat{\beta}) = \sigma^2(\mathbf{X}'\mathbf{X})^{-1}$.
5. Define $\mathbf{D} = \mathbf{T}\mathbf{X}$ where $\mathbf{T}$ denotes the $n \times q$ diagonal matrix with the first m_1 elements equal to $1/\sigma_1$, the next m_2 elements $1/\sigma_2$, ..., the last m_n elements $1/\sigma_n$. Define $\mathbf{y}^+ = \mathbf{T}\mathbf{y}$. Then OLS applied to $\mathbf{D}$ and $\mathbf{y}^+$ yields $\hat{\beta} = (\mathbf{D}'\mathbf{D})^{-1} \mathbf{D}' \mathbf{T}\mathbf{y} = (\mathbf{X}'\mathbf{T}'\mathbf{T}\mathbf{X})^{-1} \mathbf{X}'\mathbf{T}'\mathbf{T}\mathbf{y}$. Since $\mathbf{T}' = \mathbf{T}$ and $\mathbf{T}'\mathbf{T} = [\mathbf{cov}(\mathbf{y})]^{-1}$, we get $\hat{\beta} = (\mathbf{X}'[\mathbf{cov}(\mathbf{y})]^{-1}\mathbf{X})^{-1}\mathbf{X}'[\mathbf{cov}(\mathbf{y})]^{-1}\mathbf{y}$, which equals the WLS estimator.
6. $\hat{\beta} = \mathbf{W}\mathbf{y}$ with $\mathbf{W} = (\mathbf{X}'[\mathbf{cov}(\mathbf{y})]^{-1}\mathbf{X})^{-1}\mathbf{X}'[\mathbf{cov}(\mathbf{y})]^{-1}$ yields
   $$\mathbf{cov}(\hat{\beta}) = \mathbf{W}\,[\mathbf{cov}(\mathbf{y})]\,\mathbf{W}'$$
   $$= (\mathbf{X}'[\mathbf{cov}(\mathbf{y})]^{-1}\mathbf{X})^{-1}\mathbf{X}'[\mathbf{cov}(\mathbf{y})]^{-1}\mathbf{cov}(\mathbf{y})((\mathbf{X}'[\mathbf{cov}(\mathbf{y})]^{-1}\mathbf{X})^{-1}\mathbf{X}'[\mathbf{cov}(\mathbf{y})]^{-1})'$$
   $$= (\mathbf{X}'[\mathbf{cov}(\mathbf{y})]^{-1}\mathbf{X})^{-1}\mathbf{X}'[\mathbf{cov}(\mathbf{y})]^{-1}\mathbf{X}(\mathbf{X}'[\mathbf{cov}(\mathbf{y})]^{-1}\mathbf{X})^{-1}$$
   $$= (\mathbf{X}'[\mathbf{cov}(\mathbf{y})]^{-1}\mathbf{X})^{-1}.$$
7. $\hat{\beta} = \mathbf{L}\mathbf{y}$ with $\mathbf{L} = (\mathbf{X}'\mathbf{X})^{-1}\mathbf{X}'$. So $\mathbf{cov}(\hat{\beta}) = \mathbf{L}\, \mathbf{cov}(\mathbf{y})\, \mathbf{L}'$.
8. See disk.

9.
$$\hat{\sigma}_i^2 = \frac{\sum\limits_{j=1}^{m_i} (y_{ij} - \bar{y}_i)^2}{(m_i - 1)}$$

$$= \frac{\sum\limits_{j=1}^{m_i} \left\{ \sum\limits_{h=0}^{q-1} \beta_h x_{ih} + \epsilon_{ij} - \sum\limits_{j=1}^{m_i} \left(\sum\limits_{h=0}^{q-1} \beta_h x_{ih} + \epsilon_{ij} \right) / m_i \right\}^2}{(m_i - 1)}$$

$$= \frac{\sum\limits_{j=1}^{m_i} \left\{ \sum\limits_{h=0}^{q-1} \beta_h x_{ih} + \epsilon_{ij} - \sum\limits_{h=0}^{q-1} \beta_h x_{ih} - \bar{\epsilon}_i \right\}^2}{(m_i - 1)}$$

$$= \frac{\sum\limits_{j=1}^{m_i} \{ \epsilon_{ij} - \bar{\epsilon}_i \}^2}{(m_i - 1)} .$$

10. No: the 'acceptance' interval becomes wider in the Bonferroni approach.
11. See disk.

CHAPTER 8

1. Apply (3.59).
2. $(\partial \bar{w} / \bar{w}) / (\partial \lambda / \lambda) = \partial \ln(\bar{w}) / \partial \ln(\lambda) = \beta_1$.
3. $\dfrac{\partial \hat{y}}{\partial x_2} = \hat{\gamma}_2 + \hat{\gamma}_{24} x_4$. If $\hat{\gamma}_{24} > 0$ then complementary inputs x_2 and x_4. If $\hat{\gamma}_{24} = 0$ then
   independence. If $\hat{\gamma}_{24} < 0$ then substitution between x_2 and x_4.
4. See disk.

CHAPTER 9

1. $2^7 = 128$.
2.

Combination	x_1	x_2	ρ	s
1	−	−	0.5	1
2	+	−	0.8	1
3	−	+	0.5	3
4	+	+	0.8	3

3. $y_i = \beta_0 + \beta_1 x_{i1} + \beta_2 x_{i2} + \beta_3 x_{i3} + \beta_{12} x_{i1} x_{i2} + \beta_{13} x_{i1} x_{i3} + \beta_{23} x_{i2} x_{i3} + \underline{\epsilon}$.

4. $\partial E(\underline{y}) / \partial x_1 = \beta_1 + \beta_{12} x_2$, so $\left[\dfrac{\partial E(y)}{\partial x_1} \right]_{x_2 = 1} = \beta_1 + \beta_{12}$.

5. Equations (9.3) and (9.4) yield for $j = 1$
   $E(\hat{\underline{\beta}}_1) = \{ E(\underline{y}_2) - E(\underline{y}_1) \} / 2$.

Equation (9.2) yields

$E(\underline{y}_2) = E(y \mid x_1 = +1, \ x_2 = -1, \ x_3 = -1) = \beta_0 + \beta_1 - \beta_2 - \beta_3$

and

$E(\underline{y}_1) = E(y \mid x_1 = x_2 = x_3 = -1) = \beta_0 - \beta_1 - \beta_2 - \beta_3.$

So $E(\hat{\underline{\beta}}_1) = 2\beta_1/2 = \beta_1.$

6. (a) One factor at a time design for $k=2$ gives

$$\mathbf{X} = \begin{bmatrix} +1 & -1 & -1 \\ +1 & +1 & -1 \\ +1 & -1 & +1 \end{bmatrix}. \text{ So } \mathbf{X}' = \begin{bmatrix} +1 & +1 & +1 \\ -1 & +1 & -1 \\ -1 & -1 & +1 \end{bmatrix}, \ (\mathbf{X}'\mathbf{X}) = \begin{bmatrix} 3 & -1 & -1 \\ -1 & 3 & -1 \\ -1 & -1 & 3 \end{bmatrix},$$

$$(\mathbf{X}'\mathbf{X})^{-1} = \begin{bmatrix} 0.50 & 0.25 & 0.25 \\ 0.25 & 0.50 & 0.25 \\ 0.25 & 0.25 & 0.50 \end{bmatrix} \text{ and } (\mathbf{X}'\mathbf{X})^{-1}\mathbf{X}' = \begin{bmatrix} 0.0 & 0.5 & 0.5 \\ -0.5 & 0.5 & 0.0 \\ -0.5 & 0.0 & 0.5 \end{bmatrix}.$$

(b) See $(\mathbf{X}'\mathbf{X})^{-1}$.

7. $\text{var}(\hat{\underline{\alpha}}_1) = \text{var}(\underline{y}_2 - \underline{y}_1) = \text{var}(\underline{y}_2) + \text{var}(\underline{y}_1) = 2\sigma^2.$

$\text{var}(\hat{\underline{\alpha}}_j) = \text{var}\{(\underline{y}_2 + \underline{y}_4 - \underline{y}_1 - \underline{y}_3)/2\}$

$\qquad = \{\text{var}(\underline{y}_2) + \text{var}(\underline{y}_4) + \text{var}(\underline{y}_1) + \text{var}(\underline{y}_3)\}/4 = \sigma^2.$

8. (a) Table 9.7 with elimination of the columns for x_6 and x_7.

(b) $1 + 5 + (5 \times 4)/2 = 16.$

(c) Write out $n \times q$ matrix $\mathbf{X}$ with $n = 2^{5-1}$ and $q = 1 + 5 + 5*4/2$; check: $\mathbf{X}$ is orthogonal.

9. See disk.

10. Combine $E(y)$ of Table 9.8 with the formulae for $\hat{\gamma}_1$ and $\hat{\gamma}_2$ in (9.17) and (9.18).

11. Three groups (w_1, w_2, w_3) each consisting of 30 individual factors. Full factorial with three group factors yields (see Table 9.1(2)):

Combination	w_1	w_2	w_3	x_1	x_{30}	x_{31}	x_{60}	x_{61}	x_{90}
1	−	−	−	−	−	−	−	−	−
2	+	−	−	+	+	−	−	−	−
⋮									
8	+	+	+	+	+	+	+	+	+

12. See disk.

CHAPTER 10

1. (a) $\bar{w}$ (average per day).

(b) Yes: *independent* random numbers fed into the *same* computer program.

2. Confidence interval length decreases because denominator $\sqrt{m}$ increases and $t_{m-1}^{\alpha/2}$ decreases.

3. See disk.

4. See disk.

5. $\text{var}(\bar{\underline{w}}) = \text{var}\left(\dfrac{1}{m}\sum_{t=1}^{m}\underline{w}_t\right) = \dfrac{1}{m^2}\,\text{var}\left(\sum_{t=1}^{m}\underline{w}_t\right)$

$$= \frac{1}{m^2} \left\{ \sum_{t=1}^{m} \text{var}(\underline{w}_t) + 2 \sum_{t=1}^{m-1} \sum_{t'=t+1}^{m} \text{cov}(\underline{w}_t, \underline{w}_{t'}) \right\}$$

$$= \frac{1}{m^2} \left\{ m\sigma_w^2 + 2 \sum_{t=1}^{m-1} \sum_{t'=t+1}^{m} \text{cov}(\underline{w}_t, \underline{w}_{t'}) \right\}$$

$$= \frac{\sigma_w^2}{m} \left\{ 1 + \frac{2}{m} \sum_{t=1}^{m-1} \sum_{t'=t+1}^{m} \rho_{t-t'} \right\} = \frac{\sigma_w^2}{m} \left\{ 1 + \frac{2}{m} \sum_{t=1}^{m-1} (m-t)\rho_t \right\}.$$

6. See disk.
7. See disk.
8. See disk.
9. $E(\hat{\underline{p}}_c) = \frac{1}{n} \sum_{t=1}^{n} E(\underline{v}_t)$ with $E(\underline{v}_t) = 0 \ P(\underline{w} > c) + 1 \ P(\underline{w} \leqslant c) = p_c$.
10. Binomial with $\text{var}(\hat{\underline{p}}_c) = p_c(1 - p_c)/n$.
11. See disk.
12. See disk.
13. See disk.
14. The responses are independent differences $\underline{d} = \underline{x} - \underline{y}$ (with $\underline{x}$ and $\underline{y}$ correlated). Degrees of freedom: $m - 1$.
15. Identically distributed: $\text{var}(\underline{x}_1) = \text{var}(\underline{x}_2) = \sigma^2$
    Independent: $\text{cov}(\underline{x}_1, \underline{x}_2) = 0$.
    Hence: $\text{var}(\underline{\bar{x}}) = \frac{1}{4}(2\sigma^2) = \sigma^2/2$.
16. (a) Independent.
    (b) Independent.
    (c) Dependent: negative correlation.
    (d) Dependent: negative correlation.
    (e) Independent.
    (f) Independent.
    (g) No antithetics: m replicates; see (10.4).
        Antithetics: $m/2$ independent replicates: degrees of freedom of t in (10.4) is halved. However, $\text{var}\{(\underline{\bar{w}}_1 + \underline{\bar{w}}_2)/2\}$ through $\text{var}\{(\underline{\bar{w}}_{19} + \underline{\bar{w}}_{20})/2\}$ decrease. Also see disk.
17. It is given that $\bar{y} > \mu_y$. So $(\mu_y - \bar{y}) < 0$. $\bar{y}$ and $\underline{x}$ are negatively correlated (low traffic means high $\bar{y}$ and low x): $\beta_o < 0$. Hence $\beta(\mu_y - \bar{y}) > 0$. Hence $x_0 > x$.
18. See disk.
19. See disk.
20. See disk.

CHAPTER 11

1. See disk.

Author Index

Subject Index

NOW AVAILABLE

Solutions to exercises that require computer programming are available on 3.5 inch disks for your IBM PC (and most compatibles).

The large exercises are compiled and the small exercises can be compiled by the Turbo Pascal Compiler. No special graphics card is required.

Order the disk today priced £12.50/$28.50 (VAT inclusive) by using the form below. Alternatively you can telephone your credit card order on (0243) 829121, Customer Service Department, John Wiley & Sons Ltd.

If you have any queries please contact:

Helen Ramsey
John Wiley & Sons Ltd
Baffins Lane
Chichester
West Sussex
PO19 1UD
England

Affix
Stamp
here

Customer Service Department
John Wiley & Sons Ltd
Shripney Road
Bognor Regis
West Sussex
PO22 9SA
England